DATE DUE

NO 12 '96	AP 16 01		
DE 12 '96	NO 13 01		
OC 28 '97	OC 17 '01		
OC 7 '98			
OC 67 '98	AP 21 '04		
NO 3 '98	MY 19 '04		
	MY 19 '04		
DE 18 '98	MY 2 '05		
MR 9 '99	JE 8 '05		
MR 29 '99	NO 9 '05		
AP 19 '99	NO 30 05		
MY 27 '99			
AG 5 '00			
MY 31 '00			
OC 27 '00			
NO 21 '00			

DEMCO 38-296

A License to Teach

A License to Teach

Building a Profession for 21st-Century Schools

Linda Darling-Hammond

Arthur E. Wise

Stephen P. Klein

Westview Press

Boulder • San Francisco • Oxford

Published in 1995 in the United States of America by Westview Press, Inc., 5500 Central Avenue, Boulder, Colorado 80301-2877, and in the United Kingdom by Westview Press, 36 Lonsdale Road, Summertown, Oxford OX2 7EW

Library of Congress Cataloging-in-Publication Data
Darling-Hammond, Linda, 1951–
  A license to teach : building a profession for 21st-century
schools / Linda Darling-Hammond, Arthur E. Wise, and Stephen P.
Klein.
     p. cm.
  Includes bibliographical references and index.
  ISBN 0-8133-8773-6. — ISBN 0-8133-2531-5 (pbk.)
  1. Teachers—Certification—Minnesota—Case studies. 2. Teachers—
Rating of—Minnesota—Case studies. 3. Teachers—Training of—
Minnesota—Case studies. 4. Examinations—Minnesota—Case studies.
I. Wise, Arthur E.   II. Klein, Stephen P., 1938–   . III. Title.
LB1772.M6D37 1995
379.1'57—dc20   94-33963
                                                                                    CIP

Printed and bound in the United States of America

The paper used in this publication meets the requirements of the American National Standard for Permanence of Paper for Printed Library Materials Z39.48-1984.

10   9   8   7   6   5   4   3   2   1

Contents

Tables and Figures

Preface

OUR RESPECT for the pioneering efforts of the Minnesota Board of Teaching (MBOT) continues. Where others seek expedience, the MBOT, with the help of Ken Peatross and Judy Wain, has set a deliberate course to produce a licensing system that will encourage the development of professional teachers. We are pleased that the Minnesota legislature recognized that foresight by providing funds for pilot residency programs and model outcomes and assessments for such programs. The Board of Teaching continues its initiatives to embed such efforts in a comprehensive licensing system grounded in knowledge-based approaches to teacher education and licensing requirements.

It is no accident that this leadership has been provided by one of the oldest professional standards boards for teachers in the nation. The tripling in the number of professional standards boards in the past few years and the many new ventures in teacher testing represent political recognition that it is time to change teacher licensing. *A License to Teach* places Minnesota's experience in the context of current reform efforts and suggests that developing and requiring a meaningful license to teach will be crucial for ensuring that teachers have the knowledge they need as a foundation for twenty-first-century schools.

This book grows out of our work together during several years at the RAND Corporation as well as our individual work in several years since then. Some of the early work was published in two reports issued by RAND's Center for the Study of the Teaching Profession: *Licensing Teachers: Design for a Teaching Profession* by Arthur E. Wise and Linda Darling-Hammond (RAND, R-3576-CSTP [Center for the Study of the Teaching Profession], November 1987), and *The Teaching Internship: Practical Preparation for a Licensed Profession* by Linda Darling-Hammond, Tamar Gendler, and Arthur E. Wise (RAND, R-3927-MBOT/CSTP, June 1990). The initial RAND project was supported by the Minnesota Board of Teaching, supplemented by a grant from the Conrad N. Hilton Foundation. Although the impetus for the study came from Minnesota, the results are applicable to other states. The report's findings should be of interest to anyone concerned with improving the professional preparation of teachers and the quality of education.

Linda Darling-Hammond
Arthur E. Wise
Stephen P. Klein

Acknowledgments

WE THANK former RAND colleagues Barnett Berry, Tamar Gendler, Brian Stetcher, and Harriet Tyson, whose related work informed several chapters of this book. We also thank Shirley Lithgow and Nancy Rizor who supported those efforts. Gary Griffin of the University of Arizona and Gary Sykes at Michigan State University reviewed earlier drafts of chapters of this book. We thank all of these individuals for their help in sharpening our thoughts and presentation. For any remaining errors of fact or interpretation, we hold each other accountable.

L.D-H.
A.E.W.
S.P.K.

Licensing Teachers:
The Need for Change

To BORROW A LINE from Rodney Dangerfield, teacher licensing in most states gets no respect. The traditional system of "certification" based upon completion of specified courses in state-approved programs of study has left most practitioners, members of the public, and policymakers unconvinced that licensing standards separate out those who can teach responsibly from those who cannot. Despite the many examples to the contrary, the conventional wisdom among many veteran practitioners is that the teacher education courses they experienced too rarely helped them in their practice. Most members of the public continue to think of professional training requirements for teachers as weaker than those of other professions such as medicine (NCATE, 1993). And many policymakers' suspicions lead them to create special routes into teaching that avoid teacher education and standard licensing because they believe these are unnecessary (Darling-Hammond, 1992).

In part because of this lack of credibility, teaching is now the only state-licensed occupation that continues to grant "emergency certificates" to untrained practitioners when vacancies need to be filled (Bacharach, 1985). This practice would not continue if all major constituents felt that licensing standards and processes effectively captured the important knowledge and skills teachers must have in order to serve students well.

All of these concerns have stimulated rethinking of teacher licensing. Equally important is the growing realization that the intense national quest to improve education for students requires attention to the knowledge and skills of teachers. The ongoing school reform movement of the last decade has riveted renewed attention on the capacities of teachers to teach a more demanding curriculum to the increasingly diverse groups of learners who are present—and who must become successful—in American schools.

1

A New Mission for Teaching

Efforts to restructure America's schools to meet the demands of a knowledge-based economy are redefining the mission of schooling and the job of teaching. Because the great masses of students need to be educated for thinking work rather than for low-skilled factory tasks, and educational success is a necessity rather than a luxury for a chosen few, schools are being pressured to change. Rather than merely "offering education," schools are now expected to ensure that all students learn and perform at high levels. Rather than merely "covering the curriculum," teachers are expected to find ways to support and connect with the needs of all learners (Darling-Hammond, 1990a). Furthermore, they are expected to prepare all students for thinking work—for framing problems; finding, integrating, and synthesizing information; creating new solutions; learning on their own; and working cooperatively.

This new mission for education requires substantially more knowledge and radically different skills for teachers. The kind of teaching required to meet these demands for more thoughtful learning cannot be produced through teacher-proof materials or regulated curricula. In order to create bridges between common, challenging curriculum goals and individual learners' experiences and needs, teachers must understand cognition and the many different pathways to learning. They must understand child development and pedagogy as well as the structures of subject areas and a variety of alternatives for assessing learning (Shulman, 1987; Darling-Hammond, 1990b).

If all children are to be effectively taught, teachers must be prepared to address the substantial diversity in experiences children bring with them to school—the wide range of languages, cultures, exceptionalities, learning styles, talents, and intelligences that in turn requires an equally rich and varied repertoire of teaching strategies. In addition, teaching for universal learning demands a highly developed ability to discover what children know and can do, as well as how they think and how they learn, and to match learning and performance opportunities to the needs of individual children. This mission for teaching defies the single, formulaic approach to delivering lessons and testing results that has characterized the goals of much regulation of teaching, many staff development programs, and a number of teacher testing and evaluation instruments. The capacities teachers need to succeed at the twenty-first century agenda for education can only be widely acquired throughout the teaching force by major reforms of teacher preparation and major restructuring of the systems by which states and school districts license, hire, induct, support, and provide for the continual learning of teachers (Wise and Darling-Hammond, 1987).

Because of widespread concerns for school improvement that have characterized the school reform era, teacher licensing has undergone major changes in states across the nation during the past decade. As policymakers, practitioners, and the public have sought greater assurance that licensed teachers are well prepared for their work, new requirements for teacher education and certification have been promulgated with substantial zeal and alacrity (Darling-Hammond and Berry, 1988). These include basic skills and subject-matter tests in a great many states and at least rudimentary tests of pedagogical knowledge in some.

Nonetheless, even these new requirements are not accepted as meaningful and credible by many policymakers, who have simultaneously enacted loopholes to their states' newly enacted standards—and by members of the profession, who frequently have not been involved in creating the standards. There is a growing sense that additional efforts are required to create licensing standards and systems that are defensible and meaningful, that are acceptable to the profession and the public, and that will actually improve teaching practice.

New Directions in Licensing

In this book we describe many of the efforts currently underway to develop and implement more meaningful standards for teaching. These include the move toward performance-based standards for teacher licensing, companion efforts to develop more sophisticated and authentic assessments for teachers, and the development and integration of national standards for teacher education, licensing, and certification. These national efforts are being led by the new National Board for Professional Teaching Standards (NBPTS), established in 1987 as the first professional body in teaching to set standards for the advanced certification of highly accomplished teachers; the Interstate New Teacher Assessment and Support Consortium (INTASC), a consortium of states working together on National Board–compatible licensing standards and assessments; and the National Council for Accreditation of Teacher Education (NCATE), which has been strengthening standards for teacher education programs, recently incorporating the performance standards developed by INTASC.

We propose an approach to licensing teachers that we believe will better meet social demands for education and will support the improved preparation of teachers for more effective practice. The foundation for this proposal is an earlier project we undertook to design the structure for a professional system for licensing teachers in Minnesota and to develop and test options for specific components of that system. Minnesota's experience is significant, as it was the first state in the nation to define performance-based licensing standards for teachers that are to be assessed in a structured internship and performance assessment system. This task was undertaken by the Minnesota Board of Teaching, one of only three professional standards boards that existed prior to the late 1980s.

This system, which directly assesses what teachers know and can do, will replace the traditional methods of requiring graduation from an approved program or tallying specific courses and then licensing a teacher based on successful course completion. It also stands in contrast to first-generation approaches to teacher testing, emphasizing performance assessments of teaching knowledge and skill rather than the multiple-choice tests of basic skills and subject-matter knowledge used by most states (Darling-Hammond and Berry, 1988).

Assessment through a careful and systematic review of on-the-job performance in a structured internship program, supplemented by evaluation of performance on realistic and appropriately complex teaching tasks, provides the possibility of more successfully judging prospective teachers' readiness to teach. This approach should also support the development of teacher education programs organized more explicitly around the attainment of important teaching abilities.

Ultimately, altering the process by which teachers are prepared for and inducted into teaching can provide the impetus for deeper structural changes in the recruitment and responsibilities of teachers. As has occurred in other professions, as teachers receive more rigorous training, their voice, effectiveness, and responsibilities within schools should increase, and the public (including potential recruits) should increasingly recognize teaching as a challenging, vital career requiring expertise and talent.

Since the MBOT adopted performance-oriented licensing standards in 1987, a number of other states have started down the same path. Eighteen states have been involved in drafting model licensing standards that are performance-based rather than defined by inputs (INTASC, 1992), and a number of other states—including Arkansas, California, Kentucky, Maine, New York, Ohio, and Texas—have recently moved to adopt such standards. Some states, including New York and California, have also launched internship programs for prospective and/or beginning teachers. Meanwhile, the development of new, more professionally credible and performance-oriented assessments for licensing teachers is underway in states such as Connecticut, New York, Texas, and California. This trend is also reflected in changes being made by testing companies to seek to make their teacher assessment instruments more performance-oriented and more grounded in a complex knowledge base for teaching.

Launching a New System in Minnesota

Throughout the 1980s, the Minnesota Board of Teaching (MBOT) led one of the most progressive movements in the nation to strengthen the preparation and licensure of teachers, beginning with studies of teacher education and support for exemplary teacher education programs and extending to the design of a system to assess the skills of prospective and beginning teachers. Following the release of a state task force report in 1986, *Minnesota's Vision for*

Teacher Education: Stronger Standards, New Partnerships (MBOT, 1986), released jointly by the Board of Teaching and the Higher Education Coordinating Board, the MBOT adopted rules to redesign teacher education programs to
implement a "research based, results-oriented curriculum." The board also received legislative authorization to implement new systems of teacher education and approval focused on performance outcomes that reflect the skills
teachers need in order to be effective (MBOT, 1992).

As part of its initial efforts to conceptualize a more effective and meaningful
licensing system, the Minnesota Board of Teaching worked with the RAND
Center for the Study of the Teaching Profession to develop a new design
for assessing the performance of beginning teachers (Wise and Darling-
Hammond, 1987; Darling-Hammond, Gendler, and Wise, 1990). Modeled after
licensing systems in other professions, the design provides for prospective
teachers to complete a carefully designed and supervised internship program
operating under state guidelines in local school districts. This internship occurs after candidates have completed liberal arts and professional education
courses and assessments of basic skills and professional teaching knowledge.
Successful completion of the internship is to be a prerequisite for taking a final
state examination of teaching skills based on performance assessments of
contextualized, complex teaching tasks.

In 1992 the Minnesota Board of Teaching created a comprehensive plan for
establishing outcomes-based teacher education programs, a restructured licensing system with new assessments, and pilot professional development
schools within which the internships would occur. In addition to the required
internship in a professional development school, the plan calls for an examination of pedagogical knowledge prior to the internship and an examination
of teaching skills after the internship. The board hopes for full implementation
by the year 2000, depending upon legislative authorizations and appropri-
ations.

This design, developed from a study of licensing in other professions, is a
substantial departure from traditional and recent approaches to teacher licensing. It represents an effort to support more conceptually and practically
useful and valid approaches to teacher preparation and to provide the public
with a higher level of assurance that novice teachers are prepared to practice
responsibly.

In the course of our research leading to these proposals, we studied Minnesota's current teacher preparation and licensing systems; evaluated other
states' assessment practices for preservice and in-service teachers, as well as
for licensing systems; examined new approaches to teacher testing; and reviewed licensing examinations in other professions. We also investigated efforts to define the knowledge base for teaching and assessed the possibilities
and limits of various taxonomies and techniques for defining and measuring
teaching skills.

Based on this research, we developed a framework for assessing the knowledge, skills, and dispositions of prospective teachers. Working with Minnesota teachers, we then developed prototype standards and tasks for sample components of this assessment framework as a model for more thorough development and, ultimately, implementation. In this book we describe our work in Minnesota, including the structure of the proposed assessment system, the standards and criteria for establishing internship programs, and prototypes for the proposed tests of professional knowledge and teaching skills.

The New Generation of Teacher Assessments

Placing the Minnesota work in a broader context, we also examine emerging conceptions of teacher knowledge and performance as they are being articulated by a number of other states and professional organizations, exploring how these relate to teacher assessment. We describe related assessment development initiatives for teacher licensing in California and some of the emerging work on assessment for advanced certification of the National Board for Professional Teaching Standards, which begins from similar conceptions of teaching and teacher knowledge.

These examples of the new generation of teacher assessments and approaches to preparation and licensing have in common an understanding of teaching as *reciprocal*—that is, intimately connected to students and responsive to their needs; *complex*—dependent upon many kinds of knowledge and understanding that must be integrated and applied using analysis and judgment; and *contingent*—reliant on considerations of context, including the nature of students, subjects, goals, and situations within which these are pursued.

In the final chapters of this book we explore implementation concerns in undertaking these new approaches to teacher development and licensing, along with further work to be done in fully developing and implementing a comprehensive licensing system that can represent and well serve a responsible profession of teaching.

The Need for Licensing Reform

To those involved in the quest for better schooling, licensing represents one means of promoting educational change. Many proponents of licensing reform believe the establishment of rigorous professional standards for entry into the teaching profession will both improve the quality of teaching and help establish teaching as a respected and responsible profession. If standards create meaningful and inviolable screens to entry, it is also possible that salaries will rise to the market level needed to ensure a more steady supply of talented and well-prepared entrants.

Another argument for licensing reform is related to current education reforms that envision greater teacher responsibility in educational decisions at all levels. Restructured schools require changes in the nature of teaching work and knowledge, including a more active, integrated, and intellectually challenging curriculum and a broader range of roles for teachers in developing curriculum and assessments of student performance, in coaching and mentoring other teachers, and in working more closely with families and community agencies. Because restructured schools are also redesigning classroom organizations so that "push-in" rather than "pull-out" methods are more likely to be used for children with special needs and interdisciplinary approaches to a "thinking curriculum" are more common, teachers will need to know more about both subjects and students than they have in the past. Finally, school-based management and shared decisionmaking initiatives rely for their success on the capacity of education practitioners to make knowledgeable judgments about curriculum and assessment, school organization, and program evaluation (Lieberman, Darling-Hammond, and Zuckerman, 1991). This increased responsibility means that teachers will need to be prepared to make such decisions responsibly. Licensing standards should reflect the demands of teachers' evolving roles. Reform of licensing is thus needed to support the success of broader school reform efforts. Obviously, the goal of all of these changes is better education for schoolchildren.

Licensing changes will not produce these benefits overnight. Indeed, the investment of both the time and the money required to implement programs such as the ones described here will probably not produce noticeable results in schools for many years. However, steps in the direction of more meaningful and valid systems for licensing teachers will likely influence the preparation of teachers much sooner. These steps will also send a message that the state and the profession take seriously their obligations to safeguard the educational well-being of students by insisting on and supporting the competence of their teachers.

Standard Setting in Teaching

Over the years, the occupation of teaching has had difficulty defining standards and enforcing a common knowledge base. This has been the case partly because, in contrast to other professions that have developed throughout the twentieth century, teaching has been governed through lay political channels and government bureaucracies—state legislatures along with state boards and departments of education—rather than professional bodies charged with articulating and enforcing knowledge-based standards. A related problem has been the political inefficacy of professional standards-setting initiatives, which have been largely ignored by politicians enamored with the false hopes of creating the "one best system" (Tyack, 1974) implicit in regulating teaching.

The Problems of Political Governance

Members of state legislatures and state and local school boards have typically adopted a view of teaching as relatively simple, straightforward work conducted by semiskilled workers and controlled by prescriptions for practice. This view is reinforced by the "apprenticeship of experience" adults lived through during their years as students. When some of these adults are later charged with making decisions about the regulation of teaching, they often view questions of required knowledge and skill through the distorted, time-clouded lens of a former pupil rather than the clear and polished lens of a trained practitioner.

In addition, legislatures and state agencies have a conflict of interest in enforcing rigorous standards for entry to teaching, since they must ensure a warm body in every classroom—and prefer to do so without boosting wages—even as they are charged with defining the minimum preparation needed to teach (Darling-Hammond, 1989b). Teacher salaries have continually lagged behind the salaries of other professions that require similar educational qualifications. Consequently, "despite brief periods of surplus, there has always been a shortage of willing and qualified teachers" (Sedlak and Schlossman, 1986, p. vii). Thus, there has been a constant tension between raising standards of practice and keeping pace with the need for teachers.

> The states . . . [have] found themselves with a set of internally conflicting demands: Improve quality, but guarantee a body in every public classroom. Periodic severe shortages of teachers are much more obvious and compelling than the need for higher quality. . . . Temporary and emergency certificates ease the shortage in times of undersupply; while in times of oversupply, a glut of teachers removes any rising interest in providing incentives for the improvement of quality. The call for higher salaries is muted when many of those teaching have done little to be temporarily certified, just as it is muted when there are dozens of applicants for each vacancy. (Goodlad, 1990, pp. 94–95)

Apple (1987, p. 73) suggested that "we have built whatever excellence we have in schools on the backs of the low-paid labor of a largely women's work force." In a society that continues to measure status according to compensation, teaching as a meagerly paid, predominantly female occupation has had low prestige. Until the 1960s, teaching was an "in and out" career (Lortie, 1975), with women continually entering and leaving the profession for child-rearing purposes and many men and women staying only a short time before leaving for other pursuits. For these reasons and many others—including the differentials in resources committed to schools of education compared with other university departments and the public's ambivalence about education generally—investments in building, codifying, and transmitting a knowledge base for teaching have historically been small (Sedlak and Schlossman, 1986; Darling-Hammond, 1990b; Ebmeier, Twombly, and Teeter, 1991).

Whereas professional boards establish standards for education and entry in professions such as medicine, nursing, architecture, accounting, and law, until fairly recently such boards have been absent in teaching. Instead, hundreds of individual state mandates have controlled what is taught—as well as the standards that are used to grant a teaching license. Because regulation of entry to practice is not rigorous, regulation of practice itself has become the norm. Rules governing curriculum and testing, course requirements, procedures for tracking and promoting students, organization of instruction and schooling, and specific educational programs are promulgated by legislatures, state agencies, and lay boards of education at the national, state, and local levels (Wise, 1979).

This micromanagement of teachers' work is understandable given the laissez-faire approach to admitting individuals to teaching. Forty-six states grant emergency licenses to untrained entrants. In 1985 and 1986, more than thirty thousand emergency licenses were granted in just the few states that kept track of these numbers (Darling-Hammond, 1989b, 1990c). In addition, more than thirty states have authorized "alternative" routes to certification, some of which require only a few weeks of training prior to assumption of full responsibility as a teacher (Darling-Hammond, 1992). Shortages in specific subject areas and in locations such as central cities are a major reason for the adoption of such loopholes in regular preparation and licensing requirements. Since the public has no guarantee about what teachers can be expected to know and be able to do, the felt need to regulate practice against the prospect of incompetence creates a highly regulated occupation that often discourages highly talented candidates from entering and remaining (Darling-Hammond, 1984).

Vehicles for Setting Professional Standards

In recent years, several major reports calling for the professionalization of teaching have noted that teachers must take hold of professional standard setting if teaching is to make good on the promise of competence professions make to the public (Carnegie Forum, 1986; Holmes Group, 1986). Teacher education leaders recognize that teachers and teacher educators "must take greater control over their own destiny. A powerful place where this can be done is in standards-setting. . . . Professionals must define high standards, set rigorous expectations, and then hold peers to these standards and expectations" (Imig, 1992).

Accreditation, licensing, and advanced certification are the three major quality-control mechanisms for any profession. In the field of teaching, these three mechanisms have historically been weak, in large part because of lay governance. Although all of the established professions require graduation from an accredited school as one condition of the license to practice, most states do not require schools of education to be accredited nor do they require candidates for licensure to have graduated from such schools. NCATE accredits only approximately five hundred of more than twelve thousand institutions that prepare teachers. Meanwhile, "the generally minimal state-prescribed criteria remain subject to local and state political influences, economic conditions within the state, and historical conditions which make change difficult" (Dennison, 1992, p. A40).

Over time, each state has developed its own set of standards for every program. Thus, there are literally hundreds of sets of standards for teacher preparation—some high, some low; sometimes enforced, sometimes not. States typically have little funding or personpower for overseeing the work of education schools. Although reviews of programs are supposed to occur, they are often infrequent and perfunctory, revealing little about the actual quality of experience provided by the institutions. They are also frequently guided by standards that are poor reflections of important teaching knowledge and skill. As a consequence of this approach to regulating teacher education, too many teachers recall their teacher education courses with dismay. Teachers remember irrelevant courses taught by marginally qualified instructors. They recall that important areas of knowledge were never made available to them and that they had to learn real teaching skills in their own classrooms, on their own, through trial and error.

The historical lack of rigorous standard setting in teaching is changing, however (Wise and Leibbrand, 1993). Autonomous professional standards boards for teaching now exist in ten states, a threefold increase over the number only a few years ago. In these ten states, educators set and enforce standards for teacher preparation and licensing, rather than legislators or state boards of education setting standards, as has traditionally been the case and is still true in forty states.

In addition, new, more rigorous accreditation standards for teacher education programs are being implemented by some schools of education through the auspices of the National Council for Accreditation of Teacher Education, which strengthened its standards in 1988. The foundation of the new accreditation system is the body of growing knowledge about teaching and learning obtained from research and "wisdom of practice."

The new standards are demanding, and approximately one in five of those schools of education that have agreed to national peer review has been denied accreditation on an initial attempt under these requirements. Most telling, perhaps, is the fact that during the first three years of implementation, almost half of the schools reviewed could not pass the "knowledge-base" standard, which specifies that the school must be able to describe the knowledge base upon which its programs rest. Many schools have made appropriate changes since that time and have been successful in their second attempt at professional accreditation. Many had to secure new resources, make personnel changes, and revamp their courses.

In addition to accreditation, licensing and advanced certification are two other mechanisms that provide quality control in the established professions. Licensing is distinguished from certification in that licensing is a state function that seeks to ensure that practitioners allowed to practice in the state meet minimum standards of competence—that they are "safe" to practice. Certification is a professional function that generally indicates higher standards of accomplishment as determined by a national professional body, such as the National Board of Medical Examiners or the National Architectural Registration Board. In teaching, licensing mechanisms have traditionally been weak, and advanced certification has been non-existent. Recently, though, national efforts have been underway to strengthen both.

The creation of the National Board for Professional Teaching Standards, which is developing a performance-based assessment system to recognize advanced competence among experienced teachers, has promoted discussion of and action on national standards for teachers. Meanwhile, a set of model performance-based licensing standards that are compatible with the National Board's certification standards has been developed by an interstate consortium (INTASC) that is part of the Council for Chief State School Officers. This group is working in collaboration with teacher educators and teachers, state licensing officials, NCATE, and other stakeholders to develop a basis for performance-based standards for teacher licensing.

The Council of Chief State School Officers also adopted a resolution in 1991 to work with NCATE to evolve a common national system of accreditation "in which the predominant emphasis is given to the performance of teachers as well as what they need to know." Since in their respective states it is these individuals who run the system that is the state alternative to NCATE, the resolution is a major development. The general movement in teaching, then, is toward more professionally grounded and performance-based standards for education, licensing, and certification. These trends are analogous to those that have occurred in other professions over the past several decades.

The Rationale for Performance-Based Licensing in the Professions

Most professions have developed fairly complex systems for assessing what entering practitioners know and can do. Their licensing systems are substantially different from the system that has evolved in teaching. Rather than automatically licensing candidates who have graduated from state-approved programs, other professions license candidates based on their having passed a rigorous examination or set of examinations developed by members of the profession through their professional standards boards. (In teaching, examinations have been developed by commercial testing companies or state agencies without the benefit of a formal professional body charged with shaping the nature and content of the examinations.) In order to sit for these examinations, candidates in other professions must have graduated from accredited professional schools. In many cases, they must also have completed a supervised clinical training experience—for example, candidates must complete an internship before they sit for examinations in medicine, architecture, psychology, or engineering (Darling-Hammond, Gendler, and Wise, 1990).

This tripartite system of licensure consisting of education, supervised experience, and examination of knowledge and professional skill provides candidates with the kinds of knowledge and the public with the kinds of assurances no one component alone could offer. The education component ensures that candidates have encountered the broad base of knowledge they will need to draw upon when making decisions in diverse contexts. Experience alone cannot provide this assurance that foundational knowledge will be encountered and understood for future reference. Supervised experience allows candidates to learn the complex art of applying knowledge to specific problems of practice, to make judgments, to weigh and balance competing considerations, to develop skills and put them to use. Examinations provide an assurance that knowledge has been acquired and that a minimum level of performance can be demonstrated by all candidates before they are given permission to practice independently.

These three components of professional licensing are not universally present in teaching. Although most candidates complete a professional preparation program, emergency licensing and alternative licensing make it possible for one to enter teaching without professional education, as tens of thousands of candidates do each year. Furthermore, the extensiveness and quality of state-approved programs are highly variable. Very few teachers encounter a supervised internship. The general induction into teaching is sink or swim— an unsupervised period of first-year teaching by trial and error *after* having received a license. And although tests of basic skills and subject-matter knowledge are given in many states, examinations of professional skill have not yet been developed and made available in teaching.

The reasons most professions invest substantial effort in licensing stem from the need for quality control and for a vehicle that clearly transmits expectations about knowledge to professional preparation programs. We believe these reasons are at least as compelling in education, where failures of knowledge, skill, and commitment affect our society's most vulnerable citizens— children. We next discuss the several goals served by licensing examinations in the professions.

The Profession's Responsibility to the Public. One reason states pay attention to licensing is that professionals deliver services to clients in largely hidden transactions. The client almost inevitably knows less about what the specific services should be than does the service provider. In professional fields, inappropriate services can have dire consequences for clients. And when a member of a profession fails to provide adequate services, it reflects negatively on the other members of that profession. This is one reason that professions insist on quality control.

A major purpose of the professional examination is to determine objectively whether the prospective practitioner has an adequate understanding of professional knowledge and a sufficient ability to appropriately apply that knowledge to practical tasks. It screens out those not able to exhibit this knowledge and ability. It is hoped that a rigorous examination will ensure that members of the profession have at least a minimum level of knowledge needed for serving clients responsibly. This is a first step to establish public trust.

The Nature of Professional Practice. Assurance of practitioner knowledge and skill provides one important basis for quality control in those fields in which complexity requires nonroutine judgments based on an understanding and analysis of many, often competing considerations. Since complex decisions cannot be regulated directly by prescribing standardized practice (which would fail to meet the needs of unstandardized clients), professions seek to ensure that entrants have the knowledge, skills, and dispositions required to make decisions responsibly. The requirement that all entrants pass a licensing examination is one important way in which the state and the profession seek to assure the public that it will receive reasonably safe and effective services.

Graduation from an accredited institution is the first strategy for increasing the probability that new entrants will be well prepared. The established professions maintain a national system of required accreditation; in education, however, states do not require that institutions become accredited. Thus, only about 40 percent of institutions are professionally accredited; the remainder are state approved according to widely differing state standards and processes for evaluation. Unfortunately, state program approval in teaching does not assure minimum competency, because substantial differences exist among states and among schools within states in both their curricula and their admission and grading standards.

In the established professions, the requirement that all applicants take a licensing exam after graduation from a professionally accredited program determines that candidates have acquired at least some of the knowledge and skills needed for practice. In teaching, this assurance is even more sorely needed given the vast differences in the quality of preparation programs.

Influences on Professional Preparation. Licensing examinations can also influence curricula in the schools that prepare professionals. The examinations affect what schools teach and, thus, what students study and learn. Standards, then, focus attention in two directions: They reflect backward to teacher preparation and forward to teaching practice. Internship requirements and examinations are important means by which a profession makes an explicit statement about what is worth knowing and how it should be known and demon-strated. They exert a powerful influence on preparation and practice indepen-dent from cutoff scores or pass rates. By establishing test specifications and standards, practitioners who serve on licensing boards help to assure that new members to a profession develop some of the basic abilities required for practice.

Assessments can be constructed to simulate the complexities of practice in a more integrated fashion than the experiences students might otherwise en-counter in university classrooms. In school, students pass courses one at a time, and testwise students study the areas emphasized by their instructors. This is quite different from the demands of the practice situation, where pro-fessionals must simultaneously draw on a wide array of knowledge and skills and apply them in an integrated fashion to address new problems. If well de-veloped, a licensing examination can come closer to this experience than do many end-of-course tests by requiring applicants to demonstrate proficiency in a range of areas at the same time and without hints as to which facets of a subject will be covered. The licensing exam can, thus, also encourage students to broaden their range of knowledge and skills, such as becoming more adept at identifying problems as they would occur in real life and looking for rela-tionships among areas of knowledge. If the assessment is one with "high fidel-ity" to the actual situations encountered in practice, preparing for the exam can be a valuable educational experience.

A licensing examination also provides an alternative to heavy state regula-tion of the content, structure, and enrollments of professional preparation programs, an approach that has occurred in teaching far more than in other professions (Darling-Hammond and Berry, 1988). Professional schools and faculty welcome the use of licensing examinations with these qualities be-cause, among other things, such tools relieve them of the responsibility (and attendant pressures) of deciding who is qualified to practice; they allow for greater academic freedom than does the alternative strategy of regulating pro-grams directly; and they enable educational institutions to develop special ad-missions programs rather than being externally regulated in their admissions decisions.

Impartial Decisionmaking. Finally, an examination can serve as an impartial decisionmaker. Although tests, like other instruments, reflect values or biases in their judgments about what is worth knowing and how such knowledge is best demonstrated, these can be carefully evaluated to ensure cultural fairness and professional relevance of content. Furthermore, if scoring procedures are well developed and evaluators have been carefully trained and screened, pass-ing will be based on applicant proficiency in the areas tested rather than on extraneous considerations, such as where candidates went to school, whom they know, and their gender, race, ethnicity, or other personal characteristics.

The Limits of Licensing Tests

Some believe teacher testing alone will be sufficient to improve the overall quality of the teaching force either by eliminating incompetence or by encouraging changes in teacher education. Although we acknowledge the powerful role tests can play in articulating standards for professional knowledge and skill and in motivating changes in teacher education, we think the view that testing alone can improve teaching is problematic for two reasons.

First, we believe tests are effective motivators for change only within a larger context of reform. Salaries and working conditions will also affect who enters teaching, as will the conditions of schooling (Darling-Hammond, 1984; Sedlak and Schlossman, 1986). School organizational variables will affect the quality of education as much as will the competence of teachers. And investments in teacher education will influence programs as much as will licensing standards.

Second, the belief that testing alone can change the quality of the teaching force must be based on an assumption that the tests used are good measures of teacher qualities related to effective teaching. Available evidence regarding the worth of existing tests is not convincing. Even with more performance-oriented measures and with approaches that seek to simulate the complex tasks of teaching, however, it is impossible to fully capture in any examination the full range of knowledge, skills, and dispositions that actually comprise performance on any job. Consequently, we propose, as other professions have also, that assessments of actual performance within the context of a structured internship be a component of a licensing system, alongside evaluation of performance in high-quality preparation programs that include liberal arts and professional education.

The overarching question for such a system, more important than its components, however, is its substance: What should teachers know and be able to do? An adequate answer to this question must serve as the foundation of a performance-based licensing system in teaching.

2

What Teachers Need to Know
and Be Able to Do

THE HISTORY OF TEACHING in the United States requires that we address the question "what do teachers need to know and be able to do?" by first answering a prior question: Is there *anything* teachers need to know or be able to do? The view of teaching as semiskilled work requiring little more than basic literacy skills and the ability to follow guidelines encapsulated in texts and curriculum materials is a time-honored one. From popular cartoons illustrating teaching as a simplistic and mind-numbing activity to teacher-proof materials that assume teachers' activities can be easily programmed by directives about what to do when, the image of teaching as requiring little knowledge or skill is widespread.

Policymakers exhibit their ambivalence about whether a knowledge base for teaching exists by regularly enacting loopholes to licensing that require no teacher education. This ambivalence is the most obvious in the long-standing practice of emergency licensure in nearly all states and the recent enactment of alternative routes to teacher certification in more than thirty states. Some of these alternative certification programs require little more than a few weeks of preparation before entry into the classroom, where on-the-job supervision is supposed to occur but rarely does (Darling-Hammond, 1992). In the view of many educators, these alternatives "reflect unbelief in a knowledge base in teaching, . . . a lack of respect for schools of education . . . and mitigate against professional teaching" (Schwartz, 1988, p. 37).

Professional teaching is undermined by alternatives that avoid preparation for teachers because the defining characteristics of a profession are that it is *knowledge-based* and *client-oriented*—that is, committed to using the best available knowledge on behalf of the clients who are served. This commitment cannot be ensured when recruits do not encounter or master professional knowledge. Neither can the third characteristic of a profession be guaranteed:

that it is internally *accountable*—that is, members of the profession take responsibility for defining, transmitting, and enforcing standards of practice based on professional knowledge and ethical commitments (Darling-Hammond, 1989a). Society grants professionals permission to develop their own standards of practice rather than being managed by external regulations that determine practice. This transfer of state authority exists in exchange for assurance that the profession will allow only those who have mastered the knowledge base needed for responsible decisionmaking to practice—that is, to apply their judgment in situations that can have important influences on clients.

The knowledge professionals need in order to make sound decisions is transmitted through professional education and by initiation through supervised clinical practice under the guidance of experts. This process requires that organizations of professionals achieve a consensus about what is worth knowing and how it can best be transmitted and that they then use these judgments as the basis for regulating professional preparation programs and entry standards.

As a consequence of the historical regulation of teaching, this process of codifying knowledge and establishing standards is just beginning. Of course, there is a chicken-and-egg problem that makes this enterprise problematic. Because low standards for entry into teaching have been commonplace, the resulting unevenness in the capacities of teachers has led many to perceive—accurately—that a substantial number of teachers seem unable to make sound judgments about curriculum and teaching methods on their own. As a consequence, prescribed teaching behaviors appear to some to be necessary and warranted. And if the prescribed structures for teaching make it appear mechanical and thoughtless, unexciting and low-skilled in nature, then any need for greater knowledge and skill may seem to have been obviated by the routinized nature of the job. In addition, prospective entrants looking for more intellectually challenging work will be dissuaded from seeking it in the teaching profession. Unless these conditions are changed, it will be difficult to raise standards and maintain a large pool of talented recruits.

Although the interaction of low standards with a deskilled role for teachers has slowed progress toward standard setting, the heightened demands of schooling as we enter a new social era are clearly changing both the expectations for teachers and the requirements for teacher preparation. As reformers have stressed the need for more students to be better prepared for critical thinking and advanced disciplinary inquiry, they have also emphasized the need for teachers who possess these characteristics and who can do more than march students through textbooks, who can educate students for inquiry and invention and can reach students traditionally left behind.

At the same time, the complexity of teaching and learning has been illuminated by educational research over the past two decades. We now know that students have different learning styles and rates of development, that psychological factors—such as perceptions of self-efficacy—influence motivation and learning, and that prior experiences and learnings mediate the processing of information presented in formal instruction. In short, we know that students do not come to school as tabula rasae to be imprinted with well-defined bits of knowledge that inescapably adds up to "good education." We also know that there is no simple set of easily prescribed teaching behaviors that invariably add up to teaching effectiveness. "Effective" teaching behaviors vary for different subject areas and grade levels, for students at different developmental stages and with different cognitive and psychological characteristics, and—most important, perhaps—for different learning outcomes. The concept of teacher effectiveness is not only defined by the teaching context; it is also defined by the goals of instruction (Darling-Hammond and Hudson, 1988). As the goals of education change from the acquisition of basic skills and facts to the development of higher-order thinking and performance skills, society's conceptions of what teachers need to know and be able to do must change as well.

Teaching is an intense activity. Teachers must simultaneously juggle subject matter; the lesson's underlying cognitive, social, and affective goals; the management of time, materials, and equipment; and the needs and responses of individual students. They must be aware of how students are working and be alert to signs of misunderstanding or confusion while seizing the "teachable moment" for pursuing a key point when students are ready to grasp it. They must skillfully manage transitions among activities so as not to lose students' attention and momentum. They must attend to health and safety concerns as well as cognitive ones, understanding home and family circumstances to create appropriate classroom conditions for learning.

In addition to structuring encounters with important ideas and useful tasks, good teachers cheer up children who are discouraged, rechannel the energies of those who are aimless or nonproductive, and challenge those who are bored. They listen to students to understand what the students know and think, evaluate papers and performances, give assignments that move students forward, and provide feedback that offers constructive information and direction. They must be well organized and able to concentrate to keep all of these balls in the air at once, yet their structures must be permeable, allowing them to maintain an openness to unexpected events, problems, and opportunities.

Teachers make at least ten nontrivial decisions an hour (Berliner, 1984). Is this an appropriate question to ask Johnny? Is Susan ready to learn about paragraphing? How can I find yet another way to convey the concept of photosynthesis in a way that breaks through the students' misconceptions? Will correcting Ellen's spelling at this point discourage her from writing? How can I find out why Joe has been so withdrawn and disconnected lately? These decisions are made in the course of at least fifteen hundred interactions each day with groups of twenty-five to thirty students in a class (Berliner, 1984). And beyond all of these describable complexities of teaching is the artistry that resists codification. As Max van Manen (1984) noted in "Reflections on Teacher Experience and Pedagogic Competence":

> Teacher competence does not consist of some systematic set of teaching skills and classroom management techniques which once mastered take the mystery out of teaching children. Teacher competence is that which a teacher resorts to when he or she tactfully converts just any kind of experience to a true learning experience, and in so "doing," he or she restores the mystery of "being" a teacher (p. 147)

It is no wonder that teachers have some difficulty articulating what it is they do in a way that can be easily communicated to a lay public.

Nonetheless, answers to the questions of what teachers should know and be able to do in order to create these kinds of experiences and make sound teaching decisions are closer now than they have been in the past, partly because of a growth of knowledge derived from research on teaching and learning and partly because of changes in the governance of the teaching profession. These latter changes have enabled a consensus about teaching knowledge to be crafted by newly formed and recently strengthened professional bodies charged with defining and transmitting standards.

In this chapter we discuss both the substance of a growing consensus about teaching knowledge and the processes by which that consensus is being forged and transmitted.

The Knowledge Base for Teaching

Although legislative policies have often presumed that little special knowledge is needed for successful teaching, the weight of research over the past twenty years indicates that—even given the wide range of quality in schools of education—teachers who have completed a full preparation program for licensure are in fact more highly rated and successful with students than are teachers without full preparation (Evertson, Hawley, and Zlotnik, 1985; Ashton and Crocker, 1986, 1987; Greenberg, 1983; Haberman, 1984; Olsen, 1985). As Evertson and colleagues concluded in their research review:

> The available research suggests that among students who become teachers, those enrolled in formal preservice preparation programs are more likely to be effective than those who do not have such training. Moreover, almost all well planned and executed efforts within teacher preparation programs to teach students specific knowledge or skills seem to succeed, at least in the short run. (Evertson, Hawley, and Zlotnik, 1985, p. 8)

The importance for teacher effectiveness of preparation in both education and subject-matter courses shows up strongly in a number of specific fields that have been studied, including science (for a review see Druva and Anderson, 1983; see also Davis, 1964; Perkes, 1967–1968; Taylor, 1957); mathematics, where mathematics methods courses are particularly important (Begle, 1979; Begle and Geeslin, 1972); and vocational education (Erekson and Barr, 1985). At the elementary level, teachers' education training is related to ratings of instructional effectiveness, as well as to student achievement and interest on a wide range of tasks (LuPone, 1961; McNeil, 1974). Teachers' background in reading methods courses is positively related to students' reading achievement (Hice, 1970). And the single most important feature of early childhood programs with long-term positive effects on student performance is the extent of preparation the programs' teachers have received (Roupp et al., 1979).

The effects of teacher preparation are particularly noticeable when achievement is measured on higher-order tasks such as students' abilities to apply and interpret scientific concepts (Perkes, 1967–1968) or other higher-order thinking skills (Hansen, 1988). Given current school reforms aimed at more adaptive teaching focused more on critical thinking skills, it is important to understand how teacher preparation appears to have these positive influences on teachers' sensitivity to diverse student needs and on their ability to teach in a style conducive to higher-order learning. These influences may result partly from the fact that as prospective teachers progress through their professional education courses, they become increasingly student-centered in their attitudes and more aware of methods that support students' development and independent and critical thinking (Skipper and Quantz, 1987).

Furthermore, it seems that appropriate preparation in planning and classroom management is one of the factors that allows teachers to focus on the kind of complex teaching that is needed to develop higher-order skills. Since the novel tasks required for complex problem solving are more difficult to manage than the routine tasks associated with learning simple skills, lack of management ability can lead teachers to reduce curriculum demands in order to more easily control student work (Carter and Doyle, 1987; Doyle, 1986).

How Preparation Makes a Difference

Other studies illuminate these findings by pointing out the differences in the perceptions and practices of teachers with differing amounts and kinds of preparation. A number of studies have suggested that the typical problems of beginning teachers are lessened for those who have had adequate preparation prior to entry (Adams, Hutchinson, and Martray, 1980; Glassberg, 1980; Taylor and Dale, 1971).

Studies of teachers admitted through quick-entry alternate routes have frequently noted that the candidates have difficulty with curriculum development, pedagogical content knowledge, attending to students' differing learning styles and levels, classroom management, and student motivation (Lenk, 1989; Feiman-Nemser and Parker, 1990; Grossman, 1989, 1990; Mitchell, 1987).

Novice teachers without full training show more ignorance about student needs and differences and about the basics of teaching than do trained beginners (Rottenberg and Berliner, 1990).

A number of studies have found that in comparison to beginners who have completed a teacher education program, teachers who enter teaching without preparation are less sensitive to students, less able to plan and redirect instruction to meet students' needs (and less aware of the need to do so), and less skilled in implementing instruction (Rottenberg and Berliner, 1990; Bents and Bents, 1990; Grossman, 1988; Bledsoe, Cox, and Burnham, 1967; Copley, 1974). They are less able to anticipate students' knowledge and potential difficulties and less likely to see it as their job to do so, often blaming the students if their teaching is not successful. As Pamela Grossman (1989, p. 205) put it: "Without formal systems for induction into teaching, learning to teach is left largely to chance. Although much pedagogical knowledge has been characterized as common sense, knowledge is not hanging, ripe and fully formed, in the classroom, waiting to be plucked by inexperienced teachers."

The teacher who gives up on a child who has not learned an important skill or concept is a teacher who does not know what the child does not know. A teacher who does not understand the ways in which different children learn differently, who does not have a sense of the scaffolding of a field of knowledge or how to evaluate students' prior knowledge, and who does not have a wide repertoire of alternative representations, explanations, and modes of teaching is not going to be equipped to help all children learn. Research on cognition, learning, and subject-matter pedagogy has made strong advances that provide insights in each of these areas.

An unprepared teacher is likely to teach in the way he or she was taught. When a powerful teacher education process does not intervene, new knowledge does not have an opportunity to transform teaching across generations. Yet prospective teachers cannot profit from these insights if they have no opportunity to encounter them. As Mary Kennedy (1991b) explained:

> The improvement-of-practice problem boils down to this: if we know that teachers are highly likely to teach as they were taught and if we are not satisfied with the way they were taught, then how can we help them develop different teaching strategies? And how can we create schools and policies that will support the use of these policies?
>
> How serious is the improvement-of-practice problem? I judge it to be very serious. We are caught in a vicious circle of mediocre practice modeled after mediocre practice, of trivialized knowledge begetting more trivialized knowledge. Unless we find a way out of this circle, we will continue re-creating generations of teachers who re-create generations of students who are not prepared for the technological society we are becoming. (p. 662)

The problems of practicing without a strong teacher education intervention were reflected in a study of the performance of alternate-route candidates in Dallas (Gomez and Grobe, 1990). Although on average these candidates were rated about as well as traditional education candidates on some aspects of teaching, they were rated lower on such factors as their knowledge of instructional techniques and ability to use different instructional models. The performance of alternate-route candidates was also much more uneven than that of trained teachers, with a much greater proportion—from two to sixteen times as many—likely to be rated "poor" on each of the teaching factors evaluated. The proportions of alternate-route candidates rated "poor" ranged from 8 percent on reading instruction to 17 percent on classroom management, whereas fewer than 2 percent of trained beginners typically received "poor" ratings on any of the factors. The effects of this unevenness showed up most strongly on students' achievement in language arts, where the achievement gains of students of alternate-route teachers were significantly lower than those of students of traditionally trained teachers.

Perhaps it is not surprising that alternate-route teachers from short-term programs often experience less job satisfaction than do fully certified beginning teachers (Sciacca, 1987; Lutz and Hutton, 1989) or that they report less satisfaction with their preparation and less commitment to remaining in teaching than do other recruits (Darling-Hammond, Hudson, and Kirby, 1989; see also, regarding attrition, Lutz and Hutton, 1989; Roth, 1986, p. 5). Problems resulting from inadequate preparation headed the list of complaints of the 20 percent of Los Angeles alternate-route candidates who quit before they completed their programs in 1984 and 1985, as well as many of those who remained but voiced dissatisfaction (Wright, McKibbon, and Walton, 1987).

What Kinds of Preparation Matter

Traditionally, teacher preparation programs have been structured around a presumption that teachers need some grounding in the disciplines they will teach, in specialized education courses focused on teaching, learning, and child development, and in a supervised practice experience such as student teaching. Recent policies seeking to change teacher education and licensing have differed in the extent to which they accept these presumptions. The various policies represent differing beliefs about what teachers need to know in order to be effective.

Alternative certification programs often presume that education courses and student teaching are unnecessary, although they may require a bachelor's degree in the subject to be taught. For those routes that incorporate only brief preliminary training, the basic assumption is that subject-matter preparation is the most crucial foundation for good teaching; with modest initial guidance, it is felt that teachers will learn pedagogical skills on the job. Most of the fast-track routes postulate supervision for their already-hired beginning teachers, thus implicitly acknowledging the desirability of professional guidance for this clinical learning. However, a number of studies have found that this supervision does not often materialize for alternate-route trainees (Darling-Hammond, 1992). School districts are generally not financed or structured to provide time and opportunity for expert professionals to assume responsible supervision.

During the 1980s, a few states—Virginia, Texas, and New Jersey—sought to increase time for subject-matter preparation at the undergraduate level by limiting the number of education courses a student could take, typically to no more than eighteen credits. These approaches assumed that whereas disciplinary preparation might be important for good teaching, specific preparation regarding how to teach is not.

In other states, such as New York, Connecticut, Oregon, and Wisconsin, both disciplinary background and education preparation have been extended by requiring a bachelor's degree in a discipline plus the equivalent of a fifth year of education training or a master's degree that includes pedagogical preparation. These programs include a fairly substantial amount of study in educational foundations (child development, learning theory, and similar areas) and teaching methods, alongside an intensively supervised internship or student teaching experience. They assume that teachers need to know a great deal about learners and learning as well as subject-specific pedagogy in order to be able to teach effectively. They share a belief that clinical learning opportunities are important for prospective teachers, and they incorporate supervised clinical training into their preservice programs rather than assuming that such opportunities will materialize after the teacher has begun full-time teaching.

These differing assumptions suggest that, ultimately, the design of teacher licensing systems should rest on answers to two related questions: What kinds of knowledge and training play important roles in the development of teachers' skills and abilities, and how are these best acquired? Although definitive answers to the second question are not yet available, research on teaching and teacher effectiveness has provided many clues about how subject-matter preparation, pedagogical preparation, and opportunities for supervised practice influence teacher abilities.

The Influence of Subject-Matter Courses. Subject-matter knowledge appears to make a difference in teaching, at least up to a certain point. Byrne's (1983) summary of thirty studies found seventeen showing a positive, although not always statistically significant, relationship between teachers' subject knowledge and student achievement. Of the studies they reviewed, Ashton and Crocker (1987) found only about a third suggesting a positive relationship between these two variables. Other reviews have found inconsistent (sometimes even inverse) relationships between teachers' subject-matter knowledge as measured by the National Teacher Examinations and ratings of teacher performance (Andrews, Blackmon, and Mackey, 1980; Ayers and Qualls, 1979; Quirk, Witten, and Weinberg, 1973).

These results are likely mixed because subject-matter knowledge is a positive influence up to some level of basic competence and familiarity with the subject but is less important thereafter. For example, evidence exists that out-of-field assignment of teachers has negative effects on student achievement in mathematics (Hawk, Coble, and Swanson, 1985). When teachers with backgrounds in mathematics were compared to teachers with backgrounds in other subjects who had been assigned to teach mathematics, the lack of subject-matter competence resulted in reduced teacher effectiveness.

However, beyond some point, more subject-matter courses do not seem to make a difference. As Begle and Geeslin (1972) found, the absolute number of course credits in mathematics is not linearly related to teaching quality for mathematics teachers. And as McDiarmid, Ball, and Anderson's (1989, p. 17) review noted: "While obviously essential, a flexible understanding of subject-matter is not enough for beginning teachers. They also need to know about learners . . . and the learning process."

Furthermore, McDiarmid's (1989) review of what college students learn in their liberal arts courses confirmed that the pedagogical shortcomings of most postsecondary teaching do not supply students with useful models of active learning to apply to their own teaching. The image of the renowned university professor who knows much about his or her subject but cannot explain it to students is widely held. To know is not necessarily to be able to teach. Thus, we must be concerned with how to make the knowledge of the teacher serve the needs of the learner.

The Influence of Education Courses. A large number of studies have found positive relationships between education coursework and teacher performance in the classroom. These relationships are stronger and more consistent than those between subject-matter knowledge and classroom performance (for reviews, see Ashton and Crocker, 1987; Guyton and Farokhi, 1987). Denton and Lacina (1984) found a positive relationship between the amount of professional coursework taken by teachers and their teaching performance, including their students' achievement. Specific kinds of teacher education have also been found to produce positive effects on the later performance of teachers and their students (for reviews, see, e.g., Evertson, Hawley, and Zlotnik, 1985; Good, 1983; Butcher, 1981; Gage and Winne, 1975).

Two recent studies of midcareer and other nontraditional recruits to teaching found that their strongest recommendation was for a heavier dose of subject-specific teaching methods, including pedagogical guidance combined with more information about child and adolescent motivation, development, and cognition (Darling-Hammond, Hudson, and Kirby, 1989; Coley and Thorpe, 1985). These findings are not surprising in light of recent research suggesting the importance of subject-specific pedagogy to teacher effectiveness, particularly as it intersects with knowledge about students (Shulman, 1986; Wilson, Shulman, and Richert, 1987; see also Kennedy, 1990).

Knowledge about how to teach particular subjects has its intellectual roots in research on cognitive processes. Subject-specific pedagogy goes beyond this foundation, however. Solid understandings about how to teach reading are built on knowledge about how readers form conceptions, interact with text, and make sense of new information, words, and ideas (Anderson et al., 1984). Knowledge about mathematics teaching is built on understandings of how students develop mathematical reasoning and how they construct number concepts that they can later apply in various operations (Romberg and Carpenter, 1985). Knowledge about science teaching rests on an understanding of the misconceptions students typically hold about natural phenomena as well as on an appreciation for the structure of scientific knowledge that enables scaffolding of ideas and guidance of student inquiry (Anderson, 1991; Carey, 1986). These understandings are then joined to knowledge about teaching materials and resources that enable theoretical knowledge to come alive in purposeful, content-rich teaching and learning.

A number of capabilities and dispositions that are related to education preparation are also important to teacher performance. Research on teachers' attitudes and dispositions has found that flexibility (alternatively labeled *adaptability* or *creativity*) increases teacher effectiveness (Darling-Hammond, Wise, and Pease, 1983; Walberg and Waxman, 1983; Schalock, 1979). This finding is consistent with other research on effective teaching (discussed in the section "Characterizing Teaching Knowledge"), which suggests that an effective teacher is one who molds and adjusts his or her teaching to fit the demands of each student, topic, instructional method, and teaching goal. Given the multidimensionality, simultaneity, and immediacy of classroom events, it is not surprising that teachers who are flexible, adaptable, and creative are more effective in producing positive student learning outcomes. Studies of the development of expertise have indicated that flexibility increases as a function of both experience and preparation (Berliner, 1987, 1992; Rottenberg and Berliner, 1990; Bents and Bents, 1990).

Teachers' attitudes—specifically, their feelings of efficacy or beliefs in their ability to help students learn—have also been found to be strongly and consistently related to teacher performance and student outcomes (Berman and McLaughlin, 1977; Armor et al., 1976; Brookover, 1977; Rutter et al., 1979). Teachers who believe they can help their students achieve are more effective than teachers who are less certain of their influence. Rosenholtz (1989) demonstrated that teacher learning opportunities have important effects on teachers' sense of self-efficacy and certainty regarding their knowledge and capacity to be effective. Several studies have suggested that professional preparation enhances both teachers' sense of efficacy—their responsibility for and capacity to ensure that students learn—and their ability to respond flexibly to student needs (Grossman, 1988, 1989; Rottenberg and Berliner, 1990).

Efficacy also appears to influence teacher satisfaction and teachers' more generalized feelings about their work (Rosenholtz, 1989). In fact, teachers who lack confidence in their teaching skills have higher rates of absenteeism and attrition (Chapman, 1984; Litt and Turk, 1983). Teachers' educational background and preparation appear closely related to their confidence in their ability to teach effectively.

Thus, the interactions between teachers' preparation and what their students later experience and learn are many and complex. Based on a review of eighty-three studies from nine countries, Veenman (1984) concluded that given the common experiences of beginning teachers, programs that emphasize subject-matter training at the expense of professional education courses are not warranted.

The Influence of Guided Clinical Experience. A third component of teacher preparation is "clinical" learning: the application of knowledge about teaching in the complex, real world of classrooms. Teachers traditionally cite their supervised student teaching experience as a key element of their preparation. Although many applied skills must ultimately be learned in practice, it is clear that unsupervised on-the-job experience is, in and of itself, insufficient to support teacher learning and teacher effectiveness, as it can lead as frequently to the adoption of regressive and ineffective methods as to the acquisition of appropriate strategies (Darling-Hammond, Gendler, and Wise, 1990; Grossman, 1989; Hawley and Rosenholtz, 1984; McDonald, 1980; Ryan, 1980; NIE, 1979).

The importance of guidance in learning to teach has been confirmed by studies showing that induction support for entering teachers improves the quality of their teaching (Huling-Austin and Murphy, 1987). Beginning teachers who receive such support move more quickly from concerns about discipline and basic classroom management to concerns about instruction and student progress (Odell, 1986). Virtually all studies of alternate-routes to teacher education have noted the vital importance of high-quality, intensive supervision and related clinical learning opportunities to candidates' success and the problems that occur when such support is absent (see, e.g., Adelman, 1986; Wright, McKibbon, and Walton, 1987; Darling-Hammond, Hudson, and Kirby, 1989).

Interestingly, a state evaluation of the Los Angeles alternative certification program compared several different kinds of teaching recruits, including one group of alternate-route entrants who decided to enroll in regular university teacher education programs rather than the short alternate-route summer program while still receiving state-funded mentor support. This group far outscored any of the other recruits on every criterion of classroom effectiveness, suggesting the cumulative power of adding adequate preservice preparation to intensive on-the-job supervision (Wright, McKibbon, and Walton, 1987, p. 124).

Summary. In sum, research on teacher knowledge and preparation indicates that teacher education makes a difference in teaching effectiveness. Most research indicates that students taught by fully prepared teachers learn more than students taught by teachers who are not prepared. The extent of teacher preparation is especially important in determining the effectiveness of teachers in "school-based" subjects, such as mathematics, science, and early reading, as well as the use of teaching strategies that encourage higher-order learning and respond to students' needs and learning styles.

Furthermore, some kinds of preparation appear to make more difference than others. Standard knowledge of subject-matter is important up to a point: For example, out-of-field teachers are less effective than teachers who have been prepared to teach a given subject. However, past the level of basic subject-area preparation, most studies find that greater preparation in child development, learning theory, curriculum development, and teaching methods has a stronger influence on teacher effectiveness than does additional subject-matter preparation. In addition, intensive clinical guidance in learning to teach is extremely important to the effectiveness of beginning teachers. These findings suggest a structure for teacher licensing that includes all three components of preparation as a prerequisite for permission to practice.

Characterizing Teaching Knowledge

Given that there do appear to be areas of study and kinds of learning that contribute to teacher effectiveness, the next question is what it is that teachers understand and can do as a consequence of these experiences that ultimately makes a difference for their students. There are at least two levels to the debate about teacher knowledge and its assessment. In addition to the question of whether any body of knowledge exists that undergirds teaching, there are also disagreements about what that knowledge is and how it should be demonstrated. The disagreements have stemmed from competing conceptions of "effective" teaching and from attempts to overgeneralize research results to circumstances to which they do not apply or to reduce specific research findings to unvarying prescriptions for teacher behavior.

Early efforts to link specific teacher characteristics or teaching behaviors to student outcomes sought context-free generalizations about what leads to or constitutes effective teaching. Specific teacher behaviors were tallied in classrooms and correlated with student achievement test scores in search of the specific set of "research-based" behaviors that could be prescribed to ensure student learning. Although process-product research of this kind produced useful data suggesting that what teachers do in classrooms does affect students (see, e.g., Medley, 1979; Rosenshine and Furst, 1971; Stallings, 1977), the findings do not hold up across diverse situations, indicating that the effectiveness of particular teachers' actions varies under different circumstances (see, e.g., Doyle, 1978; Dunkin and Biddle, 1974; Shavelson and Dempsey-Atwood, 1976).

The most extensive process-product study of teacher effectiveness, the Beginning Teacher Evaluation Study conducted for California's Commission for Teacher Preparation and Licensing, demonstrated that the search for a generic set of teaching behaviors consistently associated with student achievement gains was futile. After that monumental effort, "The researchers . . . concluded that linking precise and specific teacher behavior to precise and specific learning of pupils [the original goal of the inquiry] is not possible at this time. . . . These findings suggest that the legal requirement for a license probably cannot be well stated in precise behavioral terms" (Bush, 1979, p. 15; see also McDonald and Elias, 1976).

Researchers then sought to identify the particular conditions under which specific behaviors would prove effective. Research on aptitude-treatment interactions looked at how certain teaching behaviors might be more or less effective with different types of students. This line of research suggested that effective teaching behaviors vary for students with different socioeconomic and psychological characteristics (e.g., Brophy and Evertson, 1974, 1977; Cronbach and Snow, 1977; Peterson, 1976) and for different grade levels and subject areas (Gage, 1978; McDonald and Elias, 1976). However, as Cronbach (1975) discovered, the interaction effects that may be identified from teaching research are not confined to easily translatable two-way or even three-way interactions. The number of contextual considerations teachers must take into account is far more than a single "ability" dimension of a group of students or a particular grade level. Thus, although these findings help frame important teaching principles, they cannot be used to establish specific unvarying rules of practice (Cronbach, 1975; Knapp, 1982; Shavelson, 1973).

A related finding is that teaching behaviors that have sometimes been found to be effective often bear a distinctly curvilinear relation to achievement. A behavior that is effective when used in moderation can produce significant and negative results when used too much (Peterson and Kauchak, 1982; Soar, 1972) or when applied in the wrong circumstances (see, e.g., Coker, Medley, and Soar, 1980; McDonald and Elias, 1976). This kind of finding also makes it difficult to develop rules for teaching behaviors that can be applied generally.

As research on teacher effectiveness has become more conceptually and methodologically sophisticated, researchers have come to acknowledge that the educational environment is complex and variable and that generalized rules for teacher behavior cannot replace the need for sophisticated teacher knowledge and professional judgment. Research on nonteaching variables in the educational environment has indicated that many factors other than teaching behaviors have profound effects on student learning (Centra and Potter, 1980; Anderson, 1982; McKenna, 1981) and that effective teaching must be responsive to a number of student, classroom, and school variables in ways that preclude the application of predetermined approaches to teaching (Joyce and Weil, 1972).

Researchers who have adopted an ecological perspective for investigating teaching have also pointed out that teaching and learning are characterized by reciprocal causality—what the teacher does depends on what students do, and vice versa, in a continuous set of interactions that cannot be predetermined given the variability of human behavior and experience. This reality also limits the applicability of process-product research findings. Research grounded in this perspective has found that what students do affects teachers' behaviors and that the complexity of classroom life calls for teaching strategies responsive to environmental demands. As Walter Doyle (1979) noted:

> Traditionally, research on teaching has been viewed as a process of isolating a set of effective teaching practices to be used by individual teachers to improve student learning or by policy makers to design teacher education and teacher evaluation programs. The emphasis in this tradition has been on predicting which methods or teacher behaviors have the highest general success rate, and much of the controversy over the productivity of research on teaching has centered on the legitimacy of propositions derived from available studies. . . . [The ecological approach] would seem to call into question the very possibility of achieving a substantial number of highly generalizable statements about teaching effectiveness. (pp. 203–204)

Research on the stability and generalizability of measures of teaching behaviors lends support to a context-specific view of teaching. Stability refers to the extent that a teacher's behavior as measured at one point in time correlates with measures taken at another point in time. Generalizability refers to the extent that such measures are stable across different teaching situations (e.g., different subject areas, grade levels, student ability levels). The bottom-line question is: Does a given teacher exhibit the same kinds of behavior at different points in time and within different teaching contexts? In general, the answer is no, especially with regard to low-inference measures of specific, discrete teaching behaviors (Shavelson and Dempsey-Atwood, 1976). In fact, the more knowledgeable a teacher is, the more we would expect his or her teaching to be responsive to the many considerations of subject, learners, goals, and purposes that combine to produce different judgments.

In his *Sources of a Science of Education,* John Dewey (1929) put it this way:

> Command of scientific methods and systematized subject-matter liberates individuals; it enables them to see new problems, devise new procedures, and, in general, makes for diversification rather than for set uniformity (p. 12). . . . This knowledge and understanding render [the teacher's] practice more intelligent, more flexible and better adapted to deal effectively with concrete phenomena of practice. . . . Seeing more relations, he sees more possibilities, more opportunities. His ability to judge being enriched, he has a wider range of alternatives to select from in dealing with individual situations. (pp. 20–21)

Thus, as we describe more fully in the section "Research on Teaching," we believe the large body of research on teaching supports a conception of teaching that is:

- Based on the integration of many areas of knowledge. These areas comprise three major domains—knowledge about learners and learning; knowledge about curriculum and teaching, and knowledge about society and social contexts of education.
- Characterized by the use of multiple skills, appropriately applied to particular situations, rather than by the unvarying exhibition of uniform teaching behaviors in all teaching circumstances.
- Context-dependent. The uses of knowledge and the applications of skills depend on the needs of particular students and classes as defined by instructional goals; on pedagogical demands associated with the subject-matter, instructional objectives, stages of student development, and previous learning; and on characteristics of the students individually and as a class group (cognitive styles, social and cultural attributes, social organization of the school and classroom, and similar traits).

As a consequence, our approach to building assessments of teachers' skills is based on evaluating how well prospective teachers can apply knowledge of learning, teaching, and the social context of education to the tasks of teaching—planning, instruction, diagnosis of student needs and assessment of learning, and classroom management—within the contexts of subject matter and students. We assume they must evaluate information about students' prior knowledge, approaches to learning, and interests, along with concerns for instructional goals and the classroom-school-community setting as they form judgments about appropriate courses of action.

Research on Teaching

Current research supports this view of teaching as relying on many sources of knowledge that must be applied in nonroutine circumstances demanding contextualized performance (Brophy and Evertson, 1976; Doyle, 1978; Darling-Hammond, Wise, and Pease, 1983; Good and Brophy, 1986). Studies of expertise in teaching have demonstrated that knowledge is quite contextualized and that a major aspect of expert performance is the teacher's knowledge of students in terms of their cognitive abilities and their personal styles and characteristics (Berliner, 1992; Berliner et al., 1988; Leinhardt, 1988). When planning instruction, expert teachers ask many more questions about the teaching context than do novices, taking into account the abilities, experiences, and backgrounds of the students they will teach, as well as the environment within which they will be teaching (Housner and Griffey, 1985.) Their expertise rests on their ability to create this kind of situated knowledge, a "contextually developed knowledge that is accessed and used in a way that tends to make use of characteristic features of the environment as solution tools" (Leinhardt, 1988,

p. 146). This knowledge, along with the development of relationships with students over time, enables skilled teachers to develop learning opportunities that are academically and interpersonally effective with specific groups of students (Berliner, 1992).

Studies of how teachers develop and use this "personal practical knowledge" of students and classroom situations have revealed that they reflect on classroom experiences, building a store of contextual information to use as a lens by which to interpret events and applications of other knowledge. They connect their knowledge of individual students to research-based knowledge of learning, development, and curriculum, or *pedagogical content knowledge* (Carter, 1986; Elbaz, 1983; Grossman, 1990; Grimmett and Mackinnon, 1992). As Elbaz (1983) explained:

> [Practical knowledge] encompasses first hand experience of students' learning styles, interests, needs, strengths and difficulties, and a repertoire of instructional techniques and classroom management skills. The teacher knows the social structure of the school and what it requires, of teacher and student, for survival and success; she knows the community of which the school is part, and has a sense of what it will and will not accept. This experiential knowledge is informed by the teacher's theoretical knowledge of subject matter, and of areas such as child development, learning and social theory. (p. 5)

Expert teachers also teach reciprocally, taking into account their students' responses to a lesson or series of lessons as learning unfolds. They are much more likely to implement changes in their instruction in response to social cues and evidence of student needs than are less skilled teachers (Berliner, 1992; Housner and Griffey, 1985; Hawkins and Sharpe, forthcoming). Their flexibility enables them to connect more profoundly with students and their thinking. As one expert teacher described it: "A lot of times I just put the objective in my book, and I play off the kids. . . . I sort of do a little and then they do a little. And then I do a little and they do a little. But my reaction is just that, it's a reaction. And it depends upon their action what my reaction's going to be (Borko and Livingson, 1988, quoted in Berliner, 1992, pp. 47–48)."

Finally, expert teachers are able to diagnose student needs in a multidimensional rather than a stereotypical way and can plan specific strategies to address those needs appropriately. They can construct complex representations of teaching problems, including analyses of students, situations, and subject-matter goals, and can give justifications for their teaching decisions grounded in these analyses (Peterson and Comeaux, 1987; Nelson, 1988; Berliner, 1992). Such analyses rely on constructs about curriculum and children that take many variables into account simultaneously and allow for continual revision based on new information (Bussis, Chittenden, and Amarel, 1976, p. 17).

This capacity to look at classroom events empirically and analytically is critical to the process of effective teaching. It allows teachers to continually un-

cover relevant characteristics of a situation, link them to a personal and theoretical knowledge base, and test and evaluate courses of action. As Chittenden,
Bussis, and Amarel (1976) explained:

> Translating an idea into action and experiencing its consequences counts for much
> more [than simply having a new idea] and constitutes the basis of personal (as op-
> posed to "academic") knowledge and learning. . . . If significant change is to occur, it
> requires a quality of experience that supports personal exploration, experimentation,
> and reflection. (p. 17)

The process of using knowledge and creating new knowledge through evaluation, observation, testing, and reflection on contexts and practices recalls
Shulman's (1987) model of "pedagogical reasoning," which posited a framework for teacher thinking involving comprehension, transformation, instruction, evaluation, reflection, and new comprehension. Others have pointed to
the importance of teacher reflection for engaging in social critiques of educational goals, structures, and outcomes and for evaluating the relationships between the technical and normative decisions made in teaching (Valli and Tom,
1988; Liston and Zeichner, 1987).

To be constructive, though, teacher reflection must be informed by knowledge about learning and pedagogy and grounded in instructional purposes
and concerns for the effects of one's actions on learners. The capacity to reflect in an informed and thoughtful manner is critical to the transformation of
complex knowledge into action and to the development of further knowledge
based on practice. A conception of teachers as thinking persons drawing on
many abilities, areas of understanding, and skills in exercising judgment un-
derlies all of the major professional standard-setting efforts now emerging.
Understanding the ways in which practice and reflection create the bonds between knowledge and action also suggests the importance of a structured
internship that helps teachers learn how to analyze contexts and reflect on
practice.

Sources of Knowledge About Teaching

The kind of knowledgeable and skillful teaching we have described does not
draw all of its necessary understandings solely from formal research on teaching. Shulman (1987; also Shulman and Sykes, 1986) defined at least four major
sources of teaching knowledge.

1. Scholarship in content disciplines, including knowledge of the subject
   areas being taught, research about the content area, and an understanding of the structure of the subject matter, its conceptual organization, and principles of inquiry in that domain
2. Educational materials and structures, including curriculum and
   teaching materials, tests and other assessment strategies, institutional

and governmental rules governing schooling, and other tools of the trade or contextual features teachers must manipulate in their work

3. Educational research and scholarship, including research on schooling, social organizations, human learning, diversity, development, cognitive psychology, teaching, and the effects of explicit strategies or environmental factors on learning, as well as scholarship in the areas of educational foundations

4. Wisdom of practice, including the codified and yet-to-be-codified maxims and understandings that guide the practices of able teachers and are represented in expert judgment as well as in case literature

Although the first three sources of knowledge are the most highly developed, this fourth category of knowledge about teaching has recently received a great deal of attention. Particularly because of the situated nature of teacher decisionmaking, a number of researchers have stressed the importance of case knowledge. Doyle (1990) suggested that cases in teaching are important "not simply because they convey the complexity of classroom life, but also because they are probably the form in which teachers' meanings are stored, conveyed, and brought to bear on novel instances in problem solving. . . . Such knowledge is richly imbued with the specifics of the contexts in which teaching occurs. It is case knowledge that empowers teachers to interpret situations and create solutions to classroom problems" (p. 356).

Increasingly, investigations into teaching knowledge have been conducted as extended cases or narratives inquiring into teachers' work and decisions (Bussis et al., 1976; Carter, 1992; Clandinin, 1986; Elbaz, 1983; Goldenberg and Gallimore, 1991; Grossman, 1990; Hollingsworth, Dybdahl, and Minarik, 1993). Shulman (1992) argued that a pedagogy of cases is particularly suited to teaching, because both are instances of transformation:

> Teaching is a form of transformation, in which teachers create representations of complex ideas that connect with the constructions of their students. Case methods are a particular strategy of pedagogical transformation—a strategy for transforming more propositional forms of knowledge into narratives that motivate and educate. If, however, the knowledge base and reasoning processes of teaching (or law, medicine, or other practical domain) are themselves case-based, then the use of case methods does not require a very elaborate transformation. . . . The field is itself a body of cases linked loosely by working principles, and case methods are the most valid way of representing that structure in teaching. (p. 17)

As we will see, the articulation of standards for teaching and the nature of tasks represented in emerging performance assessments both rely extensively on the idea of the richly described case that incorporates context and draws on the teacher's capacity to transform knowledge into decisions in distinctive situations.

It is increasingly clear that many forms of scholarship and inquiry contribute to the knowledge base. These different sources of knowledge are the well-springs for many types of understanding that must be used in combination when teaching decisions are made. This point was elaborated by Wilson, Shulman, and Richert (1987) with respect to one area of decisionmaking—teachers' decisions about subject-matter content:

> Teachers draw upon many types of knowledge when they are making decisions about the content of their courses. Teachers use their *content knowledge*—their understanding of the facts or concepts within a domain—as well as their grasp of the structures of the subject matter. Teachers must have knowledge of the substantive structures—the ways in which the fundamental principles of a discipline are organized. In addition, they must have knowledge of the syntactic structure of a discipline—the canons of evidence and proof that guide inquiry in the field. Teachers' *knowledge of educational aims, goals, and purposes* also contributes to pedagogical decisions. Frequently teachers use their knowledge of other content that is not within the scope of the discipline they are teaching. Teachers use *general pedagogical knowledge*—knowledge of pedagogical principles and techniques that is not bound by topic or subject-matter. Teachers also have *knowledge of learners,* including knowledge of student characteristics and cognitions as well as knowledge of motivational and developmental aspects of how students learn. Finally, teachers frequently draw upon their *curricular knowledge*—their understanding of the programs and materials designed for the teaching of particular topics and subjects at a given level. (pp. 113–114)

As we have discussed, these and other kinds of teaching decisions are contingent upon how many different variables interact in different teaching circumstances. Thus, teaching decisions cannot be evaluated or understood without full knowledge of the teaching context. In Chapter 3, we explain how this conceptualization of teaching knowledge leads us to reject a behavioral model of assessment that assumes one highly specified list of teaching behaviors to be exhibited and tallied or one set of prescriptions for best practice that can be followed independent of an understanding of context, students, and subjects. Instead, we posit an approach to assessment that attends to teacher thinking and decisionmaking in evaluating and justifying courses of action that are contextually appropriate.

Defining What Teachers Should Know and Be Able to Do

Several similar configurations of the components of a knowledge base for teaching are reflected in newly developed professional standards, research, teacher education practices, and current licensing requirements. Current thinking in each of these arenas shows substantial agreement about the major domains of knowledge required as a basis for appropriate, professional teaching. At the same time, discussions about the knowledge base for teaching have begun to emphasize the importance of helping prospective teachers develop a reflective stance toward teaching and the skills needed to evaluate and integrate knowledge as well as to assess the needs of learners and the demands of the classroom context (Henderson, 1988; Ayers, 1988; Liston and Zeichner, 1987).

Shulman (1987, p. 8) classified the elements of teaching knowledge as:

1. Content knowledge
2. General pedagogical knowledge, including principles and strategies for classroom organization and management
3. Curriculum knowledge, including materials and programs
4. Pedagogical content knowledge, an amalgam of content and pedagogy that is teachers' special form of professional understanding
5. Knowledge of learners and their characteristics
6. Knowledge of educational contexts, including the characteristics of classrooms, schools, communities, and cultures
7. Knowledge of educational ends, purposes, and values, and their philosophical and historical grounds

Other recent efforts to codify and create a taxonomy for a teaching knowledge base include the American Association of Colleges for Teacher Educators' (AACTE) *Knowledge Base for the Beginning Teacher* (Reynolds, 1989), which includes reviews of research in all of the areas outlined by Shulman and the efforts of state and national standard-setting bodies, described in the section "Professional Standards for Teaching."

Table 2.1 compares the areas of knowledge outlined in current state licensure requirements, the *Knowledge Base for the Beginning Teacher*, and Minnesota's *Vision for Teacher Education*. Comparing these with each other and with Shulman's configuration suggests that a common core of teaching knowledge exists that is widely recognized as important. Interestingly, the only major area of difference across these three conceptions of teaching knowledge is that state licensing requirements pay virtually no attention to professional knowledge and dispositions—such as the ability to collaborate with colleagues, understanding of the ethical dimensions of teaching, and legal rights and responsibilities to students—whereas the two professionally developed conceptions of teaching (from AACTE and Minnesota's Board of Teaching) emphasize these areas along with technical knowledge. In addition, Minnesota and AACTE stress the use of knowledge within teaching contexts—for example, by emphasizing subject-specific pedagogy and the functioning of classrooms as social organizations—rather than treating each of these areas of knowledge as separate.

In addition to subject-matter knowledge and liberal arts knowledge and skills, each of the knowledge base configurations fits into and across three broad areas:

1. *Knowledge about learners and learning,* including knowledge about human growth and development, motivation and behavior, learning theory, learning differences, and cognitive psychology

TABLE 2.1 Conceptions of the Teaching Knowledge Base

State Licensing Requirements: Summary of fifty states' major requirements	AACTE *Knowledge Base for the Beginning Teacher*	Minnesota's *Vision for Teacher Education*
	Knowledge About Learners and Learning	
Human Growth and Development	Learners and Learning	Human Growth and Development
Educational psychology	Knowledge of the learner	Individual development
Child development	Meeting developmental needs of students	Relationship of learning to development
Human growth and learning	Students with special needs	Individual learning styles and need
Learning differences		
	Knowledge About Curriculum and Teaching	
Curriculum and Methods	The Need for a Curricular Vision of Teaching	Knowledge of Effective Teaching
Subject area curriculum	Subject-specific pedagogy	Learning and pedagogy
Methods, materials, and techniques	Conceptions of teaching	Curriculum and resources
Methods of teaching reading	Knowledge about reading and writing	Knowledge about communication and language
Classroom management	Classroom organization and management	Organization and motivation
		Social behavior management
Evaluation and guidance	Effective classroom guidance	Evaluation and assessment
	Knowledge About Social Foundations of Education	
Schools and Society	Social and Political Contexts	Knowledge About People and Cultures
School in relation to society	The school district	People and organizations
Human and intercultural relations	Social organization of classes and schools	Cultural diversity
Organization and administration	Principles of sociology and anthropology	Social complexity
	Context, code, classroom, and culture	Social, historical, linguistic, and philosophical considerations

	Professional Knowledge	Professional Knowledge and Dispositions
Foundations of Education	Professional collaboration	Collegiality
Philosophy of education	Ethical dimensions of teaching	Professional ethics
History of education	Legal rights and responsibilities	Responsibility to students
Sociology and anthropology		
	Knowledge About Subject Matter	
Subject-matter coursework	Subject-matter knowledge for teaching	Scope and structure of discipline
		Knowledge and personal scholarship
	Knowledge About Liberal Arts	
Distributional requirements:	Knowledge, representation, and	Knowledge about epistemology
Humanities, arts, and sciences	quantitative thinking	Knowledge of scientific inquiry

Sources: Reynolds 1989, Minnesota Board of Teaching 1986.

2. *Knowledge about curriculum and teaching*, including general and content-specific pedagogical knowledge, curriculum theory, assessment and evaluation, and counseling, as well as knowledge of scientific inquiry, epistemology, communication, and language as they relate to pedagogy
3. *Knowledge about contexts and foundations of education*, including knowledge about schools and society, cultures, educational history and philosophy, principles from sociology and anthropology, legal responsibilities of teachers, and ethics

Broad as they are, the boundaries among these domains are permeable—an understanding of human growth and development (knowledge about learners) clearly influences classroom management (knowledge about teaching), as does an appreciation for community and cultural norms of social interaction (knowledge about contexts). Important questions of teaching knowledge will cut across domains. These interactions across areas of knowledge—and among the knowledge, skills, and dispositions teachers rely upon in teaching—are reflected in the standards developed by Minnesota's Board of Teaching, as well as those of the National Board for Professional Teaching Standards and the Interstate New Teacher Assessment and Support Consortium.

Professional Standards for Teaching

Minnesota's Standards

We began our project with the Minnesota Board of Teaching by grounding our work in the view of teaching expressed in Minnesota's *Vision for Teacher Education*, which articulates in performance-based terms the knowledge, skills, and dispositions desired of teachers (see Appendix A). The standards are grounded in a view that teachers should be thoughtful, creative persons who use a set of principles and strategies derived from an informed personal philosophy of education and the multiple demands of learning contexts. The standards include

- *Knowledge* about people and social organizations, cultures, epistemology, specific disciplines, human growth and development, communication and language, scientific inquiry, and research on effective learning and teaching
- *Skills* associated with assessment, planning, instruction, evaluation, social behavior management, and role modeling
- *Dispositions* toward self, toward the learner, toward teaching, and toward the profession

Thus, professional knowledge includes a grounding in the many areas that provide an understanding of students and their learning, such as physical, cognitive, and psychological development; of the nature of human intelligence, learning, and performance; and of the influences of social experience, context, and culture. It also includes an understanding of schooling, curriculum, and teaching, including social, philosophical, and historical foundations of education; of research on teaching; of pedagogical theory and practice; and of ethical requirements of teaching.

Teaching skills include the abilities to transform knowledge into actions needed for effective teaching—for example, abilities to evaluate student thinking and performance in order to plan appropriate learning opportunities; abilities to critique, modify, combine, and use instructional materials to accomplish teaching and learning goals; abilities to understand and use multiple learning and teaching strategies; abilities to explain concepts clearly and appropriately, given the developmental needs and social experiences of students; abilities to provide useful feedback to students in constructive and instructionally helpful ways, and so on.

Teaching dispositions are the orientations teachers develop to think and behave in professionally responsible ways—for example, to reflect on their teaching and its effectiveness and to strive for continual improvement; to respect and value the needs, experiences, and abilities of all learners and to strive to develop the talents of each to the greatest extent possible; to engage with learners in joint problem solving and exploration of ideas; to establish cooperative relationships with students, parents, and other teachers; to keep abreast of professional ideas; and to engage in broader professional responsibilities.

This conception of teaching knowledge, skills, and dispositions maps very closely onto those that have since been developed by the National Board for Professional Teaching Standards and by INTASC in developing model licensing standards that are board-compatible.

The National Board for Professional Teaching Standards

The NBPTS has organized its standards development around five major propositions, the content of which is more fully elaborated in the board's publications and in the standards that are being written (NBPTS, n.d.). In brief, they are:

1. Teachers are committed to students and their learning. National Board–certified teachers are dedicated to making knowledge accessible to all students. They treat students equitably, recognizing individual differences. They adjust their practice, as appropriate, based on observation and knowledge of their students' interests, abilities, skills, knowledge, family circumstances, and peer relationships. They understand how students develop and learn. They are aware of the influence of context and culture on behavior. They develop students' cognitive capacity and their respect for learning. Equally important, they foster students' self-esteem, motivation, character, civic responsibility, and their respect for individual, cultural, religious, and racial differences.

2. Teachers know the subjects they teach and how to teach those subjects to students. National Board–certified teachers have a rich understanding of the subject(s) they teach and appreciate how knowledge in their subject is created, organized, linked to other disciplines, and applied to real-world settings. Accomplished teachers command specialized knowledge of how to convey and reveal subject-matter to students. They are aware of the preconceptions and background knowledge that students typically bring to each subject and of strategies and instructional materials that can be of assistance. Their instructional repertoire allows them to create multiple paths to knowledge, and they are adept at teaching students how to pose and solve their own problems.

3. Teachers are responsible for managing and monitoring student learning. National Board–certified teachers create, enrich, maintain, and alter instructional settings to capture and sustain the interest of their students and to make the most effective use of time. Accomplished teachers call on multiple methods to meet their goals. They command a range of instructional techniques, know when each is appropriate, and can implement them as needed. They know how to motivate and engage groups of students to ensure a purposeful learning environment and how to organize instruction to allow the schools' goals for students to be met. They understand how to motivate students to learn and how to maintain their interest even in the face of temporary failure. Board-certified teachers regularly assess the progress of individual students as well as that of the class as a whole. They employ multiple methods for measuring student growth and understanding and can clearly explain student performance to parents.

4. Teachers think systematically about their practice and learn from experience. National Board–certified teachers exemplify the virtues they seek to inspire in students—curiosity, tolerance, honesty, fairness, respect for diversity, and appreciation of cultural differences—and the capacities that are prerequisites for intellectual growth: the ability to reason and take multiple perspectives, to be creative and take risks, and to adopt an experimental and problem-solving orientation. Accomplished teachers draw on their knowledge of human development, subject matter, and instruction and on their understanding of their students to make principled judgments about sound practice. Striving to strengthen their teaching, board-certified teachers critically examine their practice, seek the advice of others, and draw on educational research and scholarship to expand their repertoire, deepen their knowledge, sharpen their judgment, and adapt their teaching to new findings, ideas, and theories.

5. Teachers are members of learning communities. National Board–certified teachers contribute to the effectiveness of the school by working collaboratively with other professionals on instructional policy, curriculum development, and staff development. They can evaluate school progress and the allocation of school resources in light of their understanding of state and local educational objectives. They are knowledgeable about specialized school and community resources that can be engaged for their students' benefit and are skilled at employing such resources as needed. Accomplished teachers find ways to work collaboratively and creatively with parents, engaging them productively in the work of the school.

The NBPTS has begun its standards development within each of the more than thirty certification fields it has defined by developmental levels of students (early childhood, middle childhood, early adolescence, and late adolescence–young adulthood) and by subject areas to be taught (e.g., mathematics, science, English–language arts, generalist, and so on). Of significance in the board's propositions—and in its standards and assessments—is the extent to which the highly accomplished teachers who comprise the NBPTS have clearly broken with previous conceptions of teaching as formulaic and routine. They have rejected a view of teaching as resting on the implementation of a few basic behaviors rather than on the acquisition of a broad base of knowledge to be used strategically. In articulating standards that rest on the appropriate use of knowledge and techniques in a variety of ways on behalf of diverse student needs, the board has begun to capture the complex, contingent nature of teaching and to confront the challenge of assessing such knowledge and skills in an appropriate way. (The NBPTS's early assessments are discussed in Chapter 5 of this volume.)

This example from the standards for early adolescence English–language arts teachers provides an illustration of how the board articulates what highly accomplished teachers need to know and be able to do in a fashion that integrates understandings of learners and learning, educational goals, teaching, pedagogy, and context. Part of the elaboration for "Standard I: Knowledge of Students" states:

> Accomplished middle-grades English teachers create classrooms centered around students; in these classrooms all students take pride in their growing language facility and in their increasingly adventurous explorations of literature and other texts. . . . While they believe all students can learn, accomplished teachers are keenly aware that not all students learn in the same way. . . . Because language acquisition builds on prior achievements and experiences, accomplished English language arts teachers make it a point to find out early in the school year who their students are as individual learners—and use this knowledge to help shape decisions in the classroom.
>
> Practically everything about the young adolescent learner is grist for the middle-grades English teacher's mill, including an awareness and appreciation of the student's cultural, linguistic and ethnic heritage, family setting, prior learning experiences, personal interests, needs and goals. In particular, knowing their students entails gaining a sense of each student's capacity to read, write, speak and listen in English and/or other languages. . . . The accomplished middle-grades English teacher comple-

ments his or her knowledge of individual students with a broad perspective—gained through experience and knowledge of research—on patterns of adolescent development and language acquisition. Such teachers know that children mature according to their own internal biological clocks and that a wide variation in students' developmental stages and life experiences within the same classroom is to be expected and accommodated. (NBPTS, 1993, pp. 13–14)

The standards will be further elaborated with vignettes that provide vivid illustrations of teachers enacting the standards, consonant with the growing research base arguing for situated cases as a means of illuminating teaching knowledge in contextualized fashion.

Board-Compatible Licensing Standards

The Interstate New Teacher Assessment and Support Consortium has articulated performance-based standards for initial licensing of teachers that are intended to be compatible with those of the NBPTS. They articulate what entering teachers should know, be like, and be able to do in order to practice responsibly and develop the kinds of deeper expertise that enable highly accomplished practice. The introduction to these model standards states: "The National Board and INTASC are united in their view that the complex art of teaching requires performance-based standards and assessment strategies that are capable of capturing teachers' reasoned judgments and that evaluate what they can actually do in authentic teaching situations" (INTASC, 1992, p. 1).

The INTASC task force decided to begin its work by articulating standards for a common core of teaching knowledge that should be acquired by all new teachers, to be followed by additional specific standards for disciplinary areas and levels of schooling. Like the first tier of assessment for licensing in virtually all other professions, this "common core" is intended to outline the common principles and foundations of practice that cut across specialty areas—the knowledge of student learning and development, of curriculum and teaching, and of contexts and purposes that create a set of professional understandings, abilities, and commitments that all teachers share.

Recognizing that applications of these common understandings and commitments are manifested within specific contexts—defined by students, subjects, and school levels, among others—the task force emphasized that "common-core" standards are not analogous to generic or context-free teaching behaviors. The assessment of specific teaching decisions and actions must occur within varied contexts that will require varied responses. In some cases, these are grounded in the discipline being taught: thus, subject-specific pedagogical decisions need to be evaluated within the context of subject-specific standards. In other cases, contextual considerations must be made part of the assessment structure and response possibilities.

The NBPTS has used an inductive strategy for identifying the common core of teaching knowledge, looking for the common elements that emerge as standards are developed by committees of expert teachers in each of the specific fields. Now that standards have emerged in half a dozen fields, the common elements have become clear, and certain standards are commonly used across areas. These common elements map very closely onto the common-core principles developed by INTASC.

The INTASC task force used the national board propositions, which embody criteria for identifying excellent teaching, as the basis for exploring what beginning teachers ought to be prepared to know and be able to do in order to develop over time into a highly accomplished teacher with these capacities. Also incorporated was the work in a number of states—including California, Minnesota, New York, and Texas—that derives from a shared conception of teaching, as well as the efforts of teacher educators, including the Holmes Group of education deans and Alverno College's performance-based approach to teacher education. The resulting standards are articulated in the form of ten principles, each of which is further discussed in terms of the knowledge, dispositions, and performances it implies. The ten principles (found in INTASC, 1992) are listed below, and the standards are included in Appendix B.

Principle #1: The teacher understands the central concepts, tools of inquiry, and structures of the discipline(s) he or she teaches and can create learning experiences that make these aspects of subject-matter meaningful for students.

Principle #2: The teacher understands how children learn and develop and can provide learning opportunities that support their intellectual, social, and personal development.

Principle #3: The teacher understands how students differ in their approaches to learning and creates instructional opportunities that are adapted to diverse learners.

Principle #4: The teacher understands and uses a variety of instructional strategies to encourage students' development of critical thinking, problem solving, and performance skills.

Principle #5: The teacher uses an understanding of individual and group motivation and behavior to create a learning environment that encourages positive social interaction, active engagement in learning, and self-motivation.

Principle #6: The teacher uses knowledge of effective verbal, nonverbal, and media communication techniques to foster active inquiry, collaboration, and supportive interaction in the classroom.

Principle #7: The teacher plans instruction based upon knowledge of subject-matter, students, the community, and curriculum goals.

Principle #8: The teacher understands and uses formal and informal assessment strategies to evaluate and ensure the continuous intellectual and social development of the learner.

Principle #9: The teacher is a reflective practitioner who continually evaluates the effects of his/her choices and actions on others (students, parents, and other professionals in the learning community) and who actively seeks out opportunities to grow professionally.

Principle #10: The teacher fosters relationships with school colleagues, parents, and agencies in the larger community to support students' learning and well-being.

As is also true of the Minnesota and national board standards, the INTASC standards explicitly acknowledge that teachers' actions or performances depend on many kinds of knowledge and on dispositions to use that knowledge in particular ways. The definition of each of the principles is elaborated with a set of knowledge, dispositions, and performances that provide the basis for evaluating evidence about the achievement of the standard. These are, in turn, explicit about the kinds of considerations that are important to take into account and the areas of knowledge that should inform decisions, thus providing guidance for both preparation and assessment. The standards look beyond discrete teaching behaviors for the understandings that enable teachers to decide what to do under varying circumstances.

For example, principle #2 indicates, among other things, that teachers understand how learning occurs—how students construct knowledge, acquire skills, and develop habits of mind—and can use that knowledge, along with knowledge about physical, social, emotional, moral, and cognitive development, in structuring learning opportunities. Based on those understandings, teachers find ways to access students' thinking, prior knowledge, and experiences through discussion and written reflections. They link new ideas to already familiar ideas and make connections to students' experiences, providing opportunities for active engagement, manipulation, and testing of ideas and materials. They encourage students to assume responsibility for shaping their learning tasks. Note that the particular learning opportunities constructed and the particular actions of the teacher will vary depending on what is learned about students' experiences, prior knowledge, development, strengths, and needs. This anticipation of diverse and contingent teaching behaviors stands in direct contrast to a number of existing instruments for evaluating teachers, discussed in Chapter 3.

In addition, the standards explicitly deal with normative concerns of teaching, laying foundations for ethical considerations in teaching. This particular standard indicates that there are certain dispositions that allow teachers to act on what they know about learning and development in the interests of students, including an appreciation for individual variation, respect for the diverse talents of all learners, a disposition to use student strengths as a basis for growth and errors as an opportunity for learning, and a commitment to help them develop self-confidence and competence. These are grounded in both knowledge about what motivates learners and helps them develop new skills (e.g., building on areas of learning strength enables more effective acquisition of new skills) and in values about how children should be treated.

So, for example, using knowledge about child development to denigrate some students whose progress is slower in some respects while praising others would not be acceptable practice, because it would discourage and demotivate the students so denigrated and retard their future learning and because it violates the teacher's commitment to act in the best interests of every student. Neither would severely criticizing students when they make honest mistakes be acceptable, because lost opportunities for learning would result and because such behavior would impede the risk-taking needed for future active learning. These understandings derive from a knowledge base, but they extend beyond its technical boundaries into a domain concerned with the ethical and constructive use of knowledge in a process that has far-reaching consequences for students.

The Implications of Performance-Based Standards for Licensure

An important attribute of all of these standards is that they are *performance-based*—that is, they describe what teachers should know, be like, and be able to do rather than listing courses teachers should take in order to be awarded a license. This shift toward performance-based standard setting is in line with the approach to licensing taken in other professions and with the changes already occurring in a number of states. This approach should clarify what the criteria are for assessment and licensing, placing more emphasis on the abilities teachers develop than on the hours they spend taking classes. Ultimately, performance-based licensing standards should enable states to permit greater innovation and diversity in how teacher education programs operate by assessing their outcomes rather than merely regulating their inputs or procedures.

Zeichner (1993) noted that although focusing on outcomes, the INTASC and NBPTS standards differ in important ways from earlier, failed attempts to institute competency-based teacher education (CBTE) in the 1970s. Whereas the earlier efforts sought to break down teacher behaviors into tiny, discrete skill bits, articulating literally hundreds of desired competencies to be individually assessed, these recent efforts are defined at a broader level, communicating a vision about what teachers should know and be able to do and resting on expert judgments to evaluate the ways in which they demonstrate their capacity to do it. Thus, rather than fragmenting and trivializing teacher knowledge and performances, these efforts use research about good practice to define the *kinds* of knowledge and understandings teachers should demonstrate in an integrated fashion rather than the specific, minute behaviors they should exhibit one by one on demand. The view of teaching articulated in the new performance-based standards demands, as the INTASC (1992) report suggested, "that teachers integrate their knowledge of subjects, students, the community and curriculum to create a bridge between learning goals and learners' lives" (p. 8).

Changes in current state licensing and approval requirements are much needed if the vision of teaching offered by current reforms is to be realized. Many of the understandings about what teachers should understand and be able to do are completely absent from current state licensing requirements and program approval standards. For example, the view of teaching knowledge as complex and contingent, as rooted in an understanding of learning and the many different paths it takes, along with an appreciation for human motivation, multiple intelligences, and diverse modes of performance, is not well represented in many states' licensing and program approval standards. Requirements for secondary school teachers across the country almost completely ignore cognitive and developmental psychology, theories of learning and intelligence, and understanding of human motivation, behavior, and performance. These kinds of learning are only expected superficially of most "regular" elementary school teachers in many states. They have become somewhat more serious, although not universal, expectations for teachers in special education and for counselors.

Similarly, there is little expectation in current requirements that teachers must understand the structure of knowledge within disciplines so that they can organize instruction in a way that allows students to understand fundamental concepts and acquire conceptual frameworks that are the basis for disciplinary learning. Almost no state-approval process ensures that teachers will learn about the assessment of learning—not just so that they can interpret scores on existing tests but so they can critically examine and construct instruments for evaluating students' knowledge. Very few states require a grounding in issues associated with multicultural education and curriculum development. Current input-based regulations typically do not anticipate that this knowledge will need to be acquired in application as well as in theory, in programs that allow for the integration of subject-matter and pedagogical study, and for the study of learners and learning in clinical as well as didactic settings.

Many believe that transforming teacher education will require reshaping both education courses and the structure of teacher education programs. The Holmes Group urges the creation of professional development schools, school-university partnerships in which expert teachers join with university faculty to provide carefully structured practicum and internship experiences for prospective teachers (Holmes Group, 1990). More than one hundred such schools have been created in the past few years, based on the premise that the education of teachers must occur in an atmosphere in which theory *and* practice jointly inform their work (Darling-Hammond, 1993).

A great many schools of education are rethinking their programs and practices, reshaping coursework, designing internship programs, and creating professional development schools as part of these and other professionwide activities. Unfortunately, many of these initiatives are constrained by the traditional approach to teacher licensing, which relies heavily on state prescriptions of course offerings and regulation of teacher education programs.

Input regulations through state program approval and licensure by course taking are unlikely to facilitate major changes in the structure and content of teacher education programs. Performance-based licensing should enable states to enact rigorous assessments for determining whether teachers have the knowledge and skill needed to teach responsibly while deregulating the content and structure of teacher education programs. One proposal for such deregulation is for states to stipulate only the broad outlines of teacher education programs, such as the inclusion of certain areas of study (e.g., child development, methods of teaching) and program components (e.g., student teaching), without prescribing particular numbers of credit hours of coursework by specific areas (Zeichner, 1993). Within this framework, national accreditation of programs would provide sufficient guarantee of program quality.

The possibilities for pursuing this approach are strengthened by the creation of a program for state partnerships for performance-based licensing and accreditation through the National Council for the Accreditation of Teacher Education (NCATE), which has undertaken changes to encourage states to accept NCATE accreditation as the vehicle for enforcing professional standards. In addition, some states, such as Minnesota, are replacing course-counting approaches with licensing standards that articulate the types of knowledge and skill needed to teach. Minnesota's 1992 legislation provided that:

> The board [of teaching] shall provide the leadership and adopt rules for the redesign of teacher education programs to implement a research based, results-oriented curriculum that focuses on the skills teachers need in order to be effective. The board shall implement new systems of teacher preparation program evaluation to assure program effectiveness based on proficiency of graduates in demonstrating attainment of program outcomes. The board shall adopt rules requiring successful completion of an examination of general pedagogical knowledge and examinations of licensure-specific teaching skills (Minnesota Statutes, Section 125.05, Sec. 15, Subd. 4d, 4e)

A final implication of performance-based licensing standards is that they may, if well developed and well implemented, create a means for opening up a variety of pathways and means of preparation for entering teaching without lowering standards, as current emergency licensure provisions and many alternative certification programs do. Until the teaching profession enacts and enforces meaningful standards for licensing that are applied to every entrant, it will suffer from an inability to assure the public that all teachers have encountered and mastered a common knowledge base. However, controlling the gates to entry will be meaningless unless performance-based standards are well developed and well implemented through a comprehensive licensing system featuring high-quality assessments that adequately evaluate the most important features of teaching. If such licensure systems are created, the public may be justified in trusting that variations in the means to prepare for licensure represent responsible flexibility rather than lowered standards.

Many knotty issues must be resolved as such an assessment system is created. These issues, however they are resolved for the moment, must be the subject of an ongoing discussion that continually reevaluates what good teaching is and revises assessment tools accordingly. For example, should teaching knowledge and skills be conceived as those understandings and abilities needed to teach in most current schools, where teachers' roles are limited largely to classroom instructional activities? Or should they be conceived as the kinds of understandings that will be needed for teachers to assume the broader roles many reform plans envision—roles as curriculum developers, peer coaches, and school-level decisionmakers? Should notions of "good teaching" reflected in the teacher assessments rest on traditional practices, which are widespread but do not reflect state-of-the-art understandings of teaching and learning? Or should emerging notions of good teaching—such as those reflected in the new standards issued by the National Council of Teachers of Mathematics—be favored? As Sykes (1990, p. 19) noted in his discussion of how one justifies knowledge claims in teaching: "There is no simple and completely fair answer to the question, 'Why should a teacher know *that?*' Tough choices must be made followed by wide consultation and sensitive implementation."

As the profession engages the tough work of developing more rigorous and meaningful methods of assessing teachers, it must tackle these issues in light of the changing goals and realities it faces. In our work with Minnesota, we were guided by Minnesota's newly adopted standards for teacher education in embracing a state-of-the-art conception of "good teaching"—one oriented toward learner-centered teaching aimed at higher-order skills and understandings. Such a conception might be called *reformist* (Sykes, 1990), given its grounding in recent understandings of teaching and learning (see, e.g., Resnick, 1987) and its compatibility with the urgings of current reform reports (e.g., Carnegie Forum, 1986). Minnesota's earlier work in developing a forward-looking consensus about its aspirations for teaching made the decision an appropriate one for this context. The more recent issuance of similar standards from national professional bodies confirms that this conception of teaching is widely appropriate and points the direction for new forms of assessment based on a view of teaching as thinking work.

3

The Need for New Assessments
in Teaching

EACH DAY, teachers must apply their knowledge of subject matter, child development, cognition, group dynamics, motivation, methods of teaching, and classroom management to extremely complex situations. The quality of education children receive is largely dependent on how well their teachers have been prepared to perform these challenging tasks.

We have argued that an important strategy to encourage excellent teaching and to inspire public confidence in the quality of teachers is to ensure that all prospective teachers undergo a rigorous program of education or preparation and screening before they are permitted to operate as autonomous professionals. Such a preparation and assessment program has both internal (professional) and external (social) purposes: to increase the quality of preparation beginning teachers undergo and to justify the public's confidence in teachers as qualified experts with the knowledge, skills, and dispositions necessary to be entrusted with the development of children. The most important purpose, of course, is to increase the probability that students will be well taught.

A major unsolved problem in teacher licensing is the inability of current widely used procedures to determine when a novice teacher is ready to responsibly undertake independent, professional practice. For many years, prospective teachers faced only those hurdles associated with passing courses in an approved teacher education program. Because state-approved programs have varied so widely in their content and quality, policymakers became convinced that negotiation of these hurdles did not necessarily demonstrate that a prospective teacher was fit to practice. As a result, they have been imposing additional screens in the form of tests of basic skills, subject matter, and pedagogy. Before 1977, only three states included tests as a condition of teacher licensing. By 1986, all but four states had mandated teacher competency tests (Darling-Hammond and Berry, 1988). Currently, only three states do not test teachers for licensure.

49

Theoretically, professional requirements such as teaching tests serve two important functions—sorting and screening candidates and defining the knowledge base for defensible practice. The first function receives the most attention from policymakers and test makers. It conjures a vertical notion of standards: They go up or down. Cutoff scores may be raised or lowered to allow more or fewer people to pass. This function serves a symbolic purpose of creating selectivity in entry. It may or may not serve the substantive goal of selecting candidates based on criteria that are meaningful for performance in the field, depending on what the content of the measure is.

The second major function—and the most important one for creating professional standards—is defining the professional knowledge base. Examinations can exert substantial influence on what professionals come to know by virtue of what performances they require. When candidates prepare to take the bar examination, for example, they know they will have to study constitutional law, torts, contracts, tax law, criminal law, and so on, and they will have to demonstate their knowledge by using case law, legal procedures, and legal reasoning skills to respond in essays to case scenarios. Thus, the examination shapes the knowledge and skills lawyers acquire during legal training, regardless of the pass rates on the test.

For the most part, current teacher tests perform the first function but not the second. Most of the mandated tests are basic skills examinations and, thus, are not in the realm of professional testing. Furthermore, existing tests of general and professional knowledge assess little of what might be considered knowledge for teaching (Darling-Hammond, 1986a, 1989b; Shulman, 1987).

In recent years, policymakers and members of the profession have experienced a growing disquiet that passing the new hurdles still does not determine that a prospective teacher is indeed prepared to teach well and responsibly. Tests of basic skills and subject-matter knowledge are not designed to reveal a candidate's ability to convey that knowledge to students. In addition, the first generation of pedagogical examinations has been widely criticized as inadequate to determine teaching knowledge or skill.

Problems with Existing Tests
of Teaching

The most widely used existing tests for teacher licensing are of two main types. First, most states use paper-and-pencil standardized tests of basic skills, subject matter, or pedagogical knowledge calling primarily for multiple-choice responses. These have been developed by the Educational Testing Service in the form of the National Teacher Examinations (NTE) and by a number of states, sometimes using the services of other commercial testing firms. Second, a number of states have used performance evaluations of first-year teachers as a condition for a regular or continuing license. These evaluations use classroom observations by state evaluators or local administrators according to a check-list of designated teaching behaviors.

As we describe in the next section, neither these paper-and-pencil stan-dardized tests nor the checklist-based observations have been able to meet the goal of a licensing assessment system to represent a knowledge base and, thus, improve the quality of preparation. The currently used measures repre-sent attempts to articulate the knowledge and skills necessary for professional practice in a way that allows for reliable scoring. However, because the trans-lation of skills and knowledge into evaluation criteria has been so crude, the evaluations themselves are able neither to motivate acquisition of important information and abilities nor to validly sort those who should be permitted to practice independently from those who should not.

Shortcomings of Existing Paper-and-Pencil Tests

Most current teacher examinations ignore contextualized understanding of teaching and learning in favor of items requiring the recognition of facts with-in subject areas, knowledge of school law and bureaucratic procedures, and recognition of the "correct" teaching behavior in a situation described in a short scenario of only one or two sentences. One evaluation of the NTE test of teaching knowledge found that only 10 percent of the questions actually relied on knowledge about teaching and learning and over 40 percent were so poorly specified that they either had no clearly defensible right answer or had an answer based solely on ideology rather than on a knowledge of research (Darling-Hammond, 1986a). Of the remaining questions, 18 percent required knowledge of legal rules and bureaucratic procedures, 9 percent required fac-tual knowledge about testing terms, and 19 percent required knowledge of simple word definitions or a commonsense, careful reading of the question whose answer essentially repeated the stem.

Similarly, analyses of the professional knowledge sections of the study guides for the Arkansas Educational Skills Assessment (AESA) and the Texas Examination of Current Administrators and Teachers (TECAT) found that the tests consisted almost exclusively of definitions of vocabulary (Melnick and Pullin, 1987; Tyson-Bernstein, 1987). In both cases, the vast majority of terms were drawn from educational psychology, with a heavy emphasis on psycho-metrics and behaviorist theories. "If this is the domain of knowledge compe-tent teachers are required to know, then an analysis of the impetus for such a definition of professional knowledge is warranted," Melnick and Pullin re-marked. They noted that such a definition is not surprising, however, when test makers are psychometricians and educational psychologists rather than classroom teachers or teacher educators.

In addition, the tests currently used do not allow for demonstrations of teacher knowledge, judgment, and skills in the kinds of complex settings that characterize real teaching. They may actually discourage the use of such knowledge by positing a unidimensional philosophy of teaching that the test taker must consistently apply if he or she is to find the "best" answers to poorly defined questions (Darling-Hammond, 1986a; Shulman, 1987).

A recurring criticism of widely used standardized tests is that they present a narrow behavioristic view of teaching that so oversimplifies the nature of teacher decisionmaking that the ways in which teachers must use knowledge are misrepresented. Because the tests rely solely on multiple-choice responses to exceedingly brief statements of professional problems, they fail to represent the complexity of the decisionmaking process or the full range of the professional knowledge base (Wise and Darling-Hammond, 1987). A major problem is the failure to provide sufficient information about the context for and goals of teaching decisions to allow for a sensible answer.

Oversimplifying Teaching. An example from a previous National Teachers Examination sample test booklet (ETS, 1984) is indicative of the problem:

> Use of which of the following is most important in the beginning instruction of the young, visually impaired child?
>
> (a) Machines with lighted screens to magnify print
> (b) A large variety of large-print books
> (c) Extended periods of nondirected play
> (d) Many tactile and oral activities, or
> (e) Large-print flash cards for learning sight vocabulary

Since the question does not reveal how young the child is, the nature of the visual impairment, or the goals of instruction, there is no real way to apply professional knowledge and judgment to reach a correct answer. The desired answer (d) is not implausible, but it is not the appropriate course of action for, say, teaching early reading to a partially sighted seven-year-old child. Even were a "correct" answer clearly discernible from a more precisely framed question, it would not reveal whether the teacher could diagnose the child's needs or design an appropriate learning experience for the child.

Similarly, another question from a former NTE test of teaching knowledge (ETS, 1984) poses the following scenario that seems to imply a single, simple approach to organizing instruction:

> Research indicates that in classrooms where effective teaching and learning occur, the teacher is likely to be doing which of the following consistently?
>
> (a) Gearing instruction to the typical student at a given grade level
> (b) Carefully grouping students at the beginning of the school year and making sure that these groups remain the same throughout the year
> (c) Identifying the effective behaviors that students are likely to exhibit at a given level of development

(d) Working diligently with students to make sure that each learns all of the material for the class for the year, or

(e) Pacing instruction so that students can move ahead when they are able to or receive extra help when they need it

The question does not define what is meant by "effective teaching and learning," so it is not possible to infer which of the many competing goals for instruction ought to be the basis for making a judgment about strategies or which of several bodies of research associated with differing goals for instruction are intended to be applicable. The designated right answer (e) may not appear to be objectionable, but neither is it supported by an unambiguous body of research on how to organize students for teaching and learning activities.

The desired answer implies that individualized instructional strategies will be used, although neither the question nor the answer deals with the assumptions such a strategy makes about the nature of student grouping or the relative importance to be given to a number of academic and social learning goals. Much research on individualized instruction—which seems to be implied by (e)—has failed to find that it produces significant learning gains (Good and Brophy, 1986).

Meanwhile, some research on teaching effectiveness has concluded that whole-group instruction at a common pace fosters time-on-task and increased scores on some kinds of achievement tests (see, e.g., Waxman and Eash, 1983; Medley, 1985). Other recent research has suggested that heterogeneous groups of students engaged in cooperative learning activities are effective for many kinds of inquiry learning and for social learning, with higher-achieving students deepening their understanding as they teach other students and lower-achieving students learning more as well (Johnson and Johnson, 1985). And these two bodies of research frequently drew their conclusions based on different kinds of learning goals: mastery of basic skills and facts in the first instance and acquisition of higher-order thinking skills as well as highly developed social skills in the second. Different strategies for instruction have been found effective for these different goals (Darling-Hammond, Wise, and Pease, 1983; Good and Brophy, 1986).

The major point is that many intervening variables concerning classroom organization, teaching strategies, and instructional goals make the simplistic application of any research suspect. In this case, as in many others in which oversimplification is sought, selecting the right answer is more a matter of agreement with the test's philosophy than of having a knowledge of research (Andrews, 1984; Soar, Medley, and Coker, 1983; Palladino, 1980; Darling-Hammond, 1986a). The more one knows, the harder such questions are to answer in the way the test makers demand. As Pugach and Raths (1983) warned in the early days of teacher competency testing about the effects of such tests:

A primary problem with tests of this nature is that they tend to represent particular ideologies, namely, those of the item writers. . . . If such an examination were to be required on a statewide basis, schools, colleges, and departments of education would need to prepare their students for the test, a process that is likely to narrow the range of philosophies found in the teacher education classroom. At a time when it is increasingly recognized that a repertoire of approaches and the ability to draw on them in a variety of classroom situations is a desirable characteristic of teachers, any move that would narrow their study seems problematic.

Questions that rely on a simplistic view of teaching are not only inadequate to assess what skilled and knowledgeable teachers know, they also encourage a soft-headed approach to the preparation of teachers. In the area of educational research, consider the following question from an NTE sample test (ETS, 1984):

In general, which of the following factors has been shown in several studies to have the strongest relationship to variation in student achievement?

(a) Teacher experience
(b) School size
(c) Type of textbooks
(d) Student/teacher ratio, or
(e) Community's average income

Since many studies could be marshaled to support responses a, b, d, or e, the question is meaningless without citing the "several studies" referenced. Furthermore, the desired answer (e) is badly flawed, since those studies that have found effects of income on achievement used measures of student family income, not community income. Some of the most carefully controlled large-scale studies found that school size and teacher experience accounted for more variation in achievement among schools with similar populations than did community wealth (Ferguson, 1991; NIE, 1977). Thus, the question reveals more about the limited knowledge of the item writer than about the knowledge of teachers. Finally, by choosing the one answer that suggests that educators have little control over achievement, the test conveys an acceptance of inequality and a low level of confidence in teachers' abilities to be effective in schools in poor communities.

A final example (ETS, 1984) illustrates the test's emphasis on bureaucratic procedures. This question seems designed to assess whether the teacher will avoid embarrassment for school officials by handling sensitive situations in noninflammatory ways:

A representative of a special interest group meets a teacher out of school and indicates that the group objects to a particular textbook being used in the teacher's classroom. Of the following, which is the best response for the teacher to give the representative in order to handle the situation in a nonthreatening manner?

(a) Such a response by parents would be appropriate, but not by groups such as yours that have no close connection with public schools.
(b) Your group should write a letter to me and the principal specifying the passages that the group objects to and why.
(c) The Constitution protects a teacher's right to use any textbook that is appropriate for the purpose.
(d) Is your interest group able to propose an appropriate but less controversial textbook?
(e) Since the textbook was adopted by the school board, any comments about it should be directed to the board.

Since the question does not specify the nature of the group's concern or give a first-hand example of the text at issue, the candidate cannot sort out any of the competing considerations that might guide an authentic answer. Is the group angry that the text teaches evolution instead of creationism? Or is there a concern that portrayals of minorities are absent or stereotypic? Would the teacher's own analysis of the text reveal causes for concern? Is the text selected by the teacher? Is it the only one available in a school with few resources, or was it mandated by the school board? Does the teacher use the text heavily in his or her teaching, as a resource augmented by supplemental materials, or only on a few selected occasions? Are students asked to analyze issues from competing perspectives or to read the text as the only viewpoint on all issues? Without these kinds of information, a real answer cannot be considered. And without an explanation of his or her reasoning, a genuine evaluation of the teacher's capacity to make appropriate judgments in a difficult situation within a particular context cannot be assessed.

The desired answer (d) seems only to have the virtue of keeping the burden of dealing with such situations off of the principal or the school board (as answers (b) or (e) would entail). However, it places the teacher in a position of professional responsibility without professional authority. Very few teachers in the United States have the power to select or purchase their own textbooks. Inviting the interest group to propose another text is a disingenuous (and in that sense unprofessional) answer, since the teacher would be in no position to evaluate the merits of the proposed alternate, let alone accept or deny the proposal. Protecting the curriculum, reforming the curriculum, or participating in a worthy debate with local citizens are clearly not the concerns suggested by this test's conception of "professional" behavior. "Professionalism" here involves protecting the teacher's superiors and keeping the public at bay.

Inattention to Context. Many critics have raised concerns that by positing uniform, context-free teaching behaviors and unidimensional responses to poorly defined questions, the current measures may in fact discourage the use and acquisition of professional knowledge and moral judgment that should underlie technique (Shulman, 1987; Darling-Hammond, 1986a; MacMillan and

Pendlebury, 1985). As is true in other professions, decisions about appropriate practice are highly context-specific. However, other professions represent problems with much greater acknowledgment of the wide range of interacting variables that define context and with greater attention to the kinds of knowledge that should inform decisions. This is true even on standardized tests using multiple-choice response formats. Compare, for example, the one-sentence NTE questions cited earlier in this section with the rich, contextual information provided for this question on part 3 of the National Board of Medical Examiners (NBME) medical examinations:

> *General Information:* A 45-year-old man is admitted to the hospital because of pain in his right hip and pelvis, especially when walking. He had lost 30 pounds in weight in the past year, during which time he did not feel strong or well enough to work. Three months prior to admission, he developed an acute upper respiratory infection and noted an increase in his symptoms with generalized "pain in my bones and stiffness of my joints." At that time, he also noted generalized numbness with tingling and stiffness of his hands; he had difficulty talking because his jaws and lips became stiff, making it difficult to form words.
>
> Twenty years earlier he had had similar symptoms which he described as "pain all over." At that time, he was studied at a hospital for bone and joint disease, where he was told he had "osteoporosis." During the intervening years, he has been relatively well.
>
> *Physical examination:* Temperature is 37.0 C (98.6 F); pulse rate is 80 per minute and regular; blood pressure is 120/80 mm Hg. The patient is well developed and appears well nourished. The lungs are clear to percussion and auscultation. The heart is normal in size; there are no murmurs. The abdomen is protuberant but no masses or organs are palpable. There is tenderness in the right groin on palpation but no mass can be felt. There is 2+ edema of the legs but the extremities are otherwise normal. Neurological examination shows no abnormalities. Walking causes severe pain in the right hip and pelvis as well as pain in the feet.
>
> *Initial laboratory studies:* Results of the following tests are given in this section: hemoglobin, hematocrit, leukocyte count, erythrocyte count, urine, and roentgenogram of the chest. (excerpted from NBME, 1986)

Following the presentation of these data, the candidate is asked, in turn, to note which inquiries he or she will make of the patient (and, using a special pen that illuminates answers, is given information on another page telling what the results of those inquiries are), what additional observations or measures he or she will make (with similar feedback about findings), what additional studies he or she will undertake, and, based on the findings, what therapy he or she will advise (Wise and Darling-Hammond, 1987, pp. 65–72).

Similarly elaborate case scenarios with accompanying data can be found on licensing examinations in law and engineering and on the registration examination in architecture. In addition to providing context-rich questions, testing in other professions goes beyond multiple-choice paper-and-pencil tests of basic information. Doctors are interviewed (and sometimes observed) by a panel of their peers about past and hypothetical diagnostic and treatment decisions in specific cases; lawyers apply their legal reasoning and writing skills in essays that analyze cases and develop lines of argument; architects design structures; accountants solve problems of accounting practice. The emphasis is not primarily on finding the "right answer" but is on the candidate's ability to apply knowledge and judgment in professionally acceptable ways.

An example from the California bar examination's performance test (Klein, 1982) illustrates this approach to examining professional thinking:

TITLE: Trial Brief

TIME: 90 minutes

MATERIALS: Special Instruction Sheet
            Pleadings
            Deposition Summary
            Client interview notes
            Mini-library

In this task, you are to prepare a trial brief for submission prior to trial. This brief should be limited to the two issues specified on the Special Instruction Sheet.

Your brief should:

(1) Contain concise headings that relate the law and the facts to each other.
(2) Contain persuasive arguments that relate legal principles and factual circumstances in a way that supports your position on each issue.
(3) Resolve conflicts, if any, between legal authorities.
(4) Draw analogies and make distinctions, as appropriate, between materials in the mini-library and the circumstances of your case.
(5) Point out weaknesses in opposing counsel's likely position.
(6) Discuss policy and other implications, if any, of your and/or opposing counsel's positions.
(7) Present ideas clearly and persuasively; be well organized and concise; and employ lawyer-like terms and style.

This kind of performance task draws on many areas of knowledge about the law, as well as on skills of legal reasoning within the context of a common legal task—writing a brief. Important contextual considerations are not ignored; rather, they serve as the primary grist for analysis by the candidate. It is the capacity to evaluate and respond to these considerations that is of primary importance in the task.

By contrast, efforts to measure teaching knowledge without reference to the contextual factors and multiple bodies of knowledge that must guide teaching decisions fail to capture the essence of pedagogy while threatening to undermine effective teacher preparation. Furthermore, the traditional approach to teacher testing, which separates tests of subject matter from tests of pedagogical knowledge, is also inadequate. The interrelations between subject-matter knowledge and knowledge of learners and pedagogy make it virtually impossible to think meaningfully about teaching and content without considering learners and context. As Mary Kennedy (1991a) observed in her concluding chapter to *Teaching Academic Subjects to Diverse Learners:*

> Teachers do not teach academic subjects in the absence of diverse learners, nor do they teach diverse learners in the absence of academic subjects. The interdependence between these two objects of teaching is apparent in the chapters in this volume, for even though each author was asked to write about either an academic subject or an aspect of diverse learners, most actually wrote about both academic subjects and diverse learners. It proved hard to discuss one without considering the other; academic subjects and diverse learners are the yin and the yang of teaching—opposing and yet complementary forces. Teachers must respond to the demands of each, yet must do so within the constraints imposed by the other. (pp. 275–276)

Ultimately, the profession must develop strategies for assessing teaching that allow for contextualized evaluations of teacher judgment and skill. These evaluations should anticipate that many different teaching decisions and behaviors will occur based on the demands of the teaching situation.

Validity Issues. The limited validity of most currently used teacher tests has been reviewed elsewhere (see, e.g., Haney, Madaus, and Kreitzer, 1987; Quirk, Witten, and Weinberg, 1973). Few studies of the predictive validity of state-developed tests have been conducted. A study that examined the relationship between beginning teachers' scores on the Georgia tests of subject-matter knowledge and ratings of on-the-job performance found both positive and negative, although generally insignificant, correlations (SREB, 1982). Similarly, although NTE scores correlate with other standardized tests of general academic ability (Ayers and Qualls, 1979; Pitcher, 1962; Quirk, Witten, and Weinberg, 1973), consistent relationships between test scores and later teaching performance have not been found (Andrews, Blackmon, and Mackey, 1980; Ayers and Qualls, 1979; Quirk, Witten, and Weinberg, 1973; Summers and Wolfe, 1975).

In a recent review, Haney and colleagues found that almost no research exists confirming the predictive and construct validity of the National Teacher Examinations. They suggest that the high intercorrelations among components of the NTE Core Battery may mean that it measures general aptitude and test-taking skills rather than mastery of a professional education curriculum (Haney, Madaus, and Kreitzer, 1987; Nelson in Mitchell, 1985). Few other teacher tests have even been examined in terms of predictive validity to allow for conclusions.

It is easy to talk of raising standards for teacher preparation and entry. It is even relatively easy, as we have recently seen, to pass laws requiring more selectivity in entry, including specific tests. However, once the trappings of rigor have been adopted, the basis of confidence in a profession is that these standards can, in fact, be shown to enhance the knowledge and ability of those admitted to practice.

Teaching tests that rely on simplistic views of teaching not only inadequately assess teacher knowledge and fail to advance the development of a knowledge base but they eliminate many candidates from teaching on grounds that are tenuous. Thus, shortages are exacerbated and pressures to create loopholes are increased while the capacities of those who enter teaching are not clearly improved (Darling-Hammond, 1989b). To compound the problem, recently mandated teacher licensing tests have become barriers to entry for minorities, who pass at significantly lower rates than whites (Garibaldi, 1987; Goertz and Pitcher, 1985; Graham, 1987; Haney, Madaus, and Kreitzer, 1987). Indeed, the disparities are significantly larger than those on other commonly administered tests of general ability and achievement (Haney, Madaus, and Kreitzer, 1987), heightening questions about what the tests really measure.

In a simulation using existing data about the predictive validity of the NTE as a measure of later teaching performance and an assumed cut-score that would eliminate 10 percent of all candidates, Walter Haney, George Madaus, and Amelia Kreitzer (1987, p. 219) found that 80 percent of the rejections would be false, as compared with about 10 percent of acceptances. They concluded:

> From a public policy point of view—even accepting the proposition that the purpose of teacher tests is not to predict the degree of teacher success, but simply to protect the public from incompetent teachers—we need to examine the way in which current teacher tests affect the pool of people who do become teachers. Even if federal courts do not demand that we look at the relationship between teacher-test results and available measures of teacher quality, rational policy making demands that we look at how the screening mechanisms of current teacher tests are affecting the characteristics and qualities of the teacher corps. . . . These results indicate clearly that current teacher tests, and the manner in which cut-scores are being set on them, are differentiating among candidates far more strongly on the basis of race than they are on the basis of teacher quality (pp. 223, 227).

Thus, while reducing the supply of minority candidates, the tests fail to heighten the profession's claim to meaningful standards. Paradoxically, in the midst of initiatives to revise admissions and exit criteria for teacher education, states continue to issue tens of thousands of emergency, provisional, temporary, and alternative certificates. Fully 9 percent of new entrants to teaching in 1985 were not properly licensed (Recent College Graduates Survey, 1985, cited in Darling-Hammond, 1990c). Ironically, minority candidates are those least likely to enter teaching through these backdoor routes (Darling-Hammond, 1990c) and the most likely to be properly qualified; however, the supply of minority college students interested in teaching decreased sharply throughout the 1980s. Thus, in teaching, strategies for regulating the labor market have created a dual credentialing system that simultaneously retards efforts to improve teaching quality and decreases diversity in the teaching force.

Regardless of whether standards are being ostensibly raised or lowered, though, the substance of standards—that is, the extent and kinds of knowledge they reflect—remains outside the hands of the profession. Since tests "[transfer] control over the curriculum to the agency which sets or controls the exam" (Madaus, 1988, p. 97), and certification loopholes are created by state legislators, both the content of teacher education curricula and the endorsement of teachers are divorced from professional control.

Rather than being determined by state agencies or external testing agencies, testing in other professions is managed by members of the profession, who are charged with developing and scoring the examinations as well as defining the standards for internships and other entry requirements. This increases the chances that the assessments will be valid representations of professional tasks and modes of thinking.

By contrast, teacher tests are typically constructed by professional item writers, although advisory boards of teachers sometimes review item specifications or content categories. Meanwhile, test makers' "validation" studies of teacher tests have not attempted to discern any connection between candidates' test scores and their later teaching performance, nor have they subjected the test content to intensive professional scrutiny and modification. Instead, the approach used by test developers is to survey education program faculty members and, in some cases, practitioners, asking them to rate whether test content categories can be said to be represented in the teacher education curriculum or are perceived as important in the job of teaching.

Respondents are not asked whether the questions themselves are good representations of how teachers use knowledge or skill or whether the answers proposed represent reasonable approaches to the resolution of teaching dilemmas. The results of such surveys are not used to alter the content of the tests but, instead, to set cutoff scores for passing. Thus, test items in which educators have little confidence remain on the tests even after "validation" has been accomplished, and areas that have been ignored are not added. Equally important, this approach to test construction does not produce a coherent statement of what teachers should know and be able to do, thus providing no guidance for either professional education or teaching practice.

Edward Haertel (1991) summarized the many concerns expressed by researchers and members of the profession:

> The teacher tests now in common use have been strenuously and justifiably criticized for their content, their format, and their impacts, as well as the virtual absence of criterion-related validity evidence supporting their use.... These tests have been criticized for treating pedagogy as generic rather than subject-matter specific, for showing poor criterion-related validity or failing to address criterion-related validity altogether, for failing to measure many critical teaching skills, and for their adverse impact on minority representation in the teaching profession. (pp. 3–4)

Mismeasuring Performance

In part because of dissatisfaction with the usefulness of existing paper-and-pencil tests, during the 1980s many states turned to performance assessments of teaching skills. In nearly a dozen states, primarily in the South, beginning teachers are granted an initial license to teach when they have satisfied educational and other certification requirements. They are granted a regular or continuing license only after they have secured a teaching job and passed an on-the-job performance evaluation. However, "like the current written examinations these observational methods have been strongly criticized . . . for trivializing teaching proficiency and for reinforcing a single, narrow conception of effective teaching" (Haertel, 1991, p. 5).

The first generation of such tests of teaching skills, developed in Florida and Georgia and used throughout the southeast and elsewhere, involves observing novice teachers at work and rating their teaching behavior according to a predetermined checklist. The structure of most of these programs is similar: Assistance and assessment teams of one to three people (usually an administrator, a "mentor" teacher, and a state department or university education department representative) are to observe new teachers two or three times during the first year. Observers are usually trained to use state-developed performance observation instruments that list criteria deduced from a portion of the teaching-effectiveness literature. In some cases, new teachers are given a development plan to follow. In addition to a varying number of formative evaluations, at least one summative evaluation is required during the first year.

If new teachers fail to demonstrate the behaviors designated as indicators for the required list of competencies, they are to receive assistance from the team or attend staff development (Goertz, 1988). Those who still fail to master the competencies cannot receive a teaching license. Thus, supervision is focused on the specific behaviors required by the form rather than on actual problems of practice (Borko, 1986). As Fox and Singletary (1986) pointed out: "Few [programs] focus on the goals of developing a reflective orientation and the skills essential to self-evaluation."

This first-generation effort is correctly concerned with performance. However, the technique employed falls short of adequately discriminating between those who are and those who are not fit to practice. These early efforts suffered from three major shortcomings:

1. The rating instruments seek to promise objectivity by specifying a set of generic uniform teaching behaviors that are tallied in a small number of classroom observations. In so doing, they fail to assess the appropriateness of teaching behaviors and decisions, and they completely neglect teaching content.
2. The assessment systems do not evaluate candidates in similar job settings and performance situations.
3. Licensing assessments are made in part by employers who are also responsible for hiring and for granting tenure, thereby entangling licensing and employment decisions in conflicts of interest.

Inadequate Rating Systems. Despite the shortcomings of process-product research reviewed in Chapter 2, the conversion of teacher effects research findings to uniform rules for teacher behavior is a cornerstone of these performance-based teacher evaluation models. Many of these evaluation instruments expect the teacher to exhibit standard behaviors that are identical across classrooms, regardless of the subject matter being taught, the goals of a particular lesson, the ages or other characteristics of the students, or other features of the classroom environment. The models implicitly assume that the rules are generalizable because student outcomes are determined primarily by particular uniform teaching behaviors. By implication, the models assume either that other contextual influences on student outcomes are relatively unimportant or that these other influences do not call for different teaching behaviors in order for teaching to be effective.

At this point, research on teaching has demonstrated that the assumptions underlying such assessments of uniform teaching behaviors are seriously flawed. The subset of "effective teaching" research used to support most of these early evaluation strategies has unearthed many of its own limitations—for example, that teaching behaviors found effective in some situations are not effective or even counterproductive when used too much or under the wrong circumstances (Peterson and Kauchak, 1982; Medley, 1977; Soar, 1972). Because important context variables change the relationship between a given behavior and its outcome, effective teachers, in fact, vary their behaviors across teaching situations (Shavelson and Dempsey-Atwood, 1976; Stodolsky, 1984). As Jere Brophy and Carolyn Evertson (1976) observed:

> Effective teaching requires the ability to implement a very large number of diagnostic, instructional, managerial, and therapeutic skills, tailoring behavior in specific contexts and situations to the specific needs of the moment. Effective teachers not only must be able to do a large number of things; they also must be able to recognize which of the many things they know how to do applies at a given moment and be able to follow through by performing the behavior effectively.

However, rather than legitimizing this complexity, as professions must when they begin to codify their knowledge base and seek to establish standards for entry (Starr, 1982), the first-generation teacher assessments have reinforced conceptions of teaching as simple, cookbook-driven work.

Sometimes, the limitations of such simple applications are pointed out by additional process-product research. For example, in one study seeking to validate Georgia's Teacher Performance Assessment Instrument, two of the instrument's behaviors actually produced significant negative correlations with teachers' effectiveness as measured by student achievement gains (Ellett, Capie, and Johnson, 1981).

One behavior—the way in which the teacher "attends to routine tasks"—was significantly and negatively related to students' progress in both reading and mathematics. Another—the way in which the teacher "specifies and selects learner objectives for lessons"—was significantly and negatively related to students' progress in mathematics. Interestingly, related planning behaviors concerning the selection of procedures, materials, and assessments were also negatively related to students' mathematics progress, although not significantly. These negative relationships lead one to question whether the behavioral indicators selected were based on a notion of planning as rigid, too highly specified, or inattentive to student characteristics—all of which have been found to undermine effective teacher planning.

This example illustrates another concern about many of these instruments: that they frequently focus on attributes of teaching that are trivial but easy to measure, emphasizing such indicators as "starts class on time" and "keeps a brisk pace of instruction," along with "managing routines" and "writing behavioral objectives." In focusing on easily observed generic behaviors derived from one small subset of the body of research on teaching, the guts of teaching and learning are largely ignored. As Lee S. Shulman (1986, p. 13) noted:

> What policymakers fail to understand is that there is an unavoidable constraint on any piece of research in any discipline. To conduct a piece of research, scholars must necessarily narrow their scope, focus their view, and formulate a question far less complex than the form in which the real world presents itself in practice. This holds true for any piece of research; there are no exceptions. It is certainly true of the corpus of research on teaching effectiveness that serves as the basis for these contemporary approaches to teacher evaluation. In their necessary simplification of classroom teaching, investigators ignored one central aspect of classroom life: subject matter.

Even when studies have noted the contextual limitations of process-product research, such findings have often been ignored when research has been translated into supervision and evaluation schemes. This simplification of findings occurred so as to avoid a situation in which evaluators would have to make judgments about appropriateness. Although they were constructed to provide "objective" data ensuring high reliability by using low-inference tallies of behavior, these "evaluator-proof" rating systems seriously misrepresent both the act of teaching and the findings of research on teaching (Wise and Darling-Hammond, 1987). Meanwhile, other bodies of research—such as research on cognition, child development, motivation and behavior, subject-specific pedagogy, and effective schooling—are typically not included in the evaluation protocols focused on generic teaching behaviors (Darling-Hammond, 1986b; Darling-Hammond, Wise, and Pease, 1983; French, Hodzkom, and Kuligowski, 1990).

The Florida Performance Measurement System (FPMS) provides an important example of this approach. In addition to its use in Florida, the FPMS has been used in Kentucky, and many of its principles have been used in teacher evaluation instruments in South Carolina, North Carolina, and Texas (Hazi,

1989). Similar systems of behavioral tallies are also in use in Mississippi, Tennessee, and Virginia (French, Hodzkom, and Kuligowski, 1990). In an important sense, then, the FPMS approach represents a prototype of an evaluation model that has had widespread policy consequences, both within the state—since the instrument has been used to drive many different types of decisions about teacher certification, tenure, retention, and compensation—and outside the state, where others looking for reform guidance have found it a readily available tool for their own goals.

In the FPMS observation-based behavioral tally, the observers record the frequencies of specific behaviors in two columns—one for "effective" behaviors, the other for "ineffective." The observer does not record any other behaviors, any information about contextual factors, or any information about the behaviors of students or other individuals in the classroom; nor does any interpretive narrative accompany the tally.

What do beginning teachers who learn to teach to the FPMS actually learn? First, evidence suggests that the range of teaching concerns they are likely to encounter and consider will be much narrower than would otherwise be the case. When Hoover and O'Shea (1987) compared the postobservation conferences of supervisors who used the FPMS with those who used a more open-ended "analytical recording form," they found that a much narrower range of relevant behaviors was discussed by the FPMS users, and these focused almost exclusively on those behaviors listed on the FPMS checklist.

Among the concerns missing from such discussions are those ignored by the instrument: the teacher's content knowledge and treatment of subject matter; the relationship between teacher practices and student responses or outcomes; practices related to emerging bodies of research, such as the use of collaborative learning strategies or inductive methods for stimulating higher-order thought processes; and the teacher's performance outside of the observation context (French, Hodzkom, and Kuligowski, 1990). Nonobservable aspects of teaching using the FPMS approach include curriculum planning, the types of assignments and feedback given to students, the quality and variety of materials used, diagnostic efforts on behalf of pupils having difficulty, the depth and breadth of content covered, the coherence among lessons or units over time, interactions with parents and colleagues, and many other important dimensions of good teaching.

Teachers trained to teach to the FPMS indicators are unlikely to learn to vary their behaviors according to the needs of students and the demands of the teaching situation. In fact, as we describe later in this section, they would explicitly learn not to do so, even when research and experience indicate they should. In the process, they would likely learn to disdain complexity in both research and teaching, as the FPMS itself does. Ironically, the instrument frequently ignores or contravenes the findings presented in the substantial research summary prepared for the Florida initiative (Florida Coalition, 1983). Although the massive summary document entirely excluded some bodies of research from its purview, it did provide an honest, thoughtful, and thorough examination of the "effective teaching" research it sought to review.

For example, in a dense, nine-page discussion of the research on praise, the research document noted the differential effects of generalized and specific praise on children at different ages, of different genders, and under different circumstances. It went on to note that "even identical teacher statements made under the same circumstances and with the same intent (to provide encouragement or reinforcement) may be experienced very differently and may have very different effects in different individuals" (Florida Coalition, 1983, p. 32).

Nonetheless, the FPMS instrument provides only two behavioral indicators regarding praise to guide its tallies: "gives specific academic praise" (to be tallied as effective) and "uses general nonspecific praise" (to be tallied as ineffective). The coding manual includes the following note: "The use of general praise is pedagogically acceptable in the kindergarten and primary grades, for students have not yet learned to discount it. Even so, tally it on the right side [as an ineffective behavior]" (Florida State Department of Education, 1989, p. 7). The system, thus, consciously conveys to teachers that their use of pedagogically acceptable practices is not acceptable and that they should ignore research that suggests they should adjust their behaviors to different student responses or circumstances.

Similarly, despite substantial research that suggests the importance of linking classroom work to students' personal experiences, the FPMS codes as "ineffective" any teacher questions that "call for personal opinion or that are answered from personal experience." Here again, the coding manual notes that "these questions may sometimes serve useful or even necessary purposes; however, they should be tallied here [in the "ineffective" column] since they do not move the class work along academically" (Florida State Department of Education, 1989, p. 5b). This indicator is one example of a conception of teaching completely at odds with the standards for teaching recently developed by the National Board for Professional Teaching Standards and INTASC, as well as in states such as Minnesota that have drawn on a more comprehensive knowledge base.

The FPMS instrument is littered with such statements suggesting that beginning teachers should be trained to be insensitive to the students they teach and ignorant of a broader knowledge base on teaching. Floden and Klinzing's (1990) conclusion is on point: "Training teachers to follow a fixed set of prescriptions discourages teachers from adapting their instruction to the particular subjects and students they are teaching. Hence, the instructional effectiveness of teachers given such training is unlikely to be at a high level" (pp. 16–17).

Over the past decade, research on these early efforts has found that evaluation strategies that require teachers to demonstrate narrowly prescribed behaviors can induce a passive style of teaching that focuses on the implementation of routines rather than on an ongoing quest for effective practices suited to different needs and contexts (Darling-Hammond with Sclan, 1992; Floden and Klinzing, 1990; Gitlin and Smyth, 1990; Hoover and O'Shea, 1987; MacMillan and Pendlebury, 1985; Peterson and Comeaux, 1989). Although prescriptive programs simplify the task of evaluation, they put obstacles in the way of appropriate decisionmaking and teacher learning, causing teachers to be ineffective with many students as they focus more on *compliance* than on their own *effectiveness* (Sclan and Darling-Hammond, 1992).

Perhaps the most dramatic evidence of the results of these distortions is the fact that Michael Reynolds, Florida's 1986 Teacher of the Year (and a runner-up in NASA's Teacher in Space program) did not pass the FPMS assessment when he was being evaluated for a merit-pay award. His principal and vice-principal could not find enough of the required behaviors during the laboratory lesson they observed to qualify him for merit pay. Furthermore, they had to mark him down for answering a question with a question, a practice forbidden by the FPMS—although popular with Socrates and many other extremely effective teachers. This example is symptomatic of an especially egregious flaw of the instrument: It favors an approach to teaching that is distinctly ill suited to the development of students' critical thinking abilities and is apparently unaware of most recent research on student cognition.

Recent critiques of similar systems in Texas (Tyson-Bernstein, 1987) and South Carolina (Berry and Ginsberg, 1988) pointed out the limitations of attempts to establish context-free behavioral indicators as the basis for evaluation and the primary goal for teacher learning. They echo Shulman's (1987) concern that such initiatives are evidence of the "currently incomplete and trivial definitions of good education held by the policy community" (p. 20).

Lack of Comparability in On-the-Job Evaluation. The nature of the evaluation instrument is but one problem with these early performance appraisal schemes. The fact that beginning teachers are evaluated on the job by local school principals as the basis for a regular license poses other difficulties. That on-the-job evaluation of employees by employers may be an inadequate basis for making licensing decisions should be suggested by the fact that no other profession uses such a strategy (Wise and Darling-Hammond, 1987). Upon reflection, the reasons become clear. Teachers are not licensed to instruct a particular group of children, such as "fifth graders at Kennedy Elementary School." They are licensed instead to teach a diverse array of children across an entire state; thus, their assessment should evaluate performance in a more wide-ranging fashion than in a single classroom in which a beginning teacher happens to have been hired.

Furthermore, conditions across schools and classrooms vary, so that evaluation of candidates for licensure in these contexts puts those with superior teaching conditions—a wealth of materials, wonderful facilities, a curriculum in line with the instrument's assumptions, a supportive principal—at a distinct advantage over others. It is, in principle, unfair to make licensing decisions based on evaluations of performance that do not take differences in these factors into account, leaving candidates with unequal opportunities to exhibit their abilities.

Confusion of Employment with Licensing Decisions. Finally, using employers to make licensing decisions about already-hired employees, as states do when they ask principals to evaluate first-year teachers in this manner for a regular license, undermines the basic purpose of licensing. State licensing was created to enforce statewide standards for entry to practice that would protect consumers even if employers were willing to hire less qualified individuals. For these reasons, law firms are not allowed to license the lawyers they hire nor hospitals the doctors they employ. Public works departments cannot license their engineers. The reason for this is that the licensing process is supposed to protect the public by representing a common standard for evaluating competence to practice that overrides the variable standards of employers, who also must balance competing considerations of costs and convenience.

School administrators are in a conflict-of-interest situation when they are asked to make employment decisions about hiring, continuation, and tenure regarding the same people they must approve for a state license. One can anticipate that standards will be lower where teacher shortages exist and where schooling is of lower quality. Employers will be under pressure to pass candidates if they have difficulty filling positions. And districts may be placed in legal difficulty if they make contradictory decisions about the continued employment and licensure of a new employee. Ultimately, if states delegate their responsibility to employers, the variable standards of local districts will determine the outcomes of the licensure process (Wise and Darling-Hammond, 1987).

Efforts to Transform
Assessments of Teaching

Taking into account the feedback about their limitations, some states have modified or eliminated the beginning teacher performance evaluation programs they launched nearly a decade ago. As of 1990, Georgia's Teacher Performance Assessment Instrument was no longer used for certification decisions. Louisiana suspended its performance evaluation program for 1991–1992 when teachers overwhelmingly reported problems (Pitsch, 1991). The state's two major teachers' unions claimed that "a flawed instrument and procedures" required "teachers to address 91 items in as little as 30 minutes" (*Education Week*, March 20, 1991). In 1991 Virginia replaced its highly prescriptive

Beginning Teacher Assistance Program with a less prescriptive mentor-teacher pilot project.

In Florida, the use of the Florida Performance Measurement System was discontinued for making merit-pay awards because of a large number of problems (Darling-Hammond and Berry, 1988; Hazi, 1989). In South Carolina, where a prescriptive evaluation instrument was adopted as part of an education reform package, a majority of teachers reported that morale worsened as a result of the state's reforms (Ginsberg and Berry, 1990). In both Florida and South Carolina, new proposals to initiate professional development school models to support beginning teacher mentoring are now being considered (Sclan and Darling-Hammond, 1992).

The Emergence of New Assessments in Teaching

As a result of the kinds of criticisms detailed in the previous section, educators and policymakers have been seeking other kinds of assessments by which to make licensing decisions. States have individually and collectively begun to develop performance-oriented assessments. For example, Connecticut uses a semistructured interview in conjunction with paper-and-pencil tests as part of its licensing examination (Pecheone and Carey, 1989). The tasks that are the basis for the interviews are subject-specific (e.g., structuring a lesson about linear equations in mathematics) and developed from common tasks of teaching (e.g., presenting alternative solution strategies; evaluating student work). The assessments are grounded in four assumptions about teaching and testing:

- Teaching is a function of both content and pedagogical knowledge.
- Combining support and assessment is essential to the evaluation of professional competence.
- The tasks in the design of the assessment must represent authentic exhibitions of teacher-related activities.
- Professional judgment and expertise are key dimensions to assessing teacher performance. (Pecheone and Carey, 1989, pp. 122–123)

These assumptions differ markedly from those underlying first-generation assessments of teaching, which sought to evaluate teaching generically rather than in subject-matter and classroom context and to do so without allowing for the use of context-specific judgments on the part of either the candidates or the judges.

Other states are also beginning to experiment with new approaches. New York is piloting an assessment that will include analysis of videotaped representations of teacher performances. Connecticut has begun to develop performance tasks. A consortium of states is developing prototypes of assessments including performance tasks and portfolios. Meanwhile, the Educational Testing Service is replacing its old National Teacher Examinations with a new assessment, as are other test developers and professional associations that are striving to better represent the complexity of teaching. These initiatives reflect the growing consensus in the field that more rigorous and thoughtful tests for licensure are needed in teaching.

A major impetus for the development of new teacher assessments is the pathbreaking work of the National Board for Professional Teaching Standards. The board has developed performance assessments for certifying expert veteran teachers that include three components:

1. A portfolio developed at the school site, including videotapes of classroom teaching, samples of teacher work (plans, assignments given to students, descriptions of classroom events, and reflections on the effectiveness of teaching strategies), and samples of student work, collected and evaluated over a period of time to assess student growth in relation to teaching
2. An assessment center component, including a number of performance tasks evaluating content and pedagogical understanding, conducted over a two-day period of time and evaluated by expert teachers in the same field
3. Attestations of collegial work and professional contributions to the school community and the broader professional community from peers

These initiatives herald a new era in teacher assessment that may prove equal to the complexities of expert teaching itself. They have tackled the problem of adequately representing a complex knowledge base in a manner that allows assessment of skill in applying that knowledge intelligently. In so doing, the array of new assessment strategies has begun to establish some principles for the future development of assessments in teaching:

1. The generalizability and limitations of particular teaching principles must be acknowledged.
2. The simultaneous use of many kinds of knowledge and skill in teaching must be anticipated.
3. Teachers' reasoning processes in applying knowledge and making decisions must be assessed.

When professional examinations can achieve these goals, they will begin to serve the interests of both the profession and the public for stimulating as well as measuring good practice. Like the Connecticut initiatives, a primary goal of the assessments should be to improve teacher education and to strengthen the learning of candidates (Pecheone, et al., 1988), heightening what measurement experts increasingly emphasize as consequential validity (Shepard, 1993), or systemic validity (Frederiksen and Collins, 1989).

This extension of the notion of construct validity of a test to take into account the effects of instructional changes brought about by the introduction of the test into an educational system we shall refer to as the *systemic validity* of a test. A systemically valid test is one that induces in the education system curricular and instructional changes that foster the development of cognitive traits that the test is designed to measure (Frederiksen and Collins, 1989, p. 27)

Our efforts to develop a structure for an assessment system for teacher licensing in the state of Minnesota are based on the view that teaching and the assessment of teaching require contextualized judgment and expertise and that the system as a whole should be designed to stimulate better teacher education and teaching practice. In this, we have been guided by the three criteria presented earlier, by our understanding of teaching, and by our commitment to assessments whose consequential validity is aimed at producing the kind of teaching learner-centered education requires.

New Assessment Strategies
in Teaching

IN THIS CHAPTER, we discuss new strategies that are being developed for assessing professional skills and knowledge in teaching. We describe a number of possible evaluation techniques and assess their advantages and disadvantages. We also examine a number of approaches to teacher assessment that have recently been developed to begin to tap teacher thinking and complex performance. In Chapters 5 and 6 we describe the structure of an assessment system for licensing and provide a brief description of the assessment development work done by committees convened in Minnesota and California to generate prototype tasks for licensing tests.

New Assessment Strategies

As a consequence of the widespread dissatisfaction with existing tools for evaluating teacher competence, a range of new techniques and strategies for teacher assessment is being developed for use in licensure and certification decisions. In addition, the Holmes Group (1989, p. 19) reports that many teacher education institutions are developing new assessment methods, including reviews of teaching episodes on videotape; preparation of portfolios of lesson plans, curricular materials, and student work; and development of original instruments to measure change in attitudes, values, and knowledge. A long history of work using these approaches has been developed at Alverno College, which has been engaged in performance-based teacher education for over twenty years (Loacker and Jensen, 1988).

Performance exercises for teacher licensing or certification, along with new sources of information such as structured interviews and teacher-compiled portfolios, have been developed by the RAND Corporation for the California State Department of Education (Klein and Stetcher, 1991a, 1991b), the Teacher

Assessment Project at Stanford University (Shulman, 1991), the Connecticut State Department of Education (Pecheone and Carey, 1989), and the National Board for Professional Teaching Standards (Baratz-Snowden, 1991; Haertel, 1990, 1991). Researchers at the Center for Research on Teacher Education at Michigan State University have also developed performance exercises and interviews for assessing the knowledge of teacher education students.

Some of these tools are envisioned for use in assessment centers, such as those established for the selection of business managers and school administrators (Thornton and Byham, 1982). Performance exercises using similar strategies (e.g., simulated in-basket or analysis tasks) are also used in the licensing of other professionals, such as lawyers in California (Klein, 1984, 1986).

In addition to development of new methodological tools, these and other efforts are seeking to use traditional tools, such as paper-and-pencil examinations, in tasks that better represent the knowledge, skills, and demands of teaching. Under "Methods for Assessing Knowledge and Skill," we discuss the benefits and drawbacks of six methods of assessing knowledge and skill. We conclude that each is appropriate for different purposes and in different settings, and we suggest criteria that should be used to determine which technique is used to address which goals of a licensing assessment system.

Methods for Assessing Knowledge and Skill

A number of methods currently exist for assessing knowledge and skill, each of which has advantages and disadvantages: on-the-job evaluations, simulated teaching, interviews, portfolios, open-ended paper-and-pencil tests, and multiple-choice or other closed-ended paper-and-pencil tests.

On-the-Job Evaluation

On-the-job evaluation offers the advantage of observing the teacher in a setting where she or he can work within a more complex and familiar context (e.g., where the candidate knows the students well, knows how the particular lesson or unit fits into a larger framework, understands family or community needs and conditions). Thus, the appropriateness of teaching decisions for particular contextualized circumstances can be more fully observed and evaluated if assessment is conducted over a sustained period by evaluators familiar with the context. It also permits assessment of qualities that can only be evaluated over time, in actual situations demanding spontaneous, unguarded responses, and perhaps even under stress—for example, dispositions, attitudes, and skills, such as respect for students and colleagues, willingness to work collaboratively and to reflect on one's own practice, ability to interact effectively with parents.

Guided on-the-job evaluation based on professionally determined criteria is a promising method of assessment for use during the internship, when the internship experience can be structured to ensure certain kinds of experiences and tasks and evaluation can be sustained and wide-ranging. On-the-job evaluation is inadequate, however, as a single performance measure for licensing, particularly when it occurs in an employment setting, such as first-year teaching, that is not structured to ensure certain kinds of experiences or types of practice. Wide variations in the nature of teaching situations are even more likely in such circumstances than in an approved internship program that has been developed to meet certain prerequisites for adequate and appropriate learning environments.

If occasional samples of performance are used—for example, a few classroom observations, as is the norm in existing performance appraisal systems for licensing teachers—many aspects of teaching and of the teaching context cannot be taken into account. Since the lesson and class observed vary for each candidate, no common assessment of particular skills or strategies is really possible. The tasks observed are those that happen to occur—for example, dealing with a student who is late or distressed, focusing students on a challenging (or trivial) task, explaining a difficult (or an easy) concept using materials that are impoverished (or rich). Both the "tasks" and the teaching circumstances may vary tremendously from situation to situation. Since the observer cannot have full knowledge of the context or a means for standardizing the actual tasks observed, scoring procedures have typically been developed that are "objective" checklists of "generic" skills, divorced from content and context. Such indicators as "begins lesson promptly" and "maintains a brisk pace of instruction" are unable to tap the nature and content of instruction or the appropriateness of teaching decisions.

Efforts are underway to change the nature of assessment instruments used for on-the-job evaluation of teachers. For example, Praxis III, part of the Educational Testing Service's replacement for the old NTE, strives to examine more complex decisionmaking in classroom instruction. Its guidance to classroom assessors (who will be local teachers and administrators trained and certified by ETS) relies more on assessor judgments of appropriateness of instruction for a particular group of students than do the low-inference tally approaches critiqued in Chapter 3. As the assessors observe and rate first-year teachers or interns during one classroom period, they use a set of standards and questions to guide their observations rather than a checklist or tally sheet. The standards are in many cases more aligned with emerging professional standards than were conceptions of teaching behaviors embodied in first-generation on-the-job evaluations. For example, under "Domain A: Organizing Content Knowledge for Student Learning," standard A1 directs assessors to examine how the candidate "becomes familiar with relevant aspects of students' background knowledge and experiences," whereas standard A2 points to how the teacher "articulates clear learning goals for the lesson that are appropriate to the students" (ETS, 1992). Throughout the instrument, the question of how aspects of the observed lesson are appropriate for individuals and groups of students is raised.

However, this assessment, like the earlier approaches, is limited by its focus on direct observation of short-term events over a single class period in a classroom. Although brief preobservation and postobservation discussions are to occur, the "limits of looking" (Stodolsky, 1984) prevent the assessment from gathering rich evidence about teacher thinking, long-range planning and evaluation, or student work and progress over time. Even though criteria of appropriateness appear in the instrument, accurate judgments of appropriateness will not be possible since sufficient data about community and classroom contexts, students, and teacher thinking are not available to the assessors during their brief classroom visit and short conference. Some of the standards continue to anticipate a stylized, direct instruction approach to teaching rather than allowing for multiple methods of instruction. In addition, the generic character of the instrument and evaluation process prevents an in-depth assessment of teachers' subject-matter knowledge or subject-specific pedagogy. Because teacher behaviors and classroom situations are likely to vary, several observations would have to be made over time. One or two will not provide a sufficiently reliable basis for making a licensing decision. Finally, the reality of noncomparable settings and tasks occuring in classrooms where teachers are assessed makes truly reliable judgments that are adequate for licensing purposes problematic.

Many of these limitations are intrinsic to on-the-job assessments that rely primarily on brief classroom observations of teacher performance. A better setting for on-the-job assessment is during an internship program when extended observations of performance and collection of evidence about longer-term teaching decisions can be made. The best use of on-the-job evaluation in assessment is as one of several indicators of teacher development, where its possibilities for revealing contextualized decisionmaking and professional dispositions are exploited rather than ignored or "objectified" away. As in other professions, this requires continuous contact between interns and internship sponsors or faculty who will make such judgments. Given the necessarily unstandardized nature of on-the-job evaluation, it is best used as one component of the licensure decision in conjunction with other, more standardized assessments of skills and competence.

This is why other professions follow the practicum or internship evaluation with a structured and more standardized assessment of knowledge and skills in an examination setting. Practicum experiences can also form the basis for other examination exercises, as when candidates develop a portfolio during their internship that is itself evaluated or when records of practice (e.g., videotapes of the candidate teaching specific kinds of lessons, documentation of teaching materials or activities, teachers' and/or students' work samples) are a basis for juried evaluation or interviews that are part of the examination. These strategies are discussed further in subsequent sections.

Simulations

Simulations allow the examiner to standardize the situation—numbers and characteristics of students, type of task to be performed, quality of textbooks, nature of the lesson—in order to evaluate specific skills more precisely. A candidate might be asked to present a specific concept to a group of students or to deal with a certain type of disruption. Such a task requires that the candidate demonstrate skills, not simply describe what he or she would do. Simulations of this sort have been used in preservice microteaching exercises for the past two decades, but their usefulness as licensure tools has not yet been established. Simulations are used in some other professional examinations; for example, candidates for board certification in psychiatry are observed by a jury of examiners while they interview an actual patient and come up with an initial diagnosis.

Preliminary work on how this type of evaluation might be applied to advanced certification of teachers has been done by Professor Lee Shulman and colleagues in the Teacher Assessment Project at Stanford University. At least one of the pilot exercises they developed asks the teacher to present a lesson to a small group of students. This kind of evaluation has the advantage of allowing observation of skills as they are actually applied. The disadvantages are that such evaluation is likely to be expensive, and it requires the teacher to teach in an artificial setting where she or he is unfamiliar with the students' backgrounds, prior knowledge, and the context of the lesson.

In fact, David Berliner (1992; Berliner et al., 1988) found in conducting simulations as part of his studies of teaching expertise that the most expert teachers were particularly nonplussed at being asked to teach without the major tools they rely on to connect their work to knowledge of their students. These include an understanding of students' prior knowledge and learning styles, as well as relationships and routines created over time to work with specific students. In a study in which teachers were asked to teach a thirty-minute lesson on probability to a group of high school students they had not met before, the more expert teachers were the most unhappy. Although they had been given thirty minutes to plan, the experts claimed they needed more time to research classroom conditions and develop multiple activities. (Less skilled teachers found the planning time adequate.) Berliner noted:

> Despite the fact that, as a group, the experts were judged to be better teachers on a number of dimensions, the task triggered a good deal of anger among this group of teachers.... Our interviews revealed that experts rarely enter their classrooms without having taken all the time they need to thoroughly understand the content they will teach and to plan one or more activities to teach that content. In addition, the experts

noted that they did not know the students in this situation and that their expertise depended, in part, on knowing their students. . . . In addition, all the experts commented on the problems created by their inability to use routines. (Berliner, 1992, p. 44)

Thus, although this type of evaluation appears to simulate "real teaching," it does not allow the teacher to make contextualized judgments about the appropriateness of alternative teaching strategies, a major feature of applied teaching competence.

Candidates who feel uncomfortable performing on the spot may be penalized, even if this has no bearing on their abilities in an actual classroom. However, as we discuss throughout this section, each form of assessment is likely to favor or penalize individual candidates depending on the ways in which they are most comfortable expressing themselves. Any examination setting will create artificialities of one form or another. A balance can be sought by using a variety of strategies by which candidates respond to assessment questions or tasks. In the case of simulated teaching, the utility of this strategy depends in part on expense and in part on the extent to which decontextualized simulations contribute to an understanding of teacher competence.

Alternatives that compromise among assessment objectives might be explored. For example, candidates might be asked to teach a particular lesson with particular instructional goals to their own class during the internship, videotaping this lesson so that it can be viewed by jurors and perhaps be used as the basis for an assessment interview in which the teacher explains his or her instructional choices and teaching strategies. This maintains some standardization of content while sacrificing standardization of setting in order to regain access to an important aspect of teaching judgments—knowledge of the students being taught. Videotaping might also prove less cumbersome and less costly than creating staged classrooms with live students for assessment exercises.

An exercise such as this is part of the school-site portfolio for the Early Adolescence English–Language Arts assessment of the National Board for Professional Teaching Standards. As part of their portfolio, teachers submit a videotape and commentary concerning a postreading interpretive discussion held with a group of their own students. The nature of the lesson and the goals of instruction are specified, along with the types of documentation and commentary sought. These are designed to be tasks English teachers would commonly engage in, and the instructional goals point at higher-order skills and performance abilities for students.

In the version of the exercise that was piloted in the 1993–1994 school year, candidates were asked to prepare documentation that showed how they engage students in discussion "to help them build interpretations of a piece of literature and develop their discussion abilities." In the commentary, teachers were asked to elaborate on their understanding of students' processes of discussion and interpretation and their own role in facilitating these processes.

In contrast to on-the-job evaluations that try to apply generic criteria to whatever is going on in the classroom at the time the evaluator shows up, this approach maintains the fidelity of classroom context and allows the teacher to describe its importance in interpreting the way the lesson was structured and unfolded.

In their commentaries, teachers were asked to provide information about student context (students' prior experiences with this kind of task and their related abilities), instructional goals, other activities that preceded or followed the discussion and the role these activities played in helping students build interpretations, a copy of the piece of literature and other assignments or student activities related to this reading, and an analysis of the discussion that occurred. In their analysis, teachers discussed their role in the discussion, explaining why they approached the role as they did; described one or two routines or procedures they had established previously to help discussions run smoothly and pointed out evidence of these on the videotape; and described a particular moment on the video when one or more students demonstrated the kind of discussion that helps build interpretations. Finally, teachers evaluated the discussion in terms of the quality of interaction and how well it helped achieve their goals, as well as what they might do in a subsequent discussion to help students increase their discussion and interpretation skills.

Meanwhile, the task is sufficiently standardized to ensure that common criteria that are task sensitive and grounded in subject-specific pedagogy can be applied in evaluating performance. The parameters of the task are made clear by the way in which the task is specified (a postreading discussion with at least four students from the teacher's regular class, during a regular class meeting after the group has read the same piece of literature) and the way in which interpretive discussion is defined:

> An interpretive discussion is an exchange of ideas about the meanings of a piece of literature. Students talk about their ideas and listen to the ideas of others to build their own responses and interpretations that they support with references to the text. For example, students may hypothesize about characters' motivations or authors' intentions; they may analyze the structure of the text and how it affects them as readers; they may share their personal feelings and experiences in relationship to the text; they may retell all or parts of what they have read; they may ask questions; they may compare this piece of literature to other texts that they have read or seen to discover underlying themes. This interchange of ideas offers students opportunities to consider alternative perspectives, clarify their own understandings, and deepen their original interpretations, while at the same time providing a sense of shared meaning for the class.
>
> Although a discussion may be initiated by either the teacher or by students, the teacher can foster students' responses by using a variety of strategies. For example, teachers may ask questions and elicit student questions, pose problems, or encourage students to use strategies that were taught or demonstrated during past discussions. They rely on their knowledge of and sensitivity to how students interact, both verbally

and nonverbally, to help them manage an environment in which students feel comfortable sharing their thinking. (NBPTS, 1993b)

This definition clearly incorporates the standards written by NBPTS standards committees upon which the assessment is based. The standards are built upon knowledge about about how students develop comprehension and analysis skills, as well as abilities to communicate ideas and learn in groups, and about how teaching strategies can support students' growth in these areas. Note that this task illustrates several features of authentic performance assessments, in that it is a contextualized task commonly performed by teachers; the nature of and criteria for performance are clearly described and openly conveyed rather than hidden or secret; and developing good performance can be both a learning experience and an occasion for assessment (Glaser, 1990).

As with classroom observations, it is not clear how many such lessons would have to be videotaped to get a reliable indicator of how well a teacher performs. It is also not clear whether scores on such measures are affected by characteristics of the students or other aspects of the learning environment. These issues should be explored in future research on such assessment tasks.

Interviews

An open-ended interview format allows the candidate to describe what he or she would do in a given situation and why. It can also be used to allow the candidate to explain what he or she in fact did in an actual classroom situation (as in the videotaped lesson example described in the previous section) or in an assessment situation, such as a simulated teaching exercise. Such interviews are used in other professional licensing examinations: For example, prospective architects in California answer questions about their portfolios of work, and clinical social workers discuss a case and alternative treatment plans (Haertel, 1990, p. 283). Connecticut uses structured interviews as one component of its licensing examination for teachers. The Stanford Teacher Assessment Project used interviews in several kinds of exercises: explaining a lesson plan developed during an assessment exercise, explaining how specific materials reviewed by the candidate might be used in a specific lesson, discussing contents of a candidate's portfolio (Haertel, 1991).

Interviews allow a two-way exchange of information that can itself be part of the evaluation, since a candidate's questions may illuminate knowledge as well as his or her answers. For example, the candidate might ask for more information about a hypothetical situation presented—for example, "Have these students written a personal essay before?" "How long ago did the students study improper fractions?" "How old is the student who produced this piece of work?"—and the evaluator might use these queries as one measure of knowledge or skill.

Although there is no guarantee that the candidates would actually do what they describe as an appropriate course of action, they might be asked to demonstrate aspects of their answer: "Explain that to me as if I were a sixth grader." "What would you draw on the board then?" Such a format, used either alone or in conjunction with any of the others, also offers the examiner an opportunity to probe for the candidate's underlying knowledge and thought processes.

An example of using a structured interview approach to illuminate teacher knowledge and thinking is an exercise used in research at Michigan State University's Center for the Study of Research on Teacher Education. A number of exercises were developed to explore preservice teacher education students' thinking about teaching in several different subject areas. This excerpt is for "planning and teaching mathematics" at the elementary school level. It involves subtraction with regrouping. The interviewer shows the candidate a page from a second-grade math textbook and asks a set of questions:

1. Do you remember learning this yourself? What do you remember? [Listen for what the person considers the "this" here—e.g., subtraction, "borrowing", lining up numbers in columns.]

2. What do you think about this workbook page? . . . Do you think this is a good way to present this? Why or why not?

   Are there things you think are quite good in here?

   Some things you think are weaknesses or flaws? Why?

3. What would you say a pupil would need to understand or be able to do before they could work on this?

   Why is _____ important for this?

   Is there anything here you think might be especially hard for pupils?

4. Now here's a section from another text series.

   Can you compare the two? Does anything seem different?

   Which do you prefer? Why?

5. Can you describe a little bit about how you would approach this if you were teaching second grade? Don't feel that you have to stick to either of these pages if you have another way you'd want to work with your class, but you can use it if you choose.

   Probe as needed:

   Why would you do that?

   How did you come up with this idea/approach?

   What do you mean by _____? Can you give me an example of what you mean?

   Is there another way you can imagine doing this?

The interview goes on to ask how the candidate would know whether the students are understanding the concept and uses another prompt—a piece of work from one student—to explore the teacher's analysis of the student's knowledge and thinking. After assessing what the student does or does not understand, the candidate is asked how he or she would respond to the student's work, what he or she would have the student do next, and how he or she would go about learning anything else he or she needed to know in order to teach this concept more effectively.

This example obviously provides a wealth of information about teacher thinking and understanding in the preservice education context. Although these advantages could also be important within a licensing context, the disadvantages of structured interviews for licensing examinations may include costs of administration, difficulties in standardizing scoring, and the potential biases that can occur when face-to-face administration allows evaluators to be consciously or unconsciously influenced by a candidate's gender, race, ethnicity, or other personal characteristics. (Of course, these difficulties are also associated with simulations and on-the-job performance evaluations.) Because the interview is necessarily oral, the candidates' verbal abilities may affect scores independent of the content of their responses. Since communication skills are a prerequisite to teaching, this is not necessarily bad, but examiners must be wary of mistaking glibness for the ability to explain and of jeopardizing the chances of those who are thoughtful but not loquacious.

The expertness of examiners is crucial for this method, as it is for many of the others as well. Training and the use of multiple jurors may be needed to offset subjectivity and potential biases. For these reasons, Haertel (1990, p. 289) noted that

> Many exercises initially designed around structured interviews might be converted to a paper-and-pencil or computer-based administration. The advantages of these formats could include cost savings in administration and scoring; improved standardization of testing conditions; greater reliability and objectivity in scoring; and creation of a complete and permanent record of examinee performance that could be reviewed if ever the scoring were challenged.

Nonetheless, because of the possibilities for exploring teachers' intentions and allowing for two-way communication, some assessment exercises may be greatly enhanced by the use of interviews to probe the teacher's rationale for proposed strategies and his or her understanding of what has occurred in a given situation. Given the trade-offs, such exercises should be carefully chosen to take greatest advantage of the benefits of this method while paper-and-pencil methods are used for other components of the assessment to save on costs, increase reliability and standardization of scoring, and reduce possibilities for bias.

In Connecticut's semistructured interview for licensing in mathematics, tasks performed in the interview include structuring a unit, structuring a lesson, evaluating alternative approaches students might learn to use in solving linear equations, and evaluating student performance (Pecheone and Carey, 1989). These enable interviewers to assess the extent to which the teacher understands the mathematical and pedagogical relationship among topics; the extent to which the teacher can develop a lesson around a particular concept, tying mathematical concepts to past, present, and future learning of students; the extent to which the teacher can differentiate among various approaches as they might relate to the purposes of instruction and the characteristics of students; and the teacher's ability to analyze student understanding and errors, as well as developing strategies to address them. The interview tasks also provide several inroads for examining the teacher's own content knowledge and depth of understanding in mathematics.

Early reliability investigations of these interviews suggested that they can be scored reliably by evaluators who have had the kind of training the Connecticut State Department provided in a full-day training and practice session. Some data also suggested that scores are independent of candidates' physical characteristics, such as age, race, and gender (Grover, 1989; Pecheone and Carey, 1989). Ongoing research is examining the content and construct validity of the interview exercises, the extent to which scores are susceptible to influence based on the candidates' verbal fluency or on outside coaching or special instruction, and the extent to which they produce systemic validity—that is, efforts by the teacher preparation and mentoring system to better prepare teachers as curriculum decisionmakers (Pecheone and Carey, 1989).

Additional experience with semistructured interviews was obtained in the Teacher Assessment Project at Stanford. In an evaluation of the outcomes of two such exercises—the "Evaluation of Student Papers" and "Use of Documentary Materials" exercises for U.S. History teachers—Wilson and Wineburg (1992) demonstrated how differences in teachers' conceptions of teaching, learning, and subject matter can be illuminated using semistructured interviews. They contrasted the responses of two teachers to questions about how they graded a set of student essays and how they would use a set of primary source materials. The comparison and interpretation of responses illustrates the ways in which carefully selected interview questions can elicit information that distinguishes between very different approaches to teaching.

Portfolios

Portfolios provide the opportunity to compile records of practice that can be evaluated by experts or can serve as the basis for structured interviews concerning aspects of practice. They can include documents that derive directly from teaching—copies of lesson or unit plans, syllabi, handouts given to students, assignments, tests, samples of student work (with or without teacher feedback)—along with photographs, videotapes, or audiotapes of classroom activities ranging from bulletin boards and displays to taped lessons, conferences with students, and the like.

They can also include documents that require additional work on the part of the teacher—teacher logs or journals, detailed descriptions or analyses of lessons, student work, other teacher activities, and reflections on the outcomes of teaching activities. Portfolios can include documents that derive from the evaluations of others: notes by an observer of teaching, peer or administrator recommendations, student evaluations, and so on (Athanases, 1990; Bird and King, 1990; Haertel, 1991).

Although they provide potentially rich evidence of teacher knowledge and skills, portfolios have several drawbacks as well. Many kinds of portfolio artifacts may or may not represent the actual work of the candidate. Teachers could conceivably use "canned" lesson or unit plans available in many commercial packages or district curriculum guides, syllabi obtained from other teachers, or assignments or tests developed by others. Whereas it is possible for candidates to deliberately misrepresent their work in a portfolio, it is also true that much curriculum work is done collegially or is derived from already available sources. Although this is not necessarily a sign of "cheating," it limits the inferences licensing assessments may draw about the candidate's own abilities as they are reflected in particular artifacts of teaching.

At the same time, however, portfolio entries are likely to be used as a source for other analyses of teaching, such as teacher reflections on practice, analyses of student work, videotaped teaching episodes associated with planning or assessment documents, or further discussion of teaching intentions and outcomes in assessment center exercises or interviews. In this case, the originality of plans or teaching materials is much less important than the teachers' ability to use them effectively and to understand the effects of their use on student learning.

Other concerns that have been raised about portfolios include questions about the extent to which candidates' abilities to present a glossy showing of their accomplishments actually represent what they do in the classroom and concerns that the time needed to satisfy elaborate portfolio requirements may actually deflect teachers' attention from their students and from other teaching concerns—a concern that was voiced by candidates for Tennessee's master teacher program about the portfolio requirement. Finally, portfolios may be difficult to score in a standardized fashion. A key question that must be addressed for each item in a portfolio is what does this particular work sample represent about the teacher's knowledge, skills, dispositions, and overall competence.

Nonetheless, carefully selected portfolio requirements may be useful for licensure assessment to the extent that they are targeted on well-defined skills and abilities and can be verified as truly representative samples of the teacher's own work. It is possible that the most useful entries would be those further interpreted by the teacher in an assessment exercise, thus establishing the candidate's understanding of the material and providing a basis for evaluating his or her knowledge in particular areas.

School-site portfolios are a central part of the new National Board for Professional Teaching Standards assessments. In the two areas in which assessments are currently being piloted (Early Adolescence English–Language Arts and Early Adolescence Generalist), teachers construct portfolios that include videotapes of their teaching, with attendant commentary that establishes the instructional context, intentions, and an evaluation of the material on the tape; they submit work samples for two or three students who are followed over time, with commentary about the students, their progress, and the teaching and learning processes exemplified in their work; and they document their instruction over a sustained period of time (at least several weeks) through artifacts (e.g., lesson plans and assignments), written commentary about goals, concepts being studied, activities, and outcomes, and a thirty- to forty-minute videotaped segment of instruction from this period.

The board's approach has several advantages over early attempts to look at on-the-job teaching. First, it takes a long view of the course of instruction, documenting how teaching and learning evolve over a number of weeks and attending to how what is occurring at a given moment in time (captured in a videotape, as earlier approaches to evaluation sought to do in classroom observations) relates to what has gone on in the previous weeks and to the particular needs of students in the class. Second, it provides a variety of ways to examine teaching within the context of students and subjects and to examine whether teachers can recognize and address important contextual considerations. These strategies for tying commentary to specific, contextualized teaching events provide examiners with information regarding the rationale for curricular and pedagogical decisions. Third, the portfolio, through the samples of individual student work over time, enables an examination of how student learning is influenced by teaching, how teachers' analyses of student work and progress influence teaching decisions and practices, and how these, in turn, support or fail to support student progress. Because teachers are asked to select the students whose work is longitudinally displayed so as to represent diverse approaches to learning, the teachers' ability to recognize and support different learning styles or needs is also tapped.

The portfolios are scored by exercise, each of which includes several different sources of data. For example, the English–Language Arts portfolio includes three distinct exercises: the postreading interpretive discussion described earlier, which includes a videotape and commentary with selected artifacts; the planning and teaching exercise, which documents instruction over several weeks through statements of goals, a chronicle of daily activities, a videotape, and three commentaries; and the student learning exercise, which follows students through work samples over time, accompanied by commentaries and instructional artifacts.

Within each exercise, the several sources of evidence are evaluated in combination—as an understanding of any one relies on the others—according to a scoring scheme that asks evaluators to assess the candidates by looking for evidence of how they meet the board's standards. The search for evidence is guided through a set of specific questions tied to particular aspects of teaching that derive from the standards.

As evaluators read the evidence assembled in the portfolio, they make judgments guided by specific questions about the extent to which the teacher's thinking and examples of practice illustrate these aspects of highly accomplished teaching. In one scoring scheme that was piloted by the University of Pittsburgh developers, raters cited specific places where they found evidence in support of their judgments. For example, this excerpt of an interpretive summary of a candidate's work supports a judgment about "learner-centeredness":

> *Candidate #00001:* Candidate demonstrates knowledge of students as writers and thinkers. Candidate begins each school year by asking students to fill out autobiographical index cards, which provide data about student background and goals for the year (2). Candidate uses these cards, as well as notes and records from student conferences to tailor instruction, e.g., focusing on helping Student B with his goal to better handle long-term assignments (2, 3, 103, 104). Students A and B are described as distinct writers and learners with differing needs and goals. Candidate devotes considerable time to student conferencing and individual instruction (2). . . . Independent student project allows students opportunity to take control of their work, by choosing and refining topics, selecting their own materials, and evaluating their own progress (63–64). . . . Comments on student papers (120, 204) and language of commentary demonstrate a high degree of respect for students and their ideas (4). (Delandshere and Petrosky, 1992, p. 30)

In another case, a candidate's much lower score on the same dimension is justified by pointing to contrary evidence:

> *Candidate #00002:* Candidate tends to account for writing problems almost exclusively in terms of students' negative personality traits ("unsure of himself," "defensive," "feeling of . . . being great") (30) with little regard to the possible relationship between students' work and characteristic patterns of development of young adolescent writers and thinkers. . . . There is some evidence that her understanding of writing and thinking of young adolescents [YAs] is limited, e.g., candidate characterizes Student A's waking from a dream ending in paper 6 as unusual for YAs (2), but it is actually quite common. . . . Although students were permitted to select "a topic and style" once during this period (19, 43), skills identified by the teacher (i.e., paragraphing, word selection) were still focus of conferences and assignments. There are no other examples of candidate attending to the interests of students. (Delandshere and Petrosky, 1992, p. 31)

The board's work illustrates how standards of knowledge can be applied to open-ended, contextualized representations of work without resorting to simplistic checklists. By looking at similar tasks about which evidence is collected and presented in a structured and standardized manner, it is possible to evaluate candidates against common standards. This is made possible by assuring that similar kinds of data about teaching will be available for assessment.

Open-Ended Paper-and-Pencil Tests

Open-ended paper-and-pencil tests to evaluate knowledge or skill can offer candidates opportunities to perform many of the tasks central to teaching— planning lessons, evaluating a textbook, developing a test or an assignment for students, proposing a plan for addressing a student's particular needs—and to explain the reasons for their choices or responses (Klein and Stetcher, 1991a). Such responses can be developed in response to a videotaped scenario, a set of materials provided during the examination (e.g., students' papers, curriculum materials), or a written question.

Such tests can offer a candidate the opportunity to produce teaching "designs" (e.g., a plan for a lesson or unit), as well as elaborated responses to questions calling for complex analysis of situations within which many variables are operating and more than one appropriate answer is possible. They can provide raters with an opportunity to evaluate the candidate's ability to think pedagogically—for example, to consider important factors in reaching judgments and to plan for alternatives—in the way that essay questions on bar examinations seek to evaluate candidates' abilities to think "like a lawyer."

Open-ended written responses are common in the licensing examinations for many other professions, including essays on bar examinations and architectural designs on the architectural registration exams. Preliminary work using open-ended written response methods for the evaluation of teachers has been conducted by Shulman's Teacher Assessment Project at Stanford University, by Robert Millward at Indiana University of Pennsylvania, by the Center for Research on Teacher Education at Michigan State University, and by the RAND Corporation, among others.

This method has the advantage of allowing complex responses while preserving the anonymity of candidates, so as to avoid rater bias associated with personal characteristics of the test takers. It is also easier to produce more standardized scoring rubrics for written responses than for interviews or portfolios. As a measure of knowledge, it offers a means of asking complex questions that require synthesis and understanding by the candidate, and it can evaluate the application of knowledge to a particular problem of practice. In contrast to close-ended tests, it measures the candidate's ability to identify issues and to produce, not simply recognize, answers.

Although considerably less expensive than observations or interviews, this approach is more expensive than multiple-choice tests because experts must evaluate the candidates' responses. Because written examinations do not offer the possibility of watching the candidates teach, there is no way of knowing from the test itself whether candidates could or would put into practice what they suggest as courses of action.

Scoring may be affected by candidates' ability to express themselves in writing rather than orally or by demonstration, thus favoring some individuals over others—and possibly even some groups of teachers, such as English teachers, over others. This approach stresses writing skills more than most actual teaching activities do. This is not necessarily a purely negative feature of the method, since teachers should be competent at expressing themselves in written form; still, it suggests that this approach should be used most extensively for tasks closest to those actually conducted by teachers, for tasks that require complex responses, and probably in conjunction with other testing methods using different response modes.

The Stanford Teacher Assessment Project produced a number of tasks of this sort. A "Textbook Analysis Exercise" for U.S. History teachers, for example, asks for an essay response to an excerpt dealing with the American Revolution from a widely used U.S. History textbook. Candidates were asked to evaluate the book for adoption by an urban school district, paying special attention to three subtopics of the American Revolution: the role of minorities and women, the Boston massacre, and the issue of taxation and representation. Their essay was to "provide a candid review," considering "the soundness of the history presented; the book's appeal to students; the quality of the writing; the book's potential as a tool for enhancing social studies skills; the book's appropriateness for different kinds of students; its general strengths and weaknesses; and any other information relevant to its possible adoption" (Wilson and Wineburg, 1992, p. 26). Responses reveal a great deal about the teacher's own knowledge base in the subject area, as well as his or her pedagogical content knowledge.

Most of the tasks used in the NBPTS assessment center component are open-ended paper-and-pencil assessments. They include such tasks as analyses of texts, assessments of and responses to student work, analyses of the instruction of other teachers (represented in videotapes and teaching artifacts), and instructional planning exercises. Nearly all of the exercises developed in our work in Minnesota and California use this response mode because of its lesser cost and greater ease of development and administration.

Multiple-Choice Paper-and-Pencil Tests

Multiple-choice evaluations of content knowledge are relatively inexpensive to develop and score, and they yield highly reliable scores. Although multiple-choice methods limit the sorts of questions that can be asked and the sorts of responses that can be received, a well-constructed multiple-choice test can probe for more than factual recall. The use of complex, branched questions on the medical boards, for example, tests candidates' ability to synthesize and analyze large amounts of information in a diagnostic fashion. (See the sample set of questions in Chapter 3, for example.) Multiple-choice tests offer a practical means for measuring knowledge of particular facts, concepts, or principles, as well as the use of reasoning skills in applying knowledge to new situations. However, they are limited in their usefulness for displaying candidates' decisionmaking processes and cannot be used to evaluate performance skills. In addition, a poorly constructed multiple-choice test that demands single answers to multidimensional problems on the basis of inadequate information can trivialize knowledge and misrepresent appropriate applications.

Multiple-choice assessment is most useful for ascertaining that candidates understand certain areas of information, key concepts, and principles in a field. In some professions, multiple-choice tests are used in part to measure basic knowledge—engineering principles, the foundations of medical science, legal precedent and case law, for example. The analog in teaching would be knowledge of basic concepts fundamental to teaching—such as understanding of child development, principles of learning, cognition, motivational theory, and so on.

These same professions also use open-ended written or oral responses to measure candidates' abilities to apply knowledge and skills to problems of practice—drafts of engineering designs; computer-based, written, and interview assessments of medical skills; and essay tests of legal reasoning or production of legal briefs or memoranda. As we describe in Chapter 6, our development of prototype tests used similar distinctions in evaluating methods most useful for different assessment purposes.

Assigning Methods to Purposes

Our criteria in evaluating assessment tools use different standards for appropriateness with respect to the purpose and timing of assessment and the nature of the content to be evaluated. For example, evaluation of a candidate for the final licensing decision must use reasonably well-standardized methods that sort candidates reliably and fairly. During an internship, however, evaluation methods may be structured more flexibly to afford greater diagnostic information. In addition, some kinds of teacher attributes—for example, dispositions and interpersonal skills—will be largely invisible in a written-formal testing situation but amply displayed during the internship. (These attributes are discussed more fully in Chapter 7.)

In developing prototypes, various methods should be considered and evaluated for both utility and cost. Committees with which we worked in Minnesota, for instance, generated open-ended paper-and-pencil questions as well as performance tasks requiring open-ended paper-and-pencil responses to stimuli ranging from descriptions of situations to student papers to videotapes of classroom settings. The internship working group suggested evaluations based on observation, interview, and various focused exercises.

Although simulations and portfolios were not discussed, they are likely to find a place in the internship process. Their utility for licensing examinations will be enhanced when more extensive research and development has been conducted to establish methods for reliable scoring that can account for both nonstandardized contextual elements and common specific skills to be measured. Connecticut, Vermont, Maine, and Kentucky have already begun to develop portfolio assessments for teacher licensing or teacher education program approval. Under the auspices of INTASC, a consortium of ten states has begun joint research on and development of portfolio strategies for licensing. At some point in the near future, these strategies are likely to become a major part of states' teacher assessment processes. Ultimately, each component of the education-assessment system will need to use the evaluation format(s) most appropriate to its tripartite role of (1) articulating, (2) encouraging the acquisition of, and (3) measuring mastery of knowledge, skills, and dispositions essential to teaching.

An Architecture
for a Licensing System

NEW ASSESSMENTS for teacher licensing must be considered and developed within the context of a system of licensing that links a conception of teaching and learning to teacher preparation, testing, and licensing. In our view, an assessment system for professional preparation and licensure should accomplish three basic objectives:

1. It should reflect the knowledge and skills all professionals are expected to master as a minimum requirement for responsible practice. Responsible teachers should be able to evaluate teaching and learning circumstances and make decisions in light of knowledge about teaching and learning, about the students they serve, and about their moral obligations. The assessment system thus represents a professional consensus about what kinds of abilities and commitments provide the foundations for professional standards of practice.
2. It should be constructed so as to encourage the acquisition of the required professional knowledge, skills, and dispositions. That is, the assessment system should be designed and staged in such a way that it actually increases the probabilities that prospective teachers will acquire the desired capabilities.
3. It should reliably and validly sort those candidates who are adequately prepared for responsible independent practice from those who are not.

Although these objectives for an assessment system seem reasonably straightforward and sensible, as we have seen, for a number of social and historical reasons they have not yet been fully realized in the area of teacher licensing. Among these reasons are the regulatory structure for teacher education and licensing, which has not previously relied on the judgments of professional boards as other professions do; the consequent difficulties in achieving a consensual—and legally defensible—definition of teaching knowledge and skills; and the costs of adequate preparation and assessment.

In this chapter we outline the structure for a licensing system that can meet these three conditions, taking into account the kinds of preparation, standards, and assessments needed to ensure that licensing becomes a meaningful indicator of readiness for professional practice.

Considerations in Developing Assessments

The first objective, that the assessment system reflect a professional consensus about the knowledge and skills needed for responsible practice as a beginning teacher, points us to three desiderata:

- The assessment system should articulate a clear set of statements about what teachers need to know and be able to do that is professionally defensible and grounded in the knowledge base for teaching.
- This professional consensus about needed knowledge and skills must be well represented by the assessments.
- The assessment activities must operate as a system, not merely as a series of unrelated "off-the-shelf" measures.

These are challenges because teacher tests and other requirements, in contrast to those of other professions, have been enacted by legislatures—often hurriedly and in fragmented fashion—rather than being systematically planned and constructed by professional bodies. As a result, many existing tests are not informed by professional consensus, nor do they comprise a system that defines coherent standards for beginning teachers.

Minnesota is the first state in which a professional standards board has assumed full responsibility for conceiving and creating its own assessment system. Like other professions' examining boards, the Minnesota Board of Teaching must create a process for capturing and representing the knowledge of members of the profession in its assessments. This means both establishing conceptions of the knowledge and skills bases for teaching and developing a process that will ensure that these bases are well displayed in the tests the board adopts. The outcome-based standards developed in Minnesota, like those since developed by the INTASC consortium and the NBPTS, provide a foundation for this process. (See Appendix C.) Bringing expert teachers together to help develop and test the assessments is an essential step.

The second objective, that the assessment system actually encourage the acquisition of the required knowledge, skills, and dispositions, suggests attention to both the validity of measures and the relationship between assessment and preparation. Many current tests so poorly represent the actual abilities they purport to measure that preparing for the tests does little to encourage the acquisition of real skills. For the most part, current testing programs are structured more to screen out candidates than to encourage better training. The tests frequently serve symbolic purposes while failing to achieve the public policy purposes of improving teaching and protecting the public against incompetence.

Since we consider the encouragement of better teacher education and clinical support to be proper objectives of an assessment system, and since no assessment mechanism can fully measure all of the requisite abilities, we believe measurement must be a secondary, although indispensable, goal of the system. Inducing effective preparation and good practice is a major goal of a licensing assessment system.

This has a number of implications for the content of assessments and for the design of an assessment system. Chief among them is that an internship program is a component of an assessment system that serves training and evaluation functions of its own, as well as preparation for an examination of teaching knowledge and skill. In addition, decisions about what is tested and how it is tested should be made as much on the basis of whether test content and methods encourage the kinds of learning a state would like candidates to engage in as on the ability of test items to rank or sort candidates. This concern for consequential or systemic validity has implications for the nature of the assessments developed and for the ways in which they are validated.

The third objective, that decisions about candidates meet tests of both reliability and validity (and that the proper standard is the ability to practice responsibly without supervision), leads us to seek approaches that will surmount the shortcomings of many states' current approaches to assessment. Many paper-and-pencil tests currently in use fail the test of validity, since they are not good representations of the tasks of teaching or the reasoning process teachers must apply to problems of practice. Meanwhile, most methods for on-the-job evaluations for licensure fail the test of reliability, since they do not evaluate candidates under comparable circumstances or on comparable tasks (Wise and Darling-Hammond, 1987). Developing performance tasks that can assess candidates in comparable ways on key tasks of teaching is imperative.

The safe or responsible practice criterion—normally the primary goal of licensing—has, furthermore, not often been addressed in decisions about assessment for teacher licensing. Using this criterion to define success or failure points us to areas for assessment that look at ways in which poor teaching can be harmful (e.g., ways of interacting with children that are abusive or psychologically damaging), as well as at methods for scoring tasks that clearly identify "wrong" or "unsafe" answers while allowing for many "right" answers. Although these approaches are not yet widely used in tests for teachers, they are commonplace in tests for other professions.

Developing a Structure
for an Assessment System

The structuring task is to decide what should be evaluated, when it should be evaluated, and in what manner it should be evaluated. Developing the structure for a licensure assessment system requires at least two kinds of conceptual work. First is explicating the scaffolding for a professional education: What is included in each of its components, and how do the components fit together? Second is evaluating the construction of an assessment system: How can teaching abilities best be demonstrated and assessed? In developing a structure for a licensing assessment system, we have assumed that the following goals are important.

A Student-Centered Criterion
of Necessary Knowledge and Skill

The conceptual basis for the assessment system should be a statement of professionally defined knowledge, skills, and dispositions teachers need to serve students responsibly as independent professionals. The criterion for determining what to assess should be what *students* have a right to expect from their teachers from their first moment as teacher of record.

This is a conceptual shift in thinking about how to construct and validate teacher tests, since it explicitly grounds the goals of assessments in what students need from their teachers rather than in what the existing teacher education system currently provides. This starting point has several important implications: First, such a system is intrinsically change-oriented rather than status quo–oriented. The demands of teaching change constantly, and the assessments for licensure should keep pace with those demands. Second, as states try to figure out what kinds of preparation opportunities to require and support for teachers, they should do so against a criterion performance standard rather than against a standard that has been circularly established to measure only that which is already part of the preparation program. Finally, as the assessments are validated, they should be examined in terms of what kinds of teaching competence they select for and what kinds of learning they induce (construct and consequential validity), rather than on whether they map onto current course requirements for teachers.

A Coherent System of Guidance
to Teachers and Schools

New assessment tools should complement and not conflict with other sources of curriculum guidance and quality control, such as criteria for approving teacher education programs or other assessment mechanisms. Decisions about whether new assessments for particular purposes are warranted and what form they should take must be based on what tools are most appropriate for particular goals and how they fit within the structure of the broader system.

As part of trying to achieve complementarity and coherence, states must examine whether the ways in which they make decisions about teacher education programs and licensure are internally consistent and make changes accordingly. Although the several sets of standards we discuss in Chapter 2 are compatible with one another and with NCATE accreditation standards, the existing guidelines for teacher education approval and licensing evaluation in many states are at odds with these standards and sometimes with other sources of guidance in the same state.

For example, the licensing standards represented in Florida's Performance Measurement System, discussed in Chapter 3, are clearly at odds with the standards for licensure developed by INTASC and the NBPTS (see, e.g., Darling-Hammond with Sclan, 1992). In Florida, teachers are scored as "ineffective" if they seek to connect lessons to students' personal experiences; in the case of the NBPTS or INTASC standards, teachers would be poorly rated if they fail to connect their teaching to students' personal knowledge and experiences, since creating connections between students and subjects is a central tenet of these standards and a major concern of the research they rely upon.

Furthermore, because state legislatures and agencies have enacted testing requirements and approval guidelines in a fragmented fashion at different points in time, they are not always consistent with one another in terms of the conception of teaching they embody or the kinds of preparation they seek to inspire, even within a given state. Finally, as states undergo reforms of elementary and secondary education that influence curriculum, teaching, and assessment for students, they have typically not yet examined the implications of these desired changes in practice for teacher learning. Frequently, they are continuing to prepare teachers for a time gone by while they try to push schools into a new era. As Frazier and Callan (n.d.) noted in a guide for state leaders accompanying Goodlad's (1990) major study of teacher education:

> Many new teachers enter their first jobs unable to contribute to the reform efforts being undertaken in their schools. In schools where restructuring is occurring, this means a great waste of energy and resources, as local districts must provide further preparation to these beginners to help them become contributors to the change process. Teacher education programs thus represent an enormous investment on the part of states and institutions of higher education in keeping the schools the way they have always been. (Frazier and Callan, n.d., p. 5)

An important goal is to create a system for licensing that ensures the kind of learning for teachers that will facilitate the kinds of learning desired of children.

Careful Use of Several Sources of Evidence

Finally, the assessment system includes, but is not limited to, testing just prior to licensing; other sources of information derive from the teacher education program and the internship. Assessment should be an ongoing part of teacher preparation throughout the stage of clinical training in a supervised internship. This assessment should be pointed at the same standards as are licensing tests, and it may be structured to contribute to the examination process and licensing decision, thus strengthening confidence about the authenticity of performances evaluated and the capacity of candidates to act on what they know. At the same time, an assessment system will influence what candidates learn—and when and how they learn it. Thus, decisions about assessment should be made in the light of how they will affect teacher education and the practice of teaching.

A number of interrelated issues are central to the determination of how knowledge and skills can best be evaluated: What is to be demonstrated depends on when the evaluation occurs. How the assessment is conducted (by what method and by whom) is related to the purposes and intended outcomes of the evaluation, as well as to the nature of the content to be assessed. As we discuss later in this chapter, some assessment tools are more suitable than others for evaluating different kinds of learning and exhibitions of skill. In addition, some desirable teaching attributes are more susceptible to standardized evaluation than others. A critical task in developing an assessment system is to figure out what approaches to quality control are most appropriate for different purposes at different junctures and then to configure these tools in a coherent and sensible way so the desired outcomes are most likely to be achieved.

Parsimony in Testing

An additional consideration is how to acquire information both effectively and efficiently so important knowledge and skills are evaluated in the most expeditious manner possible. The goal of a licensing system should be quality control rather than quantity control. A new assessment system should strive to create a few good and useful measures of quality rather than many poor ones.

The current approach to setting standards for teaching in many states has been to erect a number of screens at many points in the process of teacher preparation. In some states a prospective teacher must first pass a test in order to be admitted to teacher education, must then pass a test in order to graduate from the program, and, subsequently, must pass a battery of tests (often basic skills, subject-matter knowledge, and professional knowledge examinations) in order to acquire an initial license to teach. A year later, the candidate must pass a performance assessment that evaluates on-the-job classroom performance in order to acquire a regular, continuing license. Some states have added tests for relicensure as yet another requirement during the teacher's career. The initial Holmes Group (1986) recommendations for teacher certification would have created still more stages on the path to professional teacherhood, including tests of reading, writing, subject matter, general knowledge, and the "rudiments of pedagogy" after graduating from college; examinations in pedagogy and learning following a master's degree; and "professional practice examinations" for the top tier of teachers following a doctorate.

The imposition of multiple testing requirements ensures selectivity and gives teaching the aura of professionalization; however, it is not clear that four or six or eight tests are needed to accomplish the goals of professionalization, either in terms of selection or in order to represent the knowledge base for teaching appropriately. Aside from medicine, which has staged examinations (although not as elaborate as those proposed for teaching), other professions make do with one carefully crafted, professionally administered examination for licensure. Indeed, given the widespread criticisms of current teacher tests and the costs of developing valid and useful examinations, the multiple screens route may result in a long series of poorly designed tests in lieu of a smaller number of carefully constructed, professionally defensible assessments. The potential teacher candidate who is weighing the inducements of teaching against other professional careers may demur, concluding, "alas, methinks thou dost test too much."

The costs of this approach are quite high. At every juncture at which another screen must be passed, candidates are likely to be lost, not only because of fail rates but also because the transaction costs are high. Candidates must bear monetary testing costs as well as the costs of time in preparing for and taking the tests and the psychic costs of putting their career plans on hold at each juncture while they wait for the test results. When no other college major requires tests for admission or graduation, many prospective candidates may not see the hassles associated with pursuing teaching as worth the relatively meager pecuniary benefits.

In the long run, the resolution of the supply-quality dilemma in teaching is likely to be better served by the imposition of numerically modest, defensible examinations of potential teaching ability coupled with improved assessment processes within schools of education than by the continuation of an approach that attends more to the quantity than the quality of teacher testing. We next discuss how a set of assessments mapped onto the stages of knowledge and skill acquisition in teaching could be structured.

General Structure:
Components of Professional Teaching

Professional teacher education relies upon and cultivates five kinds of abilities, which represent the knowledge and skills all teachers will be expected to master as a minimum requirement for responsible practice: (1) basic intellectual skills, (2) general liberal arts knowledge, (3) subject-matter knowledge,

(4) pedagogical and professional knowledge, and (5) teaching skills and dispositions. These abilities must be cultivated and tested in different but integrated ways, and the system as a whole must share a coherent vision. The forms of assessment that coincide with each area must be carefully designed both to encourage acquisition of this collection of knowledge, skills, and dispositions and to sort reliably and validly those candidates who are adequately prepared to practice independently from those who are not.

The first prerequisite to competent professional teaching is mastery of basic intellectual skills (1). These include such skills as the ability to read, listen, and express oneself effectively; to synthesize information, think logically, and understand different perspectives; to solve problems and interpret data. Basic liberal arts knowledge (2) and subject-matter mastery (3) are also prerequisites to professional teaching. Teachers need a broad understanding of the arts and sciences, of peoples and cultures, and of modes of inquiry to draw upon in their work, along with a deep understanding of the particular areas of study they will be called upon to teach.

Many states have sought to assess these areas of knowledge through tests of basic skills (e.g., communications and mathematics), general knowledge, and subject-matter knowledge. Such tests became popular during the early 1980s in the first wave of teacher testing legislation when concerns for teacher quality were initially raised.

Since then, most colleges of education have substantially raised their admissions requirements, and many have also increased their requirements for study in the liberal arts and sciences (Darling-Hammond and Berry, 1988). As preparation requirements are further strengthened, there should be little need for independent tests of basic skills and general knowledge, since prospective teachers will—like other professionals—have demonstrated these basic abilities prior to admission to a professional program or to graduating. Additional confirmation of teachers' abilities to access and apply their general and subject-matter knowledge and to use basic communication skills can be obtained through the construction and scoring of performance tasks in assessments of professional skills.

Thus, we concur with Minnesota's decision to accept a bachelor's degree from an accredited institution as evidence of proficiency in subject-matter and general knowledge. There, as in an increasing number of other states, all prospective teachers are required to have a grounding in the liberal arts. Prospective secondary teachers must also major in an academic discipline, whereas prospective elementary teachers must focus their studies on elementary education and a general studies curriculum.

Pedagogical and professional knowledge (4) and teaching skills and dispositions (5) are the core of professional teaching; they are the specialized knowledge, skills, and dispositions that set teaching apart from other professions.

Because these are so central to professional practice, it is appropriate that they be explicitly articulated and tested through a special assessment process. To this end, we proposed, and the MBOT endorsed, the concept of a two-part examination of professional skills and knowledge. The SKOPE (Skills and Knowledge of Professional Educators) is intended to represent a professional consensus about the knowledge and skills necessary for professional teaching, to serve as a motivating force for preparation programs to help prospective teachers master these areas, and to function as a mechanism to screen qualified candidates from those not able to practice independently.

Part 1 of this examination, covering knowledge of learning and development and educational foundations, could be taken after the completion of a teacher education program, whereas part 2, an assessment of teaching skills, would occur after an internship. Although the two parts could be taken together following an internship, there are some arguments for a staged examination, with part 1 prior to the internship and part 2 following. One argument is that taking part 1 earlier would provide a more direct connection to what has been learned during the professional education program, give an early warning of areas of further study needed prior to taking on major responsibility for clients, and offer the ability to more closely link teacher education activities to the assessment process—for example, through a portfolio developed during teacher education.

The staged option for an examination is similar to the structure for examinations in some other professions, in which initial examinations test knowledge about basic sciences and principles underlying practice and tests of clinical skills are held after an internship. For example, parts 1 and 2 of the National Board of Medical Examiners (NBME) medical examination, taken immediately after medical school, cover basic medical sciences and principles of clinical science, whereas part 3, taken after the internship, focuses on clinical skills and the ability to diagnose and treat patients within particular contexts. Similarly, after graduating from a professional program, engineering candidates take an examination in the "fundamentals of engineering," measuring basic knowledge of engineering sciences and the ability to apply them to problems. Following a period of extended "progressive experience," they may take the examination in the "principles and practices of engineering," which requires the candidate to respond to complex, contextualized problems of practice (Wise and Darling-Hammond, 1987).

Those teaching skills and dispositions that cannot be cultivated or measured by anything but long-term exposure to actual classroom situations will be developed, observed, and assessed in the course of a one-year structured internship. The internship is a means for establishing both essential skills and dispositions for autonomous practice and criteria for acceptable demonstration of their mastery. In short, all prospective teachers would be required to show mastery of the five major areas through performances of several kinds:

Area to Be Mastered	*Performance Measure*
Basic skills	Requirements for admission to teacher education
General liberal arts knowledge	BA or BS from accredited college
Subject-matter knowledge	BA or BS from accredited college
Professional knowledge	Examination of "common-core" professional knowledge
Teaching skills and dispositions	Internship assessment and Examination of Teaching Skills

One might view the progressive acquisition of knowledge and skills over the course of liberal and professional education in three stages: (1) acquiring basic or foundational knowledge and skills, (2) understanding principles for applying knowledge and combinations of skills, and (3) developing the ability to apply knowledge and perform tasks using particular skills within diverse contexts. As Fig. 5.1 suggests, these interactions between knowledge and skill acquisition occur progressively over the course of liberal education, formal teacher education, and clinical training, although there is substantial overlap. Dispositions are developed throughout the entire course of education and training. Although this representation necessarily oversimplifies the complex interactions among teachers' understandings and abilities, it serves the pragmatic function of establishing a framework for assessments.

Basic knowledge might be viewed as a set of building blocks: Knowledge about human development and subject matter in the disciplines, for example, is generally acquired in college courses within those domains. Applying that knowledge requires two additional factors that depend on analysis and judgment: the merger of several areas of knowledge and its contextualization. One must understand how knowledge about child development and knowledge about history and curriculum converge in order to apply them to a problem of curriculum development. One must also understand and take into account the teaching context in order to know whether particular principles apply in that situation. Finally, the actual ability to apply this understanding requires the ability to integrate the knowledge with a variety of developed skills—for example, skills of observation, diagnosis, and evaluation—that provide an accurate understanding of the context and student needs.

Similarly, generic skills—abilities to acquire, interpret, and communicate information, for example—serve as basic tools for more complex behavior. If they are to be usefully applied to teaching tasks, they must be further developed and combined with other knowledge and skills. For example, prospective teachers learn principles for applying communication skills when asking questions to elicit feedback from students; they develop diagnostic skills in observing and interpreting student behavior. Finally, the ability to apply these skills requires synthesizing the already complex skills with knowledge about

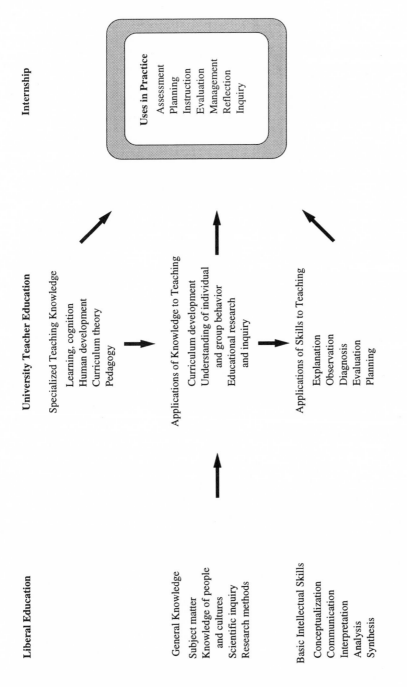

FIGURE 5.1 Developing Knowledge and Skill

learning, teaching, and context. For example, the skill required to explain a new concept to a student requires not only basic verbal ability and knowledge of subject matter but also skills in eliciting and interpreting feedback from the student, which themselves rely upon knowledge of learning and cognition.

Appropriate assessment methods will be highly sensitive to the nature (and form) of the capacities being assessed and to the stage at which prospective teachers are able to acquire and display them. Although Figure 5.1 appears to suggest that these areas of teacher knowledge and performance can be easily isolated and defined for testing at various stages, they are, in fact, closely inter-twined and are difficult, if not impossible, to disentangle. Although knowl-edge, skills, and dispositions are different from one another in "pure" form, as they are integrated and applied to theoretical and practical problems of prac-tice, the product is greater—and different in kind—than the sum of the parts.

For example, the skills associated with classroom management rest upon understandings of human behavior grounded in knowledge about motivation and group dynamics, as well as in knowledge about how to organize subject matter in coherent ways. These understandings must be activated along with abilities to manage classroom activities and discourse in ways that help create order and convey expectations. These and other understandings and abilities interact with dispositions to treat students with consideration and respect.

Furthermore, all of these aspects of teaching are manifest in real-world situ-ations that often pose tensions among valued goals. When one child is having difficulties, should the teacher attend to his or her needs at that moment or exert effort toward establishing organized group activity in the classroom? How does the teacher balance classroom needs for order and control against students' needs for openness and individual expression? How are diverse so-cial and academic goals for individuals and groups of students pursued at var-ious points in time? At what point does a challenging assignment become overwhelming or a set of manageable tasks become boring? How does the teacher find the intangible line between guiding and supporting students in their work and overmanaging that work so they are deprived of the opportu-nity to explore and learn on their own? The apparent tidiness of assessment schemes should not blind us to the messy interrelatedness of the contextual-ized understandings and actions that comprise real teaching. Furthermore, in evaluating teaching decisions and practices, it is important to keep in mind how knowledge, judgment, and skill interact to create competent teaching.

Teacher Knowledge, Judgment, and Behavior

Much of the debate about strategies for teacher evaluation has revolved around the question of how to understand and interpret teaching behaviors while acknowledging that their appropriateness depends upon different as-pects of the teaching situation: instructional goals, student needs, and contextual circumstances. In addition, assessing teacher competence for the purposes of licensure requires some understanding of how well a prospective teacher is prepared to handle a wide variety of teaching circumstances that cannot be directly observed—that is, whether the teacher has acquired the knowledge and judgment required to evaluate what strategies are appropriate in very different situations and whether she or he can apply these understandings in practice.

As Figure 5.2 suggests, readily observable teaching behaviors are but the tip of an iceberg that might be said to represent the components of teacher competence. Behaviors are informed by teacher judgments and decisions, which themselves are the products of a teacher's knowledge, beliefs, and attitudes about the contexts and purposes for education; about learners and learning; and about subject matter, curriculum, and teaching. These areas of knowledge are used, along with the beliefs and attitudes that comprise teachers' dispositions, as teachers make judgments about what they want to do based on their goals for students and subject matter.

Translating these decisions and desires into actual teaching behaviors requires many kinds of skills—for example, the ability to explain concepts

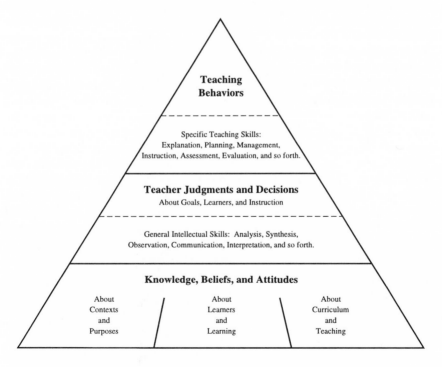

FIGURE 5.2 The Relation Among Teacher Knowledge, Judgment, and Behavior

clearly, to communicate in many ways with students and adults, to organize material for instruction, to manage classroom activities, and so on. Similarly, the ability to form reasoned judgments about how to proceed requires the use of a range of general intellectual skills that allow the transformation of knowledge and attitudes into informed decisions: skills of analysis, synthesis, interpretation of information, diagnosis of situations, and so on. Thus, general and teaching-specific skills mediate among knowledge, judgments, and actions. If these skills are well developed, they allow teachers to think and act more effectively based on what they know, believe, and intend for their students.

Although knowledge, judgment, and skills are closely related, they are manifest in different ways. Knowledge of developmental psychology, for instance, can influence instructional decisions and skill; a teacher who understands child development will be more able to create learning experiences for her or his students that take advantage of ways in which they learn easily and well. But knowledge and behavior are not identical abilities. A teacher might understand developmental theory but have no sense of how to apply it, or the teacher might have an intuitive sense of how to present material without being able to ground her or his intuition in a theoretical body of knowledge.

That knowledge and skills must both be explicitly assessed is a consequence of the fact that some aspects of teaching knowledge—such as an understanding of child development, group dynamics, or cultural diversity—may not be immediately evident in daily classroom actions but are crucial to a coherent understanding of teaching and to contextually appropriate teaching decisions. They are manifest in many places but cannot be easily disentangled from the other kinds of knowledge and skill that are also present. Although difficult to evaluate as a discrete or isolated behavior, this knowledge can be tested explicitly through questions concerning various domains of the knowledge base and through tasks that elicit teachers' rationales for their judgments about plans and actions.

At the same time, some aspects of teaching skill, such as analyzing the appropriateness of a textbook for certain teaching goals, rely on many kinds of knowledge: curriculum theory, learners and learning, methods, motivation, and human development, among others. But determining that a teacher understands these areas will not ensure that he or she will be able to analyze a textbook. This ability can only be tested through a demonstration of skill that allows the application of these areas of knowledge and the use of judgment to be shown.

A professional teacher must have both a broad base of knowledge and the ability to apply it effectively in diverse situations. If isolated skills (such as the planning of a lesson) are not grounded in a broad base of knowledge, they leave the teacher unprepared when students present particular needs that were not envisioned or problems that require further diagnosis and different strategies. On the other hand, isolated knowledge does not tell the teacher how or when to apply the principles he or she understands so well in the abstract. Teacher preparation programs must evolve in ways that help teachers acquire knowledge and skills in a thoughtful and integrated fashion.

As professional roles for teachers expand, it becomes even more essential for them to have opportunities to encounter a broad base of knowledge and to develop the skills that will enable them to make thoughtful judgments and enact these effectively. As schools increasingly aim to ensure that all students learn, teachers will be required to understand not only how to use a given curriculum but also the principles by which curricula are constructed, the circumstances under which curricular changes may be necessary, and how to develop curricula and assessments for their classroom and school. In order to perform the tasks required of professional teachers, they will need knowledge and understanding of the theories and principles that underlie specific skills, as well as the capacity to evaluate and act on the particular needs of diverse learners. In our construction of prototype assessment tasks, these intersecting applications of knowledge, judgment, and skill are addressed as interrelated and interdependent.

A licensing system that seeks to enhance the success of prospective candidates in passing rigorous assessments grounded in the demands of teaching will need to incorporate means to ensure that teacher education programs are pointed in the same direction as the new assessments. The areas of knowledge and kinds of performance described here are represented in NCATE's accreditation standards, which require that colleges ensure that candidates (1) have completed a well-planned sequence of general studies courses and experiences in the liberal arts and sciences, including theoretical, practical, and multicultural knowledge; (2) demonstrate a high level of academic competence in the areas they plan to teach, as well as in professional education courses; and (3) can integrate content and pedagogical knowledge to create meaningful learning experiences for students. In addition, the college's professional education programs must be based on established and current research and sound professional practices and must include well-planned field experiences that support students in integrating theory and practice. Finally, programs must enforce rigorous admissions standards and use multiple data sources to continually assess candidate progress and to recommend graduation. Thus, professionally accredited colleges are partners in developing and assessing teachers' abilities to integrate areas of knowledge and skill in ways that transform teacher knowledge into student understandings.

Structuring the Tests

In this section, we describe the work we did in developing the structural framework for the proposed SKOPE examinations for Minnesota. We describe first the conclusions we drew as a result of evaluating a number of conceptions of the knowledge base for professional teaching. We then describe our investigations regarding possible skills structures for the SKOPE test and propose one such structure that focuses on key tasks of teaching.

In seeking to assess knowledge, judgment, and skill, we sought to articulate the knowledge underlying the development of performance abilities. If areas of knowledge were viewed as the building blocks of teaching, then judgment and skill would comprise the understandings and abilities that permit the construction of edifices. The proposed SKOPE knowledge component would evaluate whether the teacher has the basic materials with which to make sound teaching decisions. The SKOPE skills component would evaluate whether the teacher is able to use these materials to cope with typical and critical situations that arise in practice. Although one cannot be sure from this that the teacher will be able to meet every situation successfully, one is at least assured that the raw materials and tools are available for future use.

Defining Teaching Knowledge for Assessments

In considering how to define the kinds of understandings to be included in an assessment of core teaching knowledge, we evaluated a number of formulations of the teaching knowledge base, including views of what constitutes necessary general knowledge, subject-specific knowledge, and teaching knowledge. These included major configurations reviewed in Chapter 2: Shulman's (1987) conception of the knowledge base, the components suggested by current state licensure requirements across the country, those reflected in the American Association of Colleges for Teacher Education's *Knowledge Base for the Beginning Teacher* (Reynolds, 1989) and in *Minnesota's Vision for Teacher Education.*

Some of these formulations, like Minnesota's *Vision* statement, are conceptually structured: Categories include such things as knowledge about epistemology and knowledge of people. Others, such as the formulation implied by state certification requirements, are structured by knowledge domains: Categories include, for example, courses in child development and guidance and counseling. The formulations also include knowledge about specific tasks of teaching—for example, classroom management and evaluation. Domain-based formulations help define what should be tested; concept-based formulations help define how and why certain areas of knowledge should be evaluated; task-based formulations help define the practical ends to which knowledge may be put.

In most other professions, knowledge tests are organized by domain. In law, for instance, the bar exam has domain-based parts, such as torts, contracts, and constitutional law; in architecture, the Architect Registration Examination has discrete sections such as building design and structural technology. For each domain, the profession has seminal cases, texts, and concepts that are required for its mastery; this ensures that the test itself will remain grounded in the knowledge base of the profession. In terms of test construction, this type of organization helps ensure that certain areas of basic information are sampled. These areas suggest what schools should teach and what candidates should study.

On the other hand, most applications of knowledge as well as skill will ultimately cut across any categorization of domains. For this reason, assessment development should not become a rigid, mechanical process of filling cells in matrices specifying item categories. An appreciation that multiple areas of knowledge will inform almost any response, even one that focuses primarily on a particular area, is essential to the development of tasks and scoring guides that accurately represent teacher thinking.

Conceptions of knowledge use and applications around major goals and activities of teaching, such as are represented in *Minnesota's Vision*, are useful for organizing performance assessments of teaching skill. The *Vision* statement displays the interaction between knowledge and skills by specifying not only areas of knowledge to be acquired but also principles, methods, and goals for applying these areas to specific teaching tasks. For example, teachers "must learn scientific methodology and use it systematically to identify problems and create effective learning environments. [They must] learn to interpret and apply research findings . . . on effective learning and teaching [in] defining the purpose and goals of learning activities based on designed curriculum, learner assessment, and knowledge of learning effectiveness research" (MBOT, 1986, pp. 25–28). Similarly, in the bar examination prospective lawyers must demonstrate domain-based knowledge, such as knowledge of torts or contracts, through the application of legal reasoning to a particular problem of practice. Broad knowledge of constitutional, statutory, and case law, along with analytical ability and understanding of legal principles, is necessary to answer such questions properly.

Using the configurations of teaching knowledge discussed in Chapter 2, we constructed the following categorization of teaching knowledge to guide our assessment development.

1. Knowledge about learners and learning, including knowledge about general human growth and development, motivation and behavior, learning theory, learning differences, and cognitive psychology
2. Knowledge about curriculum and teaching, including knowledge about curriculum, pedagogy, assessment and evaluation, counseling, and classroom management, as well as knowledge of scientific inquiry, epistemology, communication, and language as they relate to pedagogy

3. Knowledge about contexts and foundations of education, including knowledge about schools and society, cultures, educational history and philosophy, principles from sociology and anthropology, legal responsibilities of teachers, and ethics

This is just one of many possible configurations. It provides a good fit with Minnesota's goals and other existing configurations of the knowledge base. Further examination of competing formulations could lead to a modified structure. For any licensing system, once the basic framework for testing has been established, it defines what an assessment considers the essential knowledge base for beginning teachers. The structure of a test of teaching knowledge, once articulated, should encourage institutions of teacher education to provide their students with opportunities to encounter key ideas in the areas suggested by the test components. As a result, knowledge that professionals in the teaching field have deemed essential in order to practice should enter the curricula of teacher preparation programs throughout the state.

Unlike most current teacher tests, our proposed test of teaching knowledge does not emphasize recall of discrete, isolated facts. Instead, it aims to evaluate candidates' understanding of important principles, as well as contextual considerations that influence whether, when, and how they can be applied.

Structuring Assessments of Teaching Skills

The conception offered by *Minnesota's Vision* provides a coherent foundation for a performance assessment. (See Appendix A.) The document's seven skill clusters can be organized into five major areas: (1) assessment, (2) planning, (3) instruction, (4) evaluation, and (5) management. The remaining areas—intellectual skills and role-modeling skills—are used across teaching activities. Intellectual skills are evaluated throughout the assessment. Role-modeling skills are most likely to be evaluated during the internship.

Organizing performance assessments around the major tasks teachers must perform is consonant with practice in other professions. Prospective lawyers who sit for the California Bar Exam are asked to write and reply to memoranda, interview and brief "clients," and prepare statements and cross-examination questions. Prospective physicians taking the National Board of Medical Examiners Exam must perform simulated case analyses; prospective architects must draw actual building plans during the Architecture Registration Exam.

Because Minnesota's standards for teacher education are expressed in terms of desired outcomes as to what prospective teachers should know and be able to do, they lend themselves easily to the development of an assessment structure and specific assessment tasks and criteria. For example, *assessment skills* are described as resting upon teachers' knowledge of the students:

Teachers must be able to analyze and interpret both objective and subjective information about students' learning characteristics, attitudes, and backgrounds. Teachers must understand and respond to each student individually and personally. Therefore, teachers must:

- Be systematic in observing and interpreting learner behavior and dynamics which cause the behavior.
- Identify levels of readiness in student learning and development.
- Identify student learning style, strengths, and needs.
- Identify levels and sources of learner motivation.
- Identify relevant aspects of learner background and experience. (MBOT, 1986)

These statements of teacher skills can be used in the formulation of assessment tasks that require the demonstration of a combination of these and other abilities for the evaluation of a teaching situation or the performance of a teaching activity.

Each of these five major skill areas points in two directions: It draws on certain areas of the knowledge base that may be more broadly tested in examinations of knowledge and suggests more specific tasks that might be tested during a performance assessment. *Management skills,* for instance, draw directly on knowledge of human growth, development, and behavior, as well as group dynamics. The specified goals suggest criteria for evaluating candidates' responses to tasks: establishing behavioral expectations, diagnosing and identifying causes of counterproductive behavior, fostering learner self-discipline, employing behavioral analysis principles, altering the learning environment to promote desired social development. Management skills can be demonstrated through specific tasks—dealing with a disruptive student, developing a routine for the beginning of school, diagnosing problems within a classroom—some of which can be tested in an examination, others of which will be manifest during the internship.

Planning skills draw on knowledge of curriculum, educational goals, learners, and learning and rely on judgments about what students have learned, should learn, and are learning; they are manifest through such tasks as translating goals into curricular objectives, setting goals for individual learners, and developing lessons based on specific objectives. *Instructional skills* draw on almost every area of the knowledge base, from subject-specific pedagogy to child development. They require teachers to balance learning objectives, student characteristics, teaching strategies, and curriculum objectives and are manifest through tasks such as explaining a concept, evaluating a student's readiness to engage in a project, and probing for learner understanding. *Evaluation skills* depend on knowledge of both learners and learning, as well as subject-area and curriculum knowledge; they are manifest through tasks such as developing tests, analyzing student records, and interpreting learner behavior.

It is important to note that although we discuss common skills for teaching, we are not positing the existence of generic teaching behaviors that could be displayed and evaluated in a uniform fashion across a wide range of teaching situations. The assessments of teaching skills proposed for the Minnesota performance assessments reflect a major conclusion of teaching research of recent decades: The appropriate application of skills depends on context—that is, on varying pedagogical demands associated with, among other things, subject matter, instructional objectives, stages of student development, and previous learning. The examination system would create separate assessments in each major subject area and by school level or developmental level of students, based on the differential application of common types of skill.

Minnesota's five broad skill areas entail the use of many other types of skill—such as skills of observation, questioning, reflection, and analysis—applied to areas of knowledge (child development, cognition, curriculum) described earlier. The assessment system envisions the possibility of identifying common task "shells" representing teaching tasks that rely on certain skills, such as evaluating student work with the goal of framing future instruction, that can be the basis for similar assessment exercises across many subject areas.

Subject-specific versions of performance assessment would evaluate appropriate manifestations of skills, such as the ability of a secondary school English teacher to develop a lesson after evaluating students' first drafts of an essay, or the ability of a physical education teacher to develop an instructional plan after seeing a videotape of students engaged in a specific physical activity. Methodologically, the performance assessments will heed the lessons that current checklist-based skill evaluations ignore: namely, that effective teaching behavior varies with the situation and that generalized rules for teaching behavior cannot replace the need for highly developed teacher knowledge and judgment. Practically, the assessments will anticipate a wide range of appropriate and inappropriate responses to various tasks based on research findings and the judgment of highly knowledgeable expert professionals.

The Licensing System in Summary

The structure of the overall licensing and assessment system we envision is summarized in Table 5.1. This structure is intended to support the development of teaching knowledge and skills in a conscious manner and to evaluate them in a fashion that ensures attention to major areas of knowledge and skill, appropriately contextualized by subjects, settings, and concerns for students. In Chapter 6 we describe what some of these assessments might be like.

TABLE 5.1   Structure for a Licensing and Assessment System

1. Liberal education with an academic major

2. University-based teacher education

   - May include portfolio and other assessments of developing teacher knowledge and skill
   - Successful completion is required to sit for assessment of teaching knowledge

   Assessment of teaching knowledge

   Written and performance assessments of knowledge about
   1. learners and learning
   2. curriculum and teaching
   3. contexts and purposes

   - Successful completion is required for internship license

   Initial internship license awarded

3. Internship in a professional development school

   On-site long-term assessment of teaching skills and dispositions

   - Evaluation by on-site mentors using approved criteria
   - Successful completion required to sit for assessment of teaching skills

   Assessment of teaching skills

   Performance assessments of applied knowledge and skills in
   1. assessment
   2. planning
   3. instruction
   4. management
   5. evaluation

   - Developed by specific subject area and level (e.g., elementary education, secondary science, English)
   - Successful completion required to receive a professional teaching license

   Professional teaching license awarded

Developing Prototype Assessments for Licensing

In DEVELOPING prototypes for the performance assessments in Minnesota and for similar exercises for California, we sought explicitly to overcome some of the previously identified shortcomings of currently used teacher licensure examinations. These shortcomings include:

1. Insufficient grounding of the assessment in how teaching knowledge and teaching skills are actually used in different teaching situations
2. Use of test formats that are inadequate to assess the candidate's ability to ascertain what considerations are relevant to a situation and to demonstrate skill in applying knowledge appropriately
3. Use of assessment strategies that do not adequately control for differences in the assessment conditions, types of performance observed and assessed, and application of rating criteria (as is the case with currently used on-the-job performance assessments)
4. Inadequate attention to the construct and criterion-related validity of assessments—the extent to which the assessments actually measure the knowledge and skills of interest and the extent to which these measurements are useful indicators of later teaching performance

The approach to assessment development that we advocate has its closest analogues in the tests used by other professions, especially the performance assessments used by the California Bar, part 3 of the National Board of Medical Examiners examinations, certain sections (e.g., parts B and D) of the Architectural Registration Examination, and the "principles and practices" section of the National Council of Engineering Examiners' test. (For further discussion of these examinations, see Lareau, 1985; Wise and Darling-Hammond, 1987.)

As we have suggested, we believe the only way to develop tests that will meet the three-part task of articulating standards, encouraging the acquisition of appropriate knowledge and skills, and sorting reliably those fit for practice from those who are not is to create tasks that are authentic representations of teaching activities and judgments and to ground questions and scoring guides in the knowledge base regarding the nature of teaching and learning that has accumulated during the past several decades. Without such a grounding, an evaluation process is difficult to validate and, thus, cannot be used as a reasonable basis for licensure decisions.

In developing performance assessments, it is crucial to keep in mind at all times that questions or tasks must have clearly defined criteria for acceptable answers or good performances. The difference between responses that are professionally acceptable and those that are unacceptable should rest on a comprehensive understanding of the knowledge, skills, and dispositions that undergird professional teaching. Developers of such assessments must work closely with expert teachers to create tasks that can reveal knowledgeable and skillful teaching, and they must be careful to provide not only questions or tasks but criteria for answers as well. Similarly, the developers must remember that the test represents only one of a series of assessments within a larger system and that only those skills that are best observed through formal evaluation should be included as part of the examination.

Prototypes of Minnesota Assessments of Knowledge and Skill

In this section, we first describe general considerations involved in test development and then present sample questions and tasks developed by the two committees convened by the Minnesota Board of Teaching in spring 1989. The task descriptions created by the two committees rely primarily on existing, relatively low-cost testing technologies, under the assumption that initial efforts will be constrained to what is currently manageable in terms of development and implementation costs. Thus, they include questions, scenarios, and data (e.g., student records or examples of student work) provided through written materials or videotapes and responses provided only in writing, including essays and short-answer responses.

This pilot work was intended to create the basis for further test development but not to constrain the possibilities for assessment approaches that might be used in the near-term or longer-term future. Assessment tools may eventually include the use of computers, interactive videodisks, and other technologies and methods such as structured interviews around similar or more elaborated tasks, discussions of portfolio entries, or responses to simulated teaching. The greater costs and more unresolved technical issues associated with these methods make them less accessible for current use. In addition, the possibilities of bias associated with face-to-face assessment methods make them problematic for licensure decisions. Yet current experiments in other professions and states may eventually make a wider range of methods available and feasible. The SKOPE framework will permit their use when this occurs.

The Test Development Process

In developing prototypes for the SKOPE performance assessments, we used the model that is employed to construct performance test problems on the California Bar Examination. Specifically, the Minnesota Board of Teaching assembled a test development team consisting of teachers and teacher educators to translate abstract descriptions of skills and knowledge needed on the job into tasks that employ that knowledge and those skills in practical situations. Each of the two five-member teams worked with a test development expert who helped members of the team cast their ideas into realistic and challenging questions and task situations that require the specific use of the knowledge and skills to be tested.

The work done by the two groups, each of which met for four days in spring 1989, represents only a preliminary step in the development process. Test development is an iterative process involving the creation of both *task shells* and then individual *tasks*.

A *task* is like a single, but very complex, test item. It contains a description of the setting or context in which the situation occurs, supplemental materials that help to define and describe the situation (such as samples of student work, videoclips of classroom activities, lesson plans, scripts of classroom interactions), and specific directions to the candidate describing the nature of the response desired along with general criteria for evaluating the response.

A *task shell* is like a blueprint for generating many tasks. It contains descriptions of the characteristics of the context, the events, the materials, and the scoring criteria that represent a common class of problem or activity to be assessed rather than specific instances of items. Many tasks can be generated from the same shell by changing elements of the context, situation, or problem while still getting at the same general dimensions of performance that are of interest. Task shells are like item-generating rules, although in practice they are far less mechanical than the word *rule* implies (Klein and Stetcher, 1991b).

A test development team meets to review the knowledge domain for the test and selects from this domain the specific kinds of knowledge and understanding that will be assessed. Selection criteria focus on breadth of coverage, importance of the knowledge to practice, amenability to assessment on a licensure exam, and satisfaction of other assessment goals (e.g., eliciting whether candidates are sensitive to the diverse cultural backgrounds of students). Next, the team constructs a preliminary set of task shells that together cover the areas selected. A preliminary set of instructions and scoring criteria are also developed at this time. These criteria affect the test development process because they help to ensure that the stimulus materials have built into them the situations that will require or elicit the knowledge and skills to be tested.

A number of criteria are used to select tasks to develop further:

- The tasks represent activities teachers perform under normal conditions as part of their jobs.
- The tasks are important for competent performance, and they are performed frequently; therefore, competent performance is essential.
- Taken together, the tasks on the test should sample the full range of contexts (school, subject matter, and student types) to which the license applies, and they should represent the major functions or activities of teachers. A license is not limited to a particular classroom, grade level, or community type or to only selected features of the job. Thus, the tasks as a group should represent the various types of students as well as types of contexts within which teachers may be asked to teach.
- The tasks have both appropriate and inappropriate solutions, and the general nature of these solutions can be described in concrete terms.
- The grading criteria must be valid. There must be substantial agreement among professionals in the field as to what constitutes a good response or performance.

This last criterion is especially important. "Validity cannot be sacrificed for the sake of high reliability. What is scored must be important" (Klein and Stetcher, 1991a, p. 171). Thus, situations that are problematic and intriguing but have no consensual response are not useful starting points for tasks. Neither are situations or prompts that can be scored reliably only by attending to trivial aspects of the performance.

Once productive task possibilities have been selected, various members of the team work together in writing a first draft of all the materials needed for a concrete version of a specific task (including instructions and scoring guide). The team as a whole reviews these materials and revises them as needed.

The next step involves administering the prototype task to a few experienced teachers. The purpose of this field trial is to check for the clarity of instructions, appropriateness of time limits, whether the stimulus materials elicit the expected types of responses, and related concerns. For instance, are all of the problems that were built into the materials being recognized by the teachers? Field-test participants are also debriefed to obtain their views about what they liked and did not like about the task.

Field-test results are used to revise the shell, scoring criteria, stimulus materials, instructions, and scoring guide. The revised version is then field tested and, if necessary, revised and field tested again until an acceptable form of the task is produced. We next describe some of the assessment ideas produced by the two committees.

Examining Knowledge
About Learning and Development

Minnesota's proposed test of teaching knowledge is intended to assess "common-core" knowledge that cuts across teaching fields and provides the intellectual glue that holds the field together. Although there are good arguments for why a common examination, such as the common-core sections of other professions' licensing tests, should be constructed, there are equally good arguments for embedding knowledge of key ideas and principles in performance tasks within subject areas that also elicit demonstrations of performance skills.

The arguments for examining a common core of knowledge concern the greater possibility of including a breadth of ideas and concepts in the test and the expectation that there are some foundational ideas with which all professionals should be familiar. In addition, many states' current structures for licensing tests include an examination of core professional knowledge.

The arguments against this approach are that actual abilities to use knowledge in practice are always demonstrated within a specific context, and most teachers are prepared as specialists. We struck a middle ground, embedding knowledge of principles of teaching and learning within teaching contexts defined by subjects and students, in instances in which professional standards suggest the underlying concepts should be known to all teachers.

The knowledge committee was charged with the task of developing prototype questions in the area of human growth and development. This area fits into the larger scheme of the knowledge to be tested as indicated in Table 6.1. The area of human growth and development was selected in part because any conception of the knowledge base for teaching is likely to include it; few would argue that classroom teachers do not need a thorough knowledge of child and adolescent development if they are to work as professionals in their field. Furthermore, a reasonable degree of consensus exists on what the knowledge base on human growth and development includes. Finally, we were able to call upon a group of Minnesota teachers, counselors, and teacher educators with considerable knowledge in this area, including some with nationally recognized expertise.

To create a shared information base, we provided the knowledge committee with three sets of documents: a set offering background information about Minnesota's standards for teachers and other configurations of knowledge, skills, and dispositions important for teaching developed within the profession; documents showing how the knowledge base for human growth and development has been defined in leading college texts and assessments in related fields such as psychology; and a set providing examples of applied knowledge. This third section included three examples of how material on a given aspect of human growth and development within the context of teaching

TABLE 6.1   The Knowledge Base: Working Schema

Knowledge About Learners and Learning
   Human growth and development
   Behavior and motivation
   Cognition and learning theory
   Learner and learning characteristics and differences

Knowledge About Curriculum and Teaching
   Curriculum theory and resources
   General pedagogical principles and teaching strategies
   Assessment and evaluation
   Counseling and social behavior management
   Organizational development
   Communication, language, and technology

Knowledge About Contexts and Foundations of Education
   History and philosophy of eduction
   Schools and society
   People, social settings, and cultures
   Epistemology and ways of knowing
   Ethics and legal responsibilities

Subject-Matter Knowledge

General Liberal Arts Knowledge

---

might be presented to a beginning teacher. These included two chapters from the recently published *Knowledge Base for the Beginning Teacher* (Reynolds, 1989)—one on psychological, societal, and moral development and one on a cognitive-mediational view of learning—and a collection of six essays on motivation theory and practice. These were included to spark the imagination of the group members in developing questions that required the application of various kinds of knowledge.

The major goal of the knowledge examination group was to produce questions that required candidates to apply knowledge within specified contexts. Although a knowledge examination might include a certain number of questions that require less analysis of applications and more discussion of basic concepts and principles, it seemed appropriate to use the talents of the team to frame the more difficult application questions.

As the week progressed, it became clear that the most fruitful method of proceeding is to begin with a principle to be tested (for instance, that various causes—both developmental and pedagogical—can contribute to students' ability to master a concept) and then construct a task around it. Appendix D contains examples of the kinds of tasks that could be developed from the conceptual work completed by the committee.

The group decided to create one task shell that provides candidates with a description of a class in terms of age, subject areas, and achievement levels, along with a description of the most recent lessons conducted, including amount of time spent, concept introduced, and method used. This information could also be conveyed by giving candidates copies of lesson plans, materials used, and student assignments to tap other analytic skills. The candidate is then given evidence that the class has not yet grasped the concept being presented and is asked to evaluate what might be the causes of the problem. Tasks can be constructed to provide evidence for a variety of alternative explanations—for example: (1) The concept is too advanced for the age level of the students, (2) the students hold uncorrected misconceptions or are missing the prerequisite knowledge, (3) the pedagogical strategy is not appropriate in the context, or (4) concept and method are appropriate, but not enough time has been spent. Finally, candidates are asked to describe what alternative strategies, if any, would be likely to produce better outcomes.

In one possible task developed from this shell, a scenario for an inappropriate pedagogical strategy describes a second-grade class that has been studying fractions through a drill-and-practice strategy, individually completing worksheets each day following lectures and recitation. After three days, few can actually use fractions to solve problems. Given artifacts of the lessons and student work, the candidate must identify the mismatch between the work assigned and both the instructional outcomes desired and the developmental learning needs of the children and must propose more appropriate strategies.

In another example, a knowledgeable reading of the scenario and attendant materials reveals that eighth-grade students are being taught about a complex scientific concept (plate tectonics in this example) without sufficient scaffolding to give them a base of common knowledge, with reading materials that are too complex, and without hands-on examples, models, or active learning opportunities to aid their understanding. The candidate must identify these problems and propose more appropriate strategies.

A third example concerns a twelfth-grade U.S. History class that is asked to work in cooperative groups with two primary documents—the Magna Carta and the U.S. Constitution—to identify commonalities and differences in the ways these documents treat human rights and governmental responsibilities. The pedagogical approach is appropriate, and the materials are not too difficult; however, the one class period assigned to the task is insufficient for this kind of inquiry approach. The candidate must analyze the scenario, classroom artifacts, and student work samples to describe ways in which the assignment can be further defined and extended.

In a second sample knowledge task, candidates are asked to identify students for further assessment based on information about their behaviors and other contextual information. If they believe referral to a specialist may be needed, they must explain why. Whether they refer or adopt a wait-and-see posture, they must describe what they would do to further diagnose what is going on with the student. Descriptions include symptoms of possible dyslexia, possible severe depression, and a possible drug problem; it is the task of the candidate to recognize the symptoms from the descriptions and to associate the symptoms with some sort of specific problem.

Not all of the scenarios provide cause for referral. For example, a scenario in which a first grader reverses letters and sometimes reads words in reverse (e.g., "was" for "saw") indicates a developmental stage that is not cause for alarm. The same situation for a fourth grader should stimulate additional diagnosis.

This kind of task could also be conducted by giving candidates information in other forms—for example, a videotaped portrayal of the student, samples of student work and student records rather than a written description—thus tapping other skills of observation, data interpretation, and ability to synthesize information.

In a third task, candidates are provided with two daily plans for a first-grade class. One plan (a) includes long, uninterrupted periods of sedentary activity; the other (b) intersperses sedentary with physical activities. Candidates are asked to decide which of the two plans would be more appropriate and to explain their responses. Candidates must first recognize that plan (a) involves long periods of sedentary activity whereas plan (b) does not, recall the principle that long periods of sedentary activity are inappropriate for young children, notice that the question is framed within the context of first graders, and then combine this information to select (b) and justify their selection. Other kinds of developmental issues can be built into the prompt by including activities that are cognitively inappropriate (such as suggested readings that are clearly at a reading level and of a topical nature inappropriate for young children), teaching methods that rely too heavily on strategies such as lecture or independent seatwork, or classroom management strategies that do not demonstrate an understanding of social and emotional development at this age.

The three tasks represent different task shells that can be used as the basis for further generation of questions. In the first, combinations of the four potential pedagogical problems (or others) could be embedded within any number of specific classroom situations. In the second task, various potential grounds for further assessment could be set within the context of different scenarios offered. In the third task, different sorts of activities in different contexts could be embedded within the task prompt. Thus, in subsequent years committees need only decide upon the specific content of the question, not its structure. Furthermore, all three questions require that candidates not only know the principles being tested but also recognize situations to which they apply.

The knowledge committee produced a range of questions whose prompts include explicit factual questions, descriptions of classroom scenarios, descriptions and work samples from individual students, simulated materials (e.g., unit plans, student files, guidance counselor reports), and videotaped classroom observations. Proposed response modes include short answers, essays describing phenomena observed, essays analyzing situations or principles, and essays describing the course of action to be taken. The questions were generated on the basis of principles deemed essential knowledge for professional teachers, answered by candidates on the basis of their understanding of that knowledge, and scored on the basis of the answer's compatibility with the key principles. At the same time, the test's use of knowledge acknowledges the importance of context in application and often allows for more than one appropriate response, which can be justified by reference to relevant developmental, pedagogical, or other considerations.

Developing Performance Assessments in Secondary English–Language Arts

The task of the skills committee was to develop a set of prototypical performance task shells for secondary English–language arts teachers in the five skills areas to be tested: (1) assessment, (2) planning, (3) instruction, (4) evaluation, and (5) management. The performance assessments are to be subject-specific; that is, all of the tasks will be embedded in the candidate's subject area and within grade levels to which a license applies. In Minnesota's licensure structure, this means versions would be developed for secondary school mathematics, social studies, English–language arts, science, and foreign languages, as well as elementary school teaching, for grades 5–9, and so on. Although this is a daunting task, it is necessary if skills are to be appropriately evaluated in actual application. Elements of subject-specific pedagogical knowledge cannot be assessed in any other way.

However, because task shells may be constructed to assess skills that are common across areas (although applied differently), similar kinds of tasks are likely to appear on many, if not all, versions of the test. The substance and scoring of the tasks will vary according to the subject area and level of the candidates. In many cases, appropriate responses will differ across versions. Even where general principles exist, classroom management, for example, will be accomplished differently by a physical education teacher than by a secondary school typing teacher or a math teacher. Elementary teachers will find different approaches useful. Evaluating student work in a home economics class is likely to be different from evaluating performances in a physics class, which, in turn, will differ from evaluating learning in an elementary school reading group.

The area of secondary English and language arts was selected for prototype development for a number of reasons. First, it is one of the largest certification areas in the state of Minnesota. Second, it had received less attention than some other fields in which performance assessment was being explored at the time of our work. At that time, for example, the Stanford Assessment Project and the Connecticut assessment development efforts had worked in the areas of elementary school mathematics and secondary school history and mathematics. Secondary school English, with the exception of some interesting essay-grading exercises conducted at Michigan State University, had been relatively untouched. Third, this topic represents a subject area of medium difficulty in terms of generating consensual responses: Mathematics might have been (deceptively) easy; foreign languages, where there is debate even over how much English—if any—should be used in introducing the second language, might have been too difficult. Fourth, secondary school English and language arts was one of the subject areas for which the state of Minnesota had produced revised outcome-based licensure standards that could provide the group with guidance in determining appropriate expectations for knowledge and skills on the part of candidates. Finally, a significant body of respected literature is available on teaching English and language arts, including two chapters in the *Handbook of Research on Teaching* ("Research on Written Composition" by Marlene Scardamalia and Carl Bereiter and "Research on Teaching Reading" by Robert Calfee and Priscilla Drum) and volumes such as the *Handbook of Research on Reading* (Pearson et al., 1984) and *Research on Written Composition* (Hillocks, 1986).

As with the knowledge examination committee, the skills committee was provided with background information to create a common base of knowledge to guide it in its development process. Four kinds of information were provided: Minnesota guidelines and standards, prototypical task shells, articles on research in the five skills areas, and articles on teaching reading and writing.

The first set of papers included Minnesota's licensure standards for teachers of English and language arts, which describe the areas of mastery the state expects of candidates (see Appendix C), as well as a selection from Minnesota's *Vision for Teacher Education* (see Appendix A). The second set included five prototypical task shells from teaching (planning a discussion section, critiquing a lesson, planning instruction and developing curriculum, evaluating student papers and planning subsequent lessons, and identifying the potential sources of student disruptiveness) at various levels of detail, as well as four examples of task shells used by the California State Bar Examination (including preparing a trial brief, preparing a client for direct examination, replying to a points and authorities memo, and preparing and conducting a cross-examination).

The third set of papers included a series of articles designed to remind the group members about how knowledge about core activities and skills might be presented to a beginning teacher. For classroom management, there were two articles: one from the *Knowledge Base for the Beginning Teacher* (KBBT) on the research base underlying classroom management; the other presenting a series of case studies and exercises designed to impart these principles to beginning teachers. A KBBT article on evaluation defines the key concepts and terms necessary for a beginning teacher to understand. Another addresses learners and learning. The fourth set of papers included articles on teaching reading and writing, excerpts from the volumes mentioned earlier.

The process of constructing task shells to exemplify particular skills and applied knowledge was made much easier by the statements of Minnesota's licensure standards in terms of desired abilities for secondary English and language arts teachers. For example, teachers are expected to be able to demonstrate:

> The skill of responding specifically, constructively, and efficiently to students' writing for the purpose of revising and improving the writing; responding to considerations of audience, purpose, and context; and diagnosing problems in reasoning, form, structure, usage, and style as well as in syntax, diction, spelling, punctuation, and legibility. (Minnesota Standards for Teacher Licensure 8700.3810, Subpart 2.A(1)(i))

This skill is to be grounded in, among other things,

> - Knowledge of the elements of the writing process, the uses of writing, and research in written composition;
> - Knowledge of the methodologies for teaching writing and the importance of logic and reasoning to both the writing process and the written product; and
> - Knowledge of a variety of strategies for efficient yet effective evaluation of student writing. (Minnesota Standards, Subpart 2.A(1) d, e, f)

These specific, outcomes-based statements of expected knowledge and skills help to provide both the framework for the creation of tasks aimed at revealing particular kinds of understandings and abilities and the criteria for scoring acceptable responses.

Responding to Student Writing. As with the knowledge group, the skills group found it most expedient to begin with a principle to be tested and then to construct a scenario around it. Addressing the Minnesota standards described earlier, the group decided to examine candidates' abilities to give feedback on student papers. Among the principles embedded in the task and response are giving specific, informative feedback rather than general praise and selecting areas for improvement judiciously, in light of student development and instructional goals, without intimidating developing writers by covering the papers with red ink.

A task was constructed in which candidates are given a set of eight rough drafts of student papers on *Johnny Tremain* within the context of a lesson on topic sentences and supporting details. (The task is reproduced in Appendix E.) The papers show differential mastery of the concepts, ranging from good understanding of thesis and support to use of topic sentences with few or no supports to no thematic connection among ideas in the essay. The candidate is asked to respond to four selected papers that represent different writing problems as if they were to be handed back to the students for work on a subsequent draft. The candidate is also asked to discuss what steps he or she will take in subsequent lessons to help students continue to develop their writing.

Criteria for scoring the candidates' responses are based on the two principles described previously. The scoring materials indicate specific examples of appropriate comments and start by identifying strengths in the student's writing while posing questions for consideration in subsequent drafts. For example, "This is a good detail to support your topic sentence." "You gave one good detail to support your thesis. Can you think of others, such as how he treated Becky?" "Your topic sentence is very strong. But does the fact that Johnny burned his hand show that he is arrogant? How else can you demonstrate his arrogance?" "I can tell that you read and enjoyed the book. Could you list some of the things about Johnny that made you like him?"

The scoring criteria also give examples of inappropriate comments that are either nonspecific or nonsupportive of students' efforts. For example, "Good" without further elaboration, or "What does this have to do with anything?" Follow-up questions include asking the candidate to describe in more detail the strengths or weaknesses of specific papers and to plan the class's next few lessons and assignments on the basis of the strengths and weaknesses demonstrated in the set of papers.

This task shell provides the framework for a great number of variations. Student essays could demonstrate efforts to develop a line of argument, a sense of audience and purpose, a personal voice, persuasiveness, form and structure, grammar, research conventions, or other aspects of writing development. Problems could be written for special groups of students—for instance, students with limited English proficiency; essays could be written on any number of books at any of the secondary grade levels; and so on. In each of these cases the criteria for scoring should be based on accepted principles, such as the need for specific feedback or the inappropriateness of numerous discouraging comments. In a related task developed by a committee of teachers in California, the candidate is asked to identify the strengths and weaknesses of written teacher responses to student essays, as well as responding to the essays himself (Klein and Stetcher, 1991b).

Planning for Stages of the Writing Process. Another task developed by the California committee examines the candidate's understanding of the writing process by asking him or her to evaluate a teacher's plan that presents a series of activities and assignments whose purpose is to promote student writing. The candidate must evaluate the plan in light of contextual information about the classroom and characteristics of students and make revisions or modifications for strengthening the plan (Klein and Stetcher, 1991b).

Developing a Lesson Sequence. Other planning tasks created by the California committee include developing a lesson sequence that explores a theme shared by literary works from different genres. After reviewing the works, the candidate must develop specific student objectives that support the instructional goals and devise activities that promote the objectives: making literature accessible to all students (including limited English-proficient students), integrating the language arts, and addressing one or more supporting subskills. The candidate must provide a valid rationale for the proposed activities proposed (Klein and Stetcher, 1991b). In addition to the tasks described previously, which require candidates to demonstrate their evaluation and planning skills, the Minnesota committee developed task shells designed to tap candidates' instruction and assessment skills (in selecting an appropriate book for a particular student) and classroom management and instruction skills (in observing and managing a classroom discussion of a specific novel).

Selecting a Book for a Student. The book selection task requires that the teacher evaluate a student's interests and literacy development and connect that assessement with his or her knowledge about a number of pieces of literature—their themes, reading levels, and attractions for various kinds of readers—in order to make suggestions and justify them to the student and the assessor. This task also addresses several of the Minnesota licensing standards for English–language arts teachers, including "knowledge of a representative body of American and British literature, past and present, written for adults and for adolescents by majority and minority male and female authors, and some of the major works, in translation if necessary, of continental and non-Western authors" and "knowledge of the value of literature as an art as well as the enjoyment derived from a variety of experiences and viewpoints encountered in literature." (See Appendix C.)

Analysis of Classroom Discussion. The analysis of a classroom discussion requires that the candidate be able to identify, describe, and discuss aspects of the management of the discussion (shown in a videotaped prompt) that are useful and not useful in engaging students and moving the discussion ahead in a way that enables students to analyze motivations and plot in a piece of literature. The task can also be structured to allow the candidate to produce written responses at key points in the discussion when the videotape is stopped. At that point, candidates can describe and justify what they would do in response to a particular comment or event. The task can also be structured to allow the candidates to review a script of the discussion and to identify strengths and weaknesses of the teacher's statements and actions. To contextualize the discussion, the candidates can review artifacts that describe the previous days' lessons and assignments and the agenda for the current lesson, as well as information about the class. This kind of script or videotape strategy can also be used to evaluate candidates' understandings of specific skills, such as giving instructions or helping students to develop their oral-presentation skills by structuring the task and giving feedback (Klein and Stetcher, 1991b).

Varying Tasks Within Shells. All of these shells provide many opportunities for variations. Each shell includes a context (such as a seventh-grade heterogeneous class), materials (such as a videotape of a classroom discussion), a task (such as identifying common problems or suggesting a more appropriate technique), and scoring criteria. Each of the first three (context, materials, and task) can be varied without changing the criteria—that is, the skills and understandings being tested. In addition, each of these task shells can become a basis for tasks developed in other subject areas or at the elementary level: Giving feedback on students' work, developing an appropriate student assignment, developing lesson plans based on an assessment of students' prior work, and managing classroom discussions are activities that can be framed for other subject areas using subject-specific knowledge and pedagogy to inform the substance of the question and the criteria for scoring responses.

These tasks rely not just on general knowledge of teaching skills but on an understanding of how those skills come into play within the context of the candidate's subject area. Although this is a more challenging approach to test construction, it avoids artificial isolation of skills from the larger context within which they are embedded and increases the validity of the test itself.

Examples of Assessment Tasks in Secondary Science

The work with committees of California teachers mentioned previously also included development of prototype tasks for licensing secondary life science and general science teachers. The examples in this section illustrate how similar task shells can be constructed across subject areas (e.g., developing a lesson sequence) although the content of the actual tasks is necessarily different. There are also tasks that are grounded specifically in problems of practice that have special significance for a particular field. In this case, tasks concerned with classroom safety and with common misconceptions about scientific concepts are of special significance for science teachers. The process for developing these tasks is described more fully in Klein and Stetcher (1991a).

Teacher as Curriculum Decisionmaker. This task asks the candidates to organize activities into an effective lesson sequence. Based on contextual information about the course and the students, as well as objectives for an introductory science unit, candidates are asked to select a subset of activities from an annotated list describing the content and duration of various lectures, discussions, demonstrations, readings, laboratory activities, film and videos, worksheets, evaluation activities, and individual study. Candidates are to arrange their selected activities into a two-week lesson plan that is appropriate for the students, promotes the objectives, and incorporates effective instructional practices.

Lesson Planning. Candidates are given a reasonably well-constructed plan for a three-week science unit that describes desired outcomes for students and lessons for each day (objectives and topic, planned activities, and homework). The fifth lesson is missing. Candidates are given three detailed plans for lessons that could be used on the fifth day. They are asked to evaluate the strengths and weaknesses of each and then to design a lesson by adapting one of the alternatives or developing an entirely new plan. Finally, the candidates evaluate the strengths and weaknesses of the plan they have developed.

Classroom and Facility Safety. In this task candidates must respond to situations that are presented concerning general safety procedures, safety in specific laboratory lessons, and facility safety. In one part of the task, candidates must identify all of the safety hazards that are present in a picture of part of a science facility. This approach can be extended with new technologies. In a new interactive videodisk assessment developed by the Connectict State Department of Education, science teacher candidates evaluate safety hazards in a laboratory with the capacity to scan and zoom in for a closer look at any part of the room.

Common Misconceptions. In this task, candidates must identify common misconceptions that often underlie students' ideas about scientific concepts and design instruction that encourages students to confront and correct these misconceptions. The task presents a description of a lesson, a script of a classroom discussion in which student responses suggest certain misconceptions about the topic under discussion, and a set of student responses to a quiz that confirms these misunderstandings. The candidate must identify the misunderstandings and design a follow-up lesson to correct the students' misconceptions.

Motivating Students and Using Effective Instructional Strategies. In this task, candidates must identify a teacher's appropriate and inappropriate actions to motivate, engage, and communicate effectively with students in the course of a lesson about cell parts and functions in a racially and ethnically diverse class. Contextual information is provided about subject, grade level, students, and the lesson underway, including what is written on the board at the start of the class. In the scripts of classroom dialogue provided, candidates should recognize less than effective questioning strategies and inappropriate responses to individual students, along with some appropriate strategies.

Parent-Student Letter. The candidate must inform parents and students in writing about standard classroom practices in science and must identify the key points to be made in response to a specific situation.

Beyond Assessment:
Communicating a Conception of Teaching

Working with task development in this way helps to clarify ideas about what good teaching practice looks like and involves in the way of complex knowledge and skill. As teachers become involved in the activities of developing and scoring tasks, their own practice is also likely to be deepened by the opportunity to reflect about what is being assessed and how that reflects a standard of practice.

In addition to the kinds of criteria that are applied, perhaps one of the most useful aspects of these assessments is that they convey a clear, learner-centered conception of the activities that are part of teaching: writing parent-student letters to ensure good communication with the home, pressing further to understand why some students may not be learning as hoped, looking for strengths in student work as a basis for addressing additional needs for learning, planning lessons on the basis of careful assessment of what individual students and groups of students have learned, accessing and understanding student thinking as a basis for developing further instruction, explicitly attending to the language development and other needs of students from a variety of backgrounds and prior experiences. Although this conception of what teachers should know and be able to do guides the work of a number of well-prepared, thoughtful, and committed teachers, it does not now characterize the thinking of all—or perhaps even most—teachers. Nor does it characterize the ways in which all education programs seek to prepare would-be teachers. The great potential of performance-based licensing grounded in these standards and approaches to assessment is that it can communicate and enforce a view of teaching work and an understanding of teaching knowledge that will enable all students to be taught by teachers who will look at them, care about them, and understand them in these ways.

The Internship

UNDER THE LICENSING SYSTEM proposed and adopted by Minnesota's Board of Teaching, all prospective teachers will be required to spend one full school year working as interns under the supervision and guidance of experienced professionals before being licensed to practice independently. Because of its duration, intensity, and unique character, the internship is central to the assessment program. Many things that cannot be observed or measured in the other parts of the assessment system—dispositions, classroom-based skills, and such qualities as patience and stamina—will be cultivated and evaluated during the internship.

The internship serves two roles—educational and evaluative. Educationally, the internship will offer prospective teachers the opportunity to put theory into practice and to exercise complex decisionmaking under the supervision of experienced expert practitioners.|Guided by direct supervision, counseling, observation, reviews of practice, and formal instruction, interns will develop skills in managing the learning process by working with students and by selecting learning materials, assessment tools, and teaching strategies.\The intern will be immersed in a community of experienced practitioners and have opportunities to interact with other novices. At the same time, the intern will receive feedback from veteran teachers, both formally and informally. Guidelines for the internship program and structured evaluations will ensure that all interns are exposed to a broad range of specified experiences. They will help safeguard the rigor of the program and will allow the internship to serve, in part, as a measure of teaching dispositions and skills.

The Case for a Supervised Teaching Internship

As efforts to improve and professionalize teaching proceeded throughout the 1980s, states made major changes in the rules governing teacher preparation and licensure (Darling-Hammond and Berry, 1988). These changes include the introduction of test requirements in at least forty-six states, revisions in coursework requirements in most states, and renewed interest in strengthening supervision and clinical training for prospective or beginning teachers. As a whole, these requirements are intended to assure the public that teachers are capable before they receive a "regular" license to practice.

Even as these changes are made, though, they are not enough to ensure that beginning teachers are adequately prepared to assume the complex tasks of teaching. As have other professions, the profession of teaching is struggling with the difficult question of how candidates can be taught to use formal, abstract knowledge to inform idiosyncratic teaching decisions, how codified knowledge and theory can be applied to complex problems of practice, and how skills can be developed in practical application. The root of the question is how prospective teachers can be transformed from students of teaching into responsible practitioners, given the magnitude and complexity of the task they face.

As have other professions, teaching is examining how a supervised clinical training experience might be constructed to enrich candidates' abilities and ensure their competence before they are asked to practice autonomously. This is a matter of both improving training and increasing accountability to clients. As part of the bargain they make with society, professions promise to ensure the competence of entrants to the occupation in exchange for the right to offer particular services.

In most instances, professions have adopted requirements for a clinical internship or apprenticeship experience as part of this guarantee for two reasons. The first is that the graduate needs an internship to learn how to apply knowledge and make decisions appropriately. The second is that examinations, including performance tests, cannot completely assess the ability to use knowledge, apply skills, or demonstrate professional attitudes and dispositions. By insisting that the candidate successfully complete an internship, the profession has another measure of performance. It is valid on its face because it involves actually serving clients. But because the rating of the intern's performance in the internship is necessarily subjective and not fully standardized, it cannot be used directly for the licensing decision. The dual requirement for satisfactorily completing the internship and passing an examination balances the demands for reliability, validity, and job relevance and provides the assurance that neither alone could provide (Darling-Hammond, Gendler, and Wise, 1990).

Rationale for a Teaching Internship

As is true in other professions, written instruments for assessing teaching knowledge and skill are unable to capture fully the complexities of teaching knowledge and the context-dependent nature of teaching judgment. And because the acquisition of teaching skill is so dependent on developing judgment in complex, nonroutine situations, it cannot be adequately assessed until after the prospective teacher has had an opportunity to encounter and work through many of the common problems of teaching practice.

Before new teachers are granted a regular, continuing license, an evaluation process should identify whether they possess a range of needed teaching skills. The kinds of skills the state would like to be sure licensed teachers possess cannot be acquired through formal teacher education alone. Neither can they be effectively acquired with great certainty by independent trial and error during the initial years of practice. If a major goal of licensure is to increase the probability that those admitted to practice can indeed make appropriate decisions and execute sound teaching strategies effectively, the licensure process should require both opportunities for and evidence of learning these skills.

Other professions—such as medicine, architecture, psychology, and engineering—have accommodated similar concerns for the development of skill in practice by requiring a form of structured internship prior to licensure (described in the section "Internships in Other Professions"). In contrast, beginning teachers—with no further assistance from their college professors and few school district resources allocated for formal support—are generally left to "sink or swim" during their first years of teaching (Wise, Darling-Hammond, and Berry, 1987). Research on the experiences of beginning teachers has confirmed that the likelihood of long-term success is substantially impaired for many by the absence of expert guidance, support, and opportunities to reflect on their efforts (McDonald, 1980; Ryan, 1980; Tisher, 1978).

The Design of a Teaching Internship

If internship programs in teaching were modeled after those in other professions, they would differ from current beginning teacher programs in a number of ways.

1. The intern would not only work directly with clients but would also observe experienced professionals interacting with clients and would learn from them. Learning by modeling is a precept of an internship. Learning only by doing—that is by trial and error alone—is what beginning teachers do now, and it is much less effective.
2. The intern would assume progressive degrees of responsibility for clients.
3. The intern would receive regular supervision and guidance from practicing professionals.
4. The programs would require that all interns experience particular types of situations for decisionmaking and practice under supervision, including a range of tasks and types of clients.

Few programs for beginning teachers are structured to provide specific, supervised learning experiences for novice teachers. Usually, beginning teachers are already fully responsible for classes of students and are visited only occasionally by supervisors or evaluators. Many of the current state-mandated beginning teacher programs focus so much on evaluation that they have almost entirely forgotten the supervision and guidance aspects of induction. Because these programs are tied directly to licensure decisions, they focus on a training process for getting candidates prepared to perform to the specifications of particular evaluation instruments. However, they do little to encourage candidates to teach reflectively, to evaluate what they are doing and assess whether it is working or not working and why, to understand how to make better decisions, and to learn how to juggle the various concerns of teaching (Darling-Hammond, Gendler, and Wise, 1990; Fox and Singletary, 1986).

If teaching were to follow the lead of other professions, beginning teachers would not be evaluated for licensure on the basis of on-the-job observations. Instead, the internship would be a distinctly separate step en route to the licensing exam. By separating the formative assistance task in an internship or residency from the summative examination, it will be possible to encourage reflective teaching. It is difficult to be openly reflective and critical about one's work if one is being evaluated for licensure at the same time. Other professions have recognized this danger and have reserved the residency or apprenticeship program as a time of honest, evaluative learning experiences that enhance and encourage reflective practice.

In addition, the internship offers a setting in which one can encourage the development of ethical standards and assess, in the case of teaching, whether candidates have the kind of concern and care for children that would allow them to become honorable members of the profession. Although most professions consider ethical and moral commitments to be very important aspects of professional practice, these attributes cannot be assessed in a paper-and-pencil test. Just as some kinds of learning can only be developed in an internship program, so, too, some attitudes can only be evaluated within the context of actual practice.

By combining an assurance that all prospective teachers will undergo such training with valid assessment of beginning skills, it will be possible to assure the public that all entrants to the profession have adequately mastered the basic knowledge and skills needed to perform responsibly before they are licensed to practice independently. Finally, this approach holds promise for improving the overall quality of teaching practice by acknowledging the complexity of teaching and encouraging the acquisition of broad understanding and abilities.

Internships in Other Professions

In the course of our research, we examined the processes by which other professions prepare future practitioners. In this section, we describe and analyze the internship component of four professions' licensing procedures—engineering, psychology, architecture, and medicine—in order to understand the central features of an effective preprofessional internship. In each of these professions, the internship is embedded within a larger program of education, experience, and examination; candidates complete a formal educational program, undergo a practical exposure to the profession, and then take an examination that tests their professional skill. There are some augmentations to this scheme: In two cases (psychology and medicine) additional preservice experiential components are included in the formal education process, and in two cases (engineering and medicine) an additional examination precedes the main experiential component.

Licensing is an extremely complex subject. Terminology varies across and even within professions, and each profession offers several tiers of professional approval. Doctors may be simply licensed or be licensed and also board certified. Architects may practice without a license or may be registered and board certified. Psychologists must be licensed and may be nationally registered. Engineers may practice without a license or may be registered as professional engineers.

The requirements outlined in the following section describe the most rigorous standards in each profession—the standards required to become a professional engineer, a registered psychologist, a board-certified architect, or a board-certified doctor. Viewed as a set, these four professions illustrate both the similarities and the differences among professional licensure processes today. A brief summary of both the context and content of the internship in each profession follows. (More detailed discussion of each of the four professions is included in Darling-Hammond, Gendler, and Wise, 1990).

Basic Licensure Requirements

Engineering. Becoming licensed as a Professional Engineer in most states is a four-part process. To become an "engineer-in-training," a candidate must first graduate from a four-year accredited engineering program and then pass the Fundamentals of Engineering (FE) examination, an eight-hour multiple-choice test of basic engineering knowledge. The candidate must then practice for four years as an intern in a setting that permits assumption of a progressive degree of responsibility for engineering tasks and finally, after the internship, pass the Principles and Practice of Engineering (PE) examination—an eight-hour essay test that requires the candidate to solve actual problems in six of fourteen areas of engineering (National Council of Engineering Examiners, n.d., pp. 4–8).

Psychology. Becoming licensed as a professional psychologist in most states is a three-part process. A candidate must first complete the academic requirements of an accredited doctoral program in psychology, which generally includes—in addition to coursework—a four hundred–hour pre-dissertation practicum experience. The candidate must then practice as an intern for one or two years under supervision. American Psychological Association (APA)-accredited internships must meet professionally defined standards for administration, staff, interns, and program. Finally, the candidate must pass the Examination for Professional Practice in Psychology (EPPP)—a two hundred–item multiple-choice examination of psychological knowledge—as well as state-developed oral and essay examinations (American Association of State Psychology Boards (a); American Association of State Psychology Boards (b); American Association of State Psychology Boards (c)).

Architecture. Licensure in architecture is a three-part process. The candidate must first complete three and one-half years of architectural training in either an accredited undergraduate or graduate program. The candidate then undergoes a structured three-year internship at an architectural firm or firms, during which she or he must accrue a specified number of hours of practice and observation in fourteen task areas. Finally, the candidate must pass the Architect Registration Examination, a four-day eight-part test that includes multiple-choice and essay questions, as well as architectural design problems (NCARB, 1987a, 1987b).

Medicine. Licensure as a board-certified physician is at least a five-part process. The candidate must first complete a four-year MD program at an accredited medical school, which includes, in addition to coursework, a significant amount of field experience. The candidate then takes part 2 of the National Board of Medical Examiners' (NBME) three-part examination series. Candidates who elect the NBME route will already have taken the NBME part 1 upon completion of their second year of medical school. After passing the NBME part 2, candidates undergo one-year internships, after which they take part 3 of the NBME examination series. Candidates seeking board certification then begin a two-year to five-year residency; for each medical specialty, a structured residency program is prescribed by its regulatory board. Each specialty's regulatory board sets its own standards for a postresidency examination, but most include both an oral and a written component.

Common Features Among Internships

Despite differences in structure and degree of standardization, programs in architecture, psychology, and medicine share essential common features beyond the structural similarities of the context within which they are embedded. These represent the key features of a professional internship:

1. The intern has a special title (intern-architect, intern, resident) that denotes a special role vis-à-vis responsibilities to clients.
2. The internship takes place full time in a clinical setting.
3. The intern assumes a progressive degree of responsibility for working with clients.
4. The intern receives regular guidance and supervision from practicing professionals as well as professional educators.
5. The intern has an opportunity to observe professionals interacting with clients.
6. Didactic training accompanies clinical experience.
7. The intern is exposed to broad aspects of the field, not simply areas in which he or she has expressed interest.
8. The intern receives periodic formal evaluation.
9. Training goals for the intern outweigh service goals.
10. The intern is paid but receives less than a full professional salary.

These common features emphasize an important property of the internship: its transitional status. It is neither the last year of formal education nor the first year of fully independent work. Rather, it is a time for learning, reinforcement, and demonstration of important skills and abilities—the public's penultimate assurance of the candidate's ability to practice independently.

One final feature is present in psychology and medical internships but absent from the other professions: (11.) A critical mass of interns are placed at any given internship site to allow for peer support, structure, and an efficient use of resources. This aspect of professional internships in teaching hospitals makes it possible for an institutional ethos to develop in which the internship site organizes itself not only as a provider of services to clients, as an engineering or architecture office might, but also as a training site for future professionals so additional kinds of training experiences can be made available: ongoing seminars, cohort training and mentoring structures, and access to state-of-the-art facilities and practices. Similar benefits are hoped for in the organization of teaching internships in professional development schools, a substantial number of which have been created for enriching teaching and teacher preparation since 1986 (for a review, see Darling-Hammond, 1993).

Defining the Content of Internships

Although the central purpose of the internship is the same in all of the professions described here, each has its own way of defining the content of the internship. Requirements may be organized in at least four ways: by time spent (as in engineering), by tasks completed (as in architecture), by skills mastered (as in psychology), or by breadth of exposure (as in medicine). In actuality, each profession incorporates features of all four of these methods of organizing internship work, but for the sake of discussion, it is valuable to identify each by its primary attribute.

Time Spent. In engineering, the engineer-in-training must spend time practicing under the supervision of a professional engineer; successful completion is defined simply by having spent four years as an "intern." Some state boards examine the candidate's record to ensure that specific activities and responsibilities have been undertaken during the internship. Others leave it to the intern's employers to verify the accounting of activities offered by the intern. The engineering model provides great flexibility and makes the fewest demands upon the employer, but it leaves the internship's structure to chance and provides the intern with minimal guarantees of specific supports.

Tasks Completed. In architecture, the intern-architect must prove that he or she has spent a specified number of days performing or observing architectural practice in three major categories, such as design and construction, and fourteen smaller areas, such as building cost analysis. Successful completion is defined by having spent appropriate amounts of time on various architectural tasks. Such a model guarantees some uniformity in experience for all interns but does not necessarily account for the nature or quality of experiences provided.

Skills Mastered. In psychology, interns are generally rated on their mastery of various skills in case management, research, and assessment. Successful completion is defined by having spent both one full year working under close supervision and by having mastered certain essential skills. Such a model may offer a greater emphasis on competency (although this emphasis is limited in its effect by the fact that the ultimate judgment must simply be "pass" or "fail"), but it requires the greatest level of commitment on the part of the employer.

Breadth of Exposure. In medicine, the intern is required to participate in a range of rotation assignments, from gynecology to geriatrics to neurology; successful completion is defined both by having spent one full year having worked under close supervision and by having been exposed to a number of central domains of the profession. Such a model ensures that all professionals will have exposure to the field through experience in a number of specialized fields.

We believe each of these four ways of defining content should play some role in the structure of a teaching internship. Thus, we recommend that the program last one year (time spent), involve certain specific classroom experiences (tasks completed), include regular professional evaluation against outcome-based standards (skills mastered), and integrate specified diverse experiences (breadth of exposure). These features are discussed in detail in the following section.

Evaluation of Interns

Upon completion of the internship, each of the four professions requires some kind of summative evaluation of the intern's work. In addition, psychology, architecture, and medicine require periodic formative evaluations during the course of the internship. Although evaluation models vary across and within professions, one crucial feature is constant: Each profession relies on the cumulative judgments of veteran professionals to establish the candidate's capacity for independent practice. Although criteria are specified, not one of the professions suggests that evaluators should tally interns' behaviors during occasional observation periods. Instead, evaluations focus on patterns of skills, abilities, or tasks encountered and demonstrated over a sustained period of time.

In each of the professions, the internship is only one of three or more points at which the candidate's competence is assessed. Thus, the evaluation falls within a larger context. Candidates must also demonstrate mastery of the profession's underlying knowledge base through completion of a formal education program in a professionally accredited school and sometimes through a test of professional knowledge. In a controlled environment, they must also demonstrate mastery of the profession's fundamental duties through written and sometimes oral tests of professional skill. But the internship offers the only opportunity to observe the candidate in sustained, actual practice, and although the evaluation of the internship is neither fully standardized nor wholly objective, it is perhaps the most relevant to actual future practice.

Engineering. In engineering, two models exist for verifying the candidate's successful completion of the internship. In the first, a board of professional engineers evaluates a detailed list and description of activities submitted by the applicant and thereby determines whether the experience has been acceptable. In the second, responsibility for evaluating the candidate's experience falls on the practitioners with whom the applicant has had professional contact; each employer who has worked with the candidate is asked to fill out a form verifying the applicant's employment, experience, ability, and competency. In both of these models, the profession is self-regulating; the state trusts the board to certify the competence of potential professional engineers, and the board, in turn, trusts the practicing professional engineers of the state to prevent entrance into their ranks of anyone unfit for independent practice.

Psychology. Evaluation in psychology internships is primarily formative. Although the greatest part of the evaluation happens through informal contact between interns and their supervisors—a norm that has been established in psychology internship programs—more formal periodic evaluations are a mandated part of accredited psychology internships. The structure of the evaluation forms is left to the discretion of the individual programs, but most try to isolate essential skills—such as case management, ability to establish rapport with patients, and ability to communicate clinical data in writing and verbally—around which the supervisor is asked to evaluate the candidate's strengths and weaknesses. At the end of the internship, the internship site sends a report to the intern's graduate institution indicating whether the intern has successfully met the basic standards of professional practice and describing areas in which the intern is particularly strong or weak.

Architecture. Since the structure of the architecture internship mandates that the candidate complete activities in a specified number and range of areas, most of the evaluation process is directed toward establishing that the required diversity of experiences has actually occurred. Candidates must keep track of the amount of experience they accrue in three major areas—design and construction, construction administration, and office management—including subsets of activities within them, for example, site and environmental analysis, schematic design, and building cost analysis. Verification comes from four sources: the intern (recording), the sponsor or employer (verifying), the adviser (acknowledging), and the board (checking). No place exists on the forms for the sponsor to indicate whether the work was inadequate, satisfactory, or exemplary; it is assumed that if interns' work were of unsuitable quality, they would not have been retained as paid employees.

Medicine. The internship and residency programs in medicine emphasize formative evaluation. As in psychology, most feedback comes from the daily contact between residents and preceptors, but all programs offer more formal evaluation as well—generally on a monthly or bimonthly basis. Often, preceptors are asked to rate residents on their mastery of fundamental skills (e.g., patient management, physical diagnosis skills), knowledge (e.g., medical knowledge, knowledge of patients), and attitudes (e.g., dependability, ability to work with others). In addition, residents are frequently asked to rate their preceptors in parallel areas. The rating forms enter the resident's permanent file and at the end of the residency are used, in conjunction with other information, to determine whether the resident has satisfactorily completed the requirements of the residency. As in all of the other professions described, guided judgments by expert professionals are the basis for decisions about candidate competency.

We present these four summaries as models toward which those developing internship programs might wish to look for inspiration or critique. In the following section, we present the recommended guidelines for a teaching internship developed by the internship committee of the Minnesota Board of Teaching.

Standards for an Internship Program for Teaching

In May 1989, the Minnesota Board of Teaching convened a committee of eight practicing teachers and teacher educators to develop standards for an internship in teaching that would be part of the state's licensing process. After deliberating on the goals and needs for clinical preparation in teaching, examining and discussing internship standards from the four professions described in the previous sections, studying descriptions of program content and intern experiences, and considering examples of intern evaluation forms and procedures, the committee produced a document establishing standards for a teaching internship, which we reproduce at the end of this section.

The heart of the document is a series of standards addressing five aspects of the proposed internship program: (1) educational program, (2) interns, (3) administrative structure, (4) faculty and staffing, and (5) facilities and resources. These standards establish basic criteria programs would have to meet in order to be approved by the Minnesota Board of Teaching. (Similar standards will soon become a feature of NCATE review for those colleges of education that operate professional development schools.) Candidates will normally have taken a professional knowledge examination after completing their coursework and before beginning the internship. They will then be required to complete an approved internship program before being permitted to sit for Minnesota's performance test of teaching skills, the proposed final step in the state's licensing process.

When the program is fully implemented, internships will occur within the structure of institutionalized programs or professional development schools (sometimes also known as clinical schools or professional practice schools) that meet all standards established by the committee. However, during a transitional period (of length to be determined), candidates completing programs that meet only the basic educational program requirements (Section I of the internship standards) would be eligible for licensure.

In addition to articulating internship standards in these five areas, the document includes a discussion of preconditions for establishing a mandatory internship and provides a statement of mission, a statement of intent, and a series of definitions of terms used within the standards. A preamble stressing that the legislature must provide sufficient funding to schools and universities involved in internship programs to allow them to be held accountable for their performance opens the document. If adequate funding is not provided, the drafters agree, an internship should not be a prerequisite for licensure. This agreement was based on the realization that unfunded state evaluation requirements have frequently created situations in which prospective or beginning teachers are not supported or supervised on a regular basis but are evaluated for licensure based on inadequate information (Borko, 1986; Darling-Hammond, Gendler, and Wise, 1990; Fox and Singletary, 1986).

The document describes the mission of a licensing process for teachers: to provide the public and the profession with a high level of confidence that a new teacher is fit for responsible independent practice. Given this mission, the internship is an indispensable prerequisite for independent practice, since it offers a unique opportunity for sustained observation and coaching of prospective teachers prior to their licensure as professionals. The document goes on to define the basic terms used throughout the standards: internship, internship program, and clinical school.

The Task of Developing a Teaching Internship

The definition of a teaching internship as a component of a licensing system should rest on the development of two sets of standards: standards for evaluating interns and standards for evaluating internship programs. Most states that have enacted beginning teacher programs as a prerequisite for licensure have created an evaluation instrument or guidelines for rating the beginning teachers but have not created guidelines or methods for ascertaining what constitutes an adequate internship experience or program. Thus, frequently the educational or supervisory aspect of the experience does not occur in any systematic fashion, although rating forms are filled out.

In contrast, other professions provide detailed standards for accrediting internship programs or experiences, using these guidelines as a means of articulating the nature of the educational process and outcomes desired.[1] These professions sometimes specify the exact criteria and format for evaluating interns while at other times leaving the determination of evaluation methods in the hands of program faculty.

There are good reasons for focusing on standards for program evaluation. If internship programs are to be primarily educational experiences and are to represent a serious attempt at providing the opportunity to learn to practice under supervision, these kinds of standards are even more important for establishing quality control than are precise guidelines for evaluating the interns themselves. If the programs provide the necessary learning experiences, there is a higher probability that interns will acquire the kinds of skills and dispositions desired. Once the nature of the program is defined, along with criteria for the types of learning desired, the specific approach for evaluating an intern as having successfully completed the program may be prespecified, as in architecture, or, as in medicine and psychology, developed by the program faculty—and then approved as part of the program approval process.

The MBOT internship committee focused first on standards for establishing and evaluating programs. These resemble the kinds of standards represented in other professions' accreditation processes, such as the APA Accreditation

---

1. The term *accreditation* implies approval by a national, professional body; *approval* implies action by a state agency.

Criteria for Psychology Internships' and the Joint Commission on Accreditation of Hospitals' criteria for approving residency programs. The committee relied on existing criteria represented in the state's outcomes-based standards for teacher education as the basis for evaluating interns, leaving the development of evaluation strategies to program faculty.

In developing standards for internships, the committee considered two issues: What types of requirements for an initial internship program should be established, and what the ultimate goal for model internship programs should be. Internship standards take years to evolve, and it would be unreasonable to expect the initial teaching internship to resemble the full-fledged systems that have evolved over a longer period of time in established professions. Although the board establishes standards for the initial internship, it is also launching a number of pilot programs using a range of models for supporting beginning teachers, including some very sophisticated programs that resemble the kinds of professional development schools envisioned by the Holmes Group (1990) and others. These provide beacons for the future. Meanwhile, though, the standards developed for internship programs allow for many different approaches to supporting the development of prospective teachers while evaluating their capacities to perform in diverse, real-world settings.

Goals Embodied in the Internship Standards

The standards for the educational program, which represent the core features of an internship, describe the basic content and intention of the internship. They stress that the internship is a structured experience aimed at learning and providing opportunities for guided practice. Thus, the standards include requirements for educational supports and supervision, as well as a reduced teaching load and graduated progression of responsibilities. The internship is also based on a conscious curriculum. In contrast to the more or less haphazard experiences of most beginning teachers—even those who are assigned a mentor—the internship program is designed to ensure that novices encounter, attempt, discuss, and reflect upon certain core concepts, topics, and teaching tasks in educational settings (seminars, conferences, staff meetings, observations of other teachers) as well as in practice.

These experiences are intended to foster the development of an analytic and reflective approach to teaching rather than the rote demonstration of prespecified teaching behaviors. The conscious curriculum of the internship program is intended to help teachers learn to evaluate teaching circumstances; hypothesize, test, and apply knowledge, research, theory, and other ideas; interact with students, parents, and colleagues; reflect upon the effects of their actions and decisions; consult with other colleagues; modify strategies and practices; and grapple with uncertainties and ethical issues.

In contrast to current student teaching practices, the internship is intended to allow prospective teachers to experience and reflect upon a variety of teaching contexts in order to develop an appreciation both for the contingent nature of teaching decisions within different grade levels, subject areas, and types of communities and for a wide range of learning approaches. Thus, the internship is grounded in a view of teaching as complex and context-dependent rather than as simple and routine. It assumes that teaching requires the ability to make judgments based on many sources of information and analysis rather than simply involving the demonstration of only a few generic teaching behaviors.

The standards for *interns* address the evaluation, entry, and exit requirements for individuals in the internship program. In order to encourage a carefully planned program, as well as the peer interaction and learning that are possible with a cohort of students, programs are encouraged to admit a critical mass of interns. Making clear that the internship is an extension of formal preparation rather than a substitution for any portion of such preparation, interns must have completed all other teacher education requirements prior to entry. This both prevents the internship from being asked to serve as a substandard route to licensure (as has happened in some states' alternative certification programs) and heightens the probability that entrants will have the foundation necessary to successfully complete the challenging demands of the internship program without bringing pressures to dilute the curriculum.

Intern evaluation should address the teaching skills and dispositions articulated in Minnesota's standards for teacher education (Appendix A) as well as the ethical standards represented in the Minnesota Teachers' Code of Ethics (excerpted in Appendix F). It should be based on sustained interactions between interns and members of the program faculty and use multiple measures, such as observations, interviews and conferences, teaching products (lesson plans, examples of student assignments), self-reports, clinical supervision, and evidence from students or parents. A judgment that the intern has successfully completed the program must be made by the program director based on recommendations from the program staff. This requirement ensures that more than one professional will be involved in assessing the intern's performance, thus increasing the range of information included and reducing the subjectivity inherent in single-evaluator approaches.

Standards for *administrative structure* are intended to ensure that the program will, in fact, have the capacity to provide the desired educational experiences. These standards establish norms for the shared governance of the internship by representatives of participating schools and higher education institutions and provide for the appointment of a director, the allocation of resources (including staff time dedicated to the functions of the program), and procedures for selecting interns and staff.

Standards for *faculty and staffing* attempt to ensure that internship programs will be staffed only by outstanding professionals who are committed to the profession, to their own continued learning, and to the learning of entering teachers, and who receive the support and training necessary to permit them to do an exemplary job. Given the power of practicum experiences to shape the practice of novices, it is essential that internships provide entering teachers with positive models for practice and for reflection about practice, as well as with opportunities to receive skilled, thoughtful supervision that promotes critical thinking and inquiry rather than simplistic conclusions or dogmatism.

Standards for *facilities and resources* further detail the kinds of conditions under which productive internships allowing novices to observe and experience high-quality practices are possible.

Although *selection criteria* and procedures are to be developed by the programs rather than the state, the faculty characteristics outlined in the standards encourage programs to take account of the fact that program faculty should not only be good teachers themselves but should also have the expertise, inclination, and training to be good teachers of teachers.

Requirements for *professional development* for faculty acknowledge the need to ensure that those who work with novice teachers have opportunities to continually expand their own knowledge about teaching and learning, as well as about effective supervision.

Recommendations of Internship Task Force to Minnesota Board of Teaching Regarding Standards for Internship Programs

Preamble

Adequate funding will be provided by the legislature to schools and universities to provide the resources needed for excellent internship programs in which all participants can be accountable for their performance.

Mission

The licensing process for teachers should provide the public and the profession with a high level of confidence that a new teacher is fit for responsible, independent practice. The MBOT is instituting the internship as a key component in the licensing process to provide an opportunity for prospective teachers to acquire and demonstrate the knowledge, skills, dispositions, and ethical standards necessary for such practice. The intern must successfully complete the internship (and other licensing requirements) as a condition for being awarded a continuing professional license.

Statement of Intent

All candidates for a continuing teaching license in Minnesota shall undergo an internship. Initially, these internships may or may not occur within the structure of fully institutionalized programs or clinical schools. However, at minimum, all internships should meet the standards described in Part I herein. It shall be the policy of Minnesota to develop and institutionalize internship programs throughout the state as soon as possible and make these opportunities available to as many candidates as is practical. These programs shall meet all of the standards herein. It shall also be the policy of Minnesota to create clinical schools to serve as training sites for internship programs.

Definitions

An *internship* is a structured experience by means of which a candidate for teaching receives the supervision, opportunity for guided practice, education, assessment, and feedback needed to acquire and demonstrate the teaching knowledge, skills, and dispositions required for responsible, independent practice.

An *internship program* is a set of organized activities operated by schools and universities under a distinct administrative structure created solely for the purpose of training teacher interns. A program may be operated within a school district or across a consortium of school districts, in one or more schools, including clinical schools. Some components of a program may also operate on the campuses of higher education institutions.

Professional development schools or *clinical schools*, the educational analogue of teaching hospitals, are public schools serving the dual purpose of educating students and preparing teachers. Such schools will be staffed by a mix of highly expert professionals and teacher interns, with direct connections to a school of education. Although a variety of models may be appropriate, certain features, such as overstaffing, a commitment to high-quality education for students and interns, exhibition of state-of-the-art practice, and an atmosphere of collegiality, should be present in all such schools. Whenever possible, such schools shall be established in areas of highest need, thereby providing a stable, highly-skilled core teaching faculty to historically underserved populations.

I. The Educational Program

A. Duration. The internship shall be full-time for one academic year.
B. Instruction and Experience. By means of didactic and clinical experience, such as supervision, seminars, lectures, assigned reading, demonstration, in-class coaching and support groups, the internship

will provide opportunities (including systematic instruction and experience) for:

1. Applying knowledge to the major tasks of teaching, including diagnosing students' needs, developing learning plans, delivering instruction, evaluating student progress, managing the learning environment, and other professional duties.
2. Reflecting upon and analyzing teaching experiences.
3. Experiencing an adequate variety of teaching situations encompassed by the license, including variety in student age or grade levels, student learning characteristics, subject areas, student demographic or cultural characteristics, and types of communities. Familiarity with these diverse teaching situations can be accomplished by instruction, observation, or actual practice. To the extent that it is practically possible, familiarity should be achieved through actual practice in different settings.
4. Using and analyzing research.
5. Participating in a variety of professional activities beyond the classroom.
6. Observing other teachers.
7. Receiving systematic, ongoing assessment with procedures for intensive support as needed.
8. Instruction in professional ethics.
9. Familiarization with the operation of the entire school program, including knowledge of resources and procedures for acquiring needed services for students.

C. Curriculum. The curriculum will be guided by the common developmental needs of beginning teachers. In a progressive fashion, it should expose interns to topics appropriate to their level of training. It should support the translation of theory into practice, focusing both on applications of knowledge and practical concerns. The curriculum must be well organized, based on sound educational principles, and carried out on a regularly scheduled basis which includes organized formal instruction (prepared lectures, seminars, assigned readings, etc.) as well as less formal training (e.g., staff meetings, conferences, social interactions).

D. Essential Characteristics. In addition to systematic instruction and substantial experience in the areas listed above, a program should also provide:

1. Systematic and regular support, in the form of regularly scheduled individual supervision. As a general rule, each intern should have at least two hours of individual supervision weekly. This is in addition to teaching observations, conferences, and seminars.

2. An appropriate and progressive degree of responsibility for teaching students.
3. An optimal teaching load, such that the training functions of the internship are not overwhelmed by the service functions.

E. Descriptive Materials. Internship programs shall develop and distribute descriptive materials in which the goals and content of the program and characteristics of the student population and community setting are accurately depicted, so that interns may match the program emphasis with intern interests.

II. Interns

A. Number. Each program will determine the number of interns to be served, given the resources it has available. It is desirable that a program have a sufficient number of interns to allow for peer interaction and support, as well as adequate instruction.

B. Assessment. The program shall establish a procedure for assessing the acquisition of the skills and dispositions required of a beginning teacher by Minnesota licensing standards. These skills and dispositions must be developed and assessed in at least two diverse teaching settings, which vary by at least two dimensions listed in Part I.B.3. above, as appropriate to the specific license of the intern. The program may ascertain this acquisition by multiple measures, including:

- Observation
- Interviews and weekly conferences
- Teaching products, such as lesson plans, examples of student assignments, tests, etc.
- Self-reports by intern
- Clinical supervision
- Consumer satisfaction

C. Prerequisites. To be admitted to the program, interns must have graduated from or have completed all of the relevant didactic and practicum experiences necessary for graduation from an approved teacher education program.

D. Exit Requirements. The intern must successfully complete the internship prior to sitting for the Minnesota test of beginning teaching skills. Successful completion will be determined by the director of the program on the recommendation of the program staff. Such determination should include an attestation that the intern has developed professional dispositions and meets the ethical standards of the Minnesota Teachers' Code of Ethics. (See Appendix F.)

III. Administrative Structure

A. Director. Each program shall have a director whose major responsibility is to maintain and enhance the internship program. The director must be board-licensed or possess equivalent qualifications, and must devote a sufficient number of hours weekly to the internship program.

B. Participating Institution. Each program shall include one or more school districts and one or more teacher preparing institutions whose relevant teacher education programs are approved by the Minnesota Board of Teaching. These schools and IHEs [institutions of higher education] must meet all applicable accreditation standards.

C. Advisory Board. Each program shall have an advisory board with representatives of all participating institutions, to advise on policy decisions and facilitate close working relations.

D. Resource Allocation. The program shall have a description of the process by which institutional resources, including staff, are allocated for the educational purposes of the internship:

   1. Administrative support for the internship program shall be apparent in terms of adequacy and stability of resources and specific budgeting for training operations, including financial support for interns.

   2. All participating institutions shall recognize the internship activities of staff as part of their regular duties and shall provide the time and structures necessary to support such work.

E. Staff and Intern Selection. The program shall establish an operational system for appointment of staff, selection of interns, supervision and evaluation of interns, assurance of due process for interns and staff, and ongoing review and evaluation of the program.

F. Camaraderie. All sites, including consortia, shall encourage camaraderie among interns and should facilitate information exchange among and between interns and faculty.

IV. Faculty and Staffing

A. Selection Procedures. The director and advisory board will determine procedures for selecting faculty and staff. Staff will include personnel from both school districts and teacher education programs.

B. Staff Characteristics. The internship staff should have a strong interest in teaching and be willing to contribute the necessary time and effort to the education program. The key professional personnel, as teachers, clinical supervisors, and/or administrators, should:

   • Have adequate special training and experience
   • Participate regularly in professional activities

- Participate in their own continuing education
- Actively share teaching expertise
- Exhibit sincere interest in education research and development

C. Number and Variety. The internship program shall be staffed by qualified educators in sufficient numbers to achieve its goals and objectives. A sufficient number and variety of staff are needed to provide the interns with the instruction, supervision, and support required of the educational program (as described above).
D. Professional Development. Programs shall provide continuous professional development for staff to better enable them to carry out their internship functions.
E. Intern Assessment. It is the responsibility of the staff to actively participate in an ongoing assessment of the intern's progress.

V. Facilities and Resources

A. Site. The internship shall take place in public school settings in the state of Minnesota.
B. Program Diversity. Those sites or consortia participating in an internship program shall, independently or jointly, offer sufficient program diversity to ensure a variety of educational experiences. These sites should also serve a student body reflective of the state's diverse population.
C. Adequate Facilities. School sites or consortia providing internship programs shall have adequate facilities, equipment, and materials to provide the educational experiences and opportunities set forth in the program requirements. These include: access to an adequate library providing standard reference texts, curriculum materials, and current professional journals; sufficient space for intern instruction; adequate facilities and technologies for interns to carry out their teaching and personal education responsibilities; a student record system that facilitates both quality instruction and intern education; laboratory and classroom facilities of sufficient quality to promote professional instruction; and all other materials necessary for high quality student and intern education.

Assessment During the Teaching Internship

Although much of the assessment that occurs in a teaching internship will be ongoing and informal, embedded in the intern's work and study and shaped by the professional development school faculty, it is possible to use the internship as an extended opportunity to build some foundations for a subsequent formal assessment of teaching skills. Just as teachers who will sit for NBPTS certification spend the better part of a year assembling their school-site portfolio, so could documentations of practice be developed by requiring an internship portfolio of prospective teachers. Some of these documentations might become grist for assessment center exercises as part of the performance test—for example, semistructured interviews that explore decisions made by the prospective teacher about practices as she or he has documented them on videotape and through teaching artifacts (plans, assignments, feedback to students). Such a strategy for veteran teachers is being explored as part of the NBPTS Early Adolescence Generalist assessment.

Connecticut is also currently exploring the possibilities of requiring a portfolio developed during an internship year as a condition of licensure. The teacher portfolio would embed samples of student portfolios within it as a means for examining student progress over time as it is linked to teaching actions and decisions. These could be the source of interview examinations regarding assessments of student progress or needs and justifications for teaching decisions and future plans. Other portfolio artifacts could also be used in the assessment center to stimulate analyses of how, for example, plans and assignments could be extended to pursue additional objectives or revised for use with other groups of students. This is not dissimilar from the practice in some medical board examinations of using patient files from the candidate's internship or residency experience as the basis for interviews about why certain diagnoses or decisions were made and what other treatment strategies might be appropriate.

The use of portfolio strategies is expanding throughout teacher education. Ken Howey and Nancy Zimpher (1993) argued persuasively for the use of portfolio assessment as a developmental tool for gauging changes over time in prospective teachers'

- *Beliefs* about schooling, teaching, learning, and coming to know: from perceptions of teaching as telling and controlling to conceptions of active learning as self- and group-monitored and developmental in nature
- *Locus of concerns:* from preoccupations with creating the appearances of performance as a teacher to a focus on relationships between one's own actions and student behaviors and learning
- *Reasoning about teaching:* from unexamined assumptions to decisions that are subject to public examination, supported by many kinds of data, and cognizant of ethical consequences
- *Effectiveness:* from intermittent and uneven self-assessment to continual feedback from students and about student progress, creating ongoing evaluation embedded in instruction

Such a portfolio could be a powerful tool for enhancing the learning of prospective teachers, as well as stimulating the reflections of teacher educators in professional development schools (and other aspects of preservice teacher education programs) about the quality of their own practices. Whether this strategy is used to inform the later formal assessment of teaching skills, it is likely to provide a useful tool for structuring the assessment of developing knowledge, skills, and dispositions throughout the teacher preparation experience.

Implementation Concerns

LAUNCHING A NEW SYSTEM of licensure is a major challenge. Although the strategies proposed here are well established in other professions, they are new to teaching and will require changes in public thinking about what it means to become a professional teacher, along with investments of time, intellectual energy, and money in developing internships and assessment programs. In this chapter we discuss a number of considerations that are likely to prove important in implementing these proposals and some promising strategies for addressing them.

The work done thus far represents only the beginning of the development process. Pilot internship and residency programs already underway in Minnesota, California, and other states must be examined, further developed, and expanded. In some cases, existing mentorship programs will be adapted to the standards for internships. In other cases, new institutional arrangements creating professional development school partnerships between schools and universities will be forged. Many states already have a number of these innovations underway. The task of orchestrating their growth and development lies ahead.

Similarly, the work done thus far in developing performance assessments for licensing represents only modest initial steps. Many stages of the test development process remain, including decisions about test technologies and methods, development of tasks across all of the test areas, and studies of the reliability and validity of the instruments developed. Some of these many tasks might be usefully undertaken with other states that are also interested in this kind of assessment. The model for assessment we have proposed is one that is consistent with the changes in licensure standards and assessment goals being pursued in a number of other states. The costs of development may prove more manageable if some of them can be shared.

148

Implementing the Internship

Large numbers of practical considerations surround the proposal we have put forth in our discussion of a teaching internship. These include the questions of how the internship will be financed; what status interns will have within the school, the university, and the union; how staff for the internship should be selected, trained, and compensated; which settings would be optimal for the internship and which least satisfactory; how quickly it is feasible to envision implementation of the internship program; and ways in which we imagine the internship program affecting the current teacher education process. In our discussion, we consider briefly specific practical concerns, such as governance, responsibility for funding, and demographic trends; a much more thorough process of planning and policy development would obviously be necessary before initiating the fundamental changes described here.

Financing the Internship

One of the reasons sound supervised induction to teaching does not now occur is that no agency is financed to carry it out. Teacher education, particularly in state colleges, is financed as if it were primarily a didactic activity with few or no practical components. Funds for supervision of individual teacher candidates are meager, and, as a result, the practical preparation of teacher candidates is carried out in the low-budget enterprise known as student teaching, where supervisor caseloads are high and quality control over cooperating teachers is often nonexistent.

This situation is not rectified later in the candidate's introduction to the profession. School districts are rarely funded to provide sound, practical supervision to student teachers. Nominally and legally, supervisory responsibility for all teachers falls to principals, and occasionally, particularly when the number of beginners is very small, they may be able to provide some support. However, beginning teachers tend to cluster in particular schools, especially in cities, where turnover (and hence the number of new teachers) is high, educational resources are low, and expert veteran teachers are few and overstretched. In these cases individual supervision is curtailed by practical concerns of time and energy. In either case, though, occasional visits from a supervisor cannot offer sustained, context-specific and subject-specific guidance about daily problems of beginning practice.

The idea of expert veteran teachers serving as mentors for beginning teachers, which is gaining great currency in many states, has not yet gained commensurate financing. Mentors may receive a modest salary supplement, but they rarely receive "released time" during which they are freed from their own classes to engage in direct supervision of interns. As a result, mentoring programs as currently executed often make only modest changes in the status quo.

The constraints of financing are exacerbated by a lack of incentives to change current practice. Conventional wisdom has it that school districts are hiring fully qualified teachers when they hire new teacher education graduates. Furthermore, some districts, especially urban ones, may not capture the benefits of an increased investment in structured induction. The traditional migration pattern for teachers involves a great many new teachers starting in cities and then leaving to teach in suburban districts. Although the originating district has made an investment in teaching the beginner how to teach, the returns are captured by another, often wealthier, district.

One solution to this problem might be to ask teacher candidates to pay for their own internships as they, in effect, now pay for their own student teaching. But raising the cost of entry to teaching by requiring interns to forego income for a year-long internship does not seem like sound policy; nor is it one practiced in other professions, where interns are paid to work in supervised clinical settings. Since schools of education, school districts, and teaching interns cannot or should not finance internships, the responsibility must fall on the state, which will capture benefits even if teachers move around from local district to local district. Among the likely benefits to the state as a whole are (1) more capable teachers whose work will produce greater student success and fewer demands for funding special programs to remedy the aftereffects of poor teaching, and (2) lower rates of beginning teacher attrition from the profession.

This approach is not dissimilar from the ways in which teaching hospitals are funded. The greater cost of preparing interns and residents in such hospitals is supported substantially by external funds from several sources: higher formula rates of reimbursement from government and other third-party payers, grants from the federal and state governments for the support of medical education, and allocations to public hospitals from some municipalities and counties. All of these contributors understand that the societal benefits of preparing physicians well (and, in many cases, of serving traditionally underserved communities more effectively) are worth the additional investments that are made in these institutions.

As conceived in our proposal (and as is also true for teaching hospitals), internships need not and probably should not operate in all school districts. They should operate only in school districts that want them and can muster a critical mass of interns and marshal the intellectual resources to properly implement the program. School districts without internships would be free to hire teachers after they satisfactorily complete internships.

We turn now to four particular practical concerns.

Means of Support. The state could support internships in one of two ways: either through a grant to school districts made on the basis of a bid for funds or through state aid adjustments to districts and colleges able to develop internship programs meeting certain standards. In the former case, the state might have more leverage to shape programs, especially at the beginning. In the latter case, greater stability and predictability would follow from formula funding. The major point, however, is that the internship, as defined in this report, will require new resources to finance the time of the members of the internship staff.

Status and Compensation of Interns. As construed in this book, "intern" is a new status—neither fully a student nor a teacher. School districts will have to treat interns differently from other personnel. They must ensure that the intern is closely supervised by allocating senior personnel time to ensure such supervision. Direct supervision need not mean constant supervision. Rather, it implies that even when he or she teaches with no higher authority present, the intern is not fully responsible for the instruction he or she carries out and must have access to and claim on the expertise of a veteran teacher for planning and organizing instruction and for advice on solving problems of practice.

As is the case in some professional development schools, interns may work in a team-teaching situation in which they plan and assess their work jointly with one or several other teachers, sharing responsibility for a larger group of students. Interns may also be placed with a group of other interns in schools. Strategies for working with interdisciplinary or discipline-based cohorts of student teachers and interns may serve as models for such arrangements (see, e.g., Darling-Hammond, 1993; Lythcott and Schwartz, 1993).

Supervision and Salary. The cost of adequate supervision is high; indeed, its cost is the reason it is seldom properly carried out. In a traditionally organized self-contained classroom school, the actual cost of mentoring (as opposed to the much lower price paid to a supervising teacher in the form of a stipend) is the salary of the mentor divided by the number of interns to be supervised— generally from $3,500 to $6,500 per intern. For this reason, it may be more cost-effective to restructure schools by creating professional development school models rather than to try to accommodate mentoring arrangements in traditional egg-crate school settings.

Alternative structures might include team teaching, in which senior and junior teaching personnel jointly plan and deliver instruction to a large number of students. In this approach, one or more expert senior teachers might function as team leaders working with a group of licensed teachers and interns. Thus, for example, three teachers and three interns might be responsible for instructing 120 students. If this district has a normal teacher-pupil ratio of 1 to 20, team teaching need not increase costs. If interns are paid somewhat less than fully licensed teachers, it might decrease standard costs, allowing for a lower pupil-teacher ratio and other additional educational investments.

The determination of the intern salary level rests on two sets of considerations: compensation for work performed and supply-and-demand forces. If interns carry less than a full load (say, four courses instead of five in a high school or an 80 percent assignment relieved of extra duties in an elementary school), there is an argument for less than full compensation. This reduced load is desirable to allow for the interns' participation in seminars, consultation with supervising teachers, and other necessary learning experiences.

Even in the less desirable circumstance in which interns might be expected to carry a "full load," they should perhaps receive slightly lower compensation than that currently awarded to beginning teachers. Less than full compensation may be justified since the intern must be supervised; thus, the cost of educating students is increased by the cost of the supervision. On the basis of workload or costs of education, reduced compensation might help to finance the internship program.

But setting compensation levels is only partly related to the worth of the work of the intern and to the cost of the internship. Compensation is also determined by supply-and-demand forces. Maintaining or reducing intern compensation should also be a function of maintaining or increasing the attractiveness of teaching. In times or places of anticipated shortage, prudence may dictate that the cost of entry into teaching not be substantially increased or the benefits substantially reduced.

Union Membership. A particularly important status consideration is the eligibility of interns for union membership, an issue obviously to be confronted and settled by unions themselves. The intern's union status can make implementation of the internship program easy or problematic. If interns are full union members, two problems are created. First, senior teachers may be reluctant to take part in the evaluation of their "peers." Yet senior teachers will have the most thorough and direct knowledge of the intern's performance, and excluding them from evaluating whether the intern has satisfactorily completed the internship would render that determination less effective.

This traditional hurdle is beginning to change in an increasing number of districts in which unions have taken leadership to provide mentoring assistance and evaluation support for beginning teachers. Toledo, Ohio, Cincinnati, Ohio, and Rochester, New York, are examples of districts with well-developed mentor-intern programs in which expert veteran teachers supervise entering teachers and contribute to assessments of their competence and eligibility for retention or tenure.

In addition, if the intern is a full union member, the intern may be entitled to the full protection of the union in cases in which it is judged that he or she has not successfully completed the internship. Where this union-management adversarial relationship has not changed, it may prove a barrier to vesting the internship with the integrity that will be required to establish public trust.

It may conceivably be better for the unions to create a special (less than full) membership status for interns, something like the National Education Association's (NEA) student membership or the Toledo Federation of Teacher's treatment of interns in its intern program established in the early 1980s (Wise et al., 1984). In this example the union accepted interns as less than full members. This special status was a cornerstone of the special labor-management relation that allowed the program to become effective.

Staffing for the Internship Program

Key to the success of the program will be the selection of outstanding teachers who also have the capacity to be internship staff. The standards note that the internship staff should be composed of personnel who have actively shared their teaching expertise, exhibited sincere interest in education research and development, participated in their own education, participated regularly in professional activities, and undergone special training that ensures they are knowledgeable and skillful in teaching and supervising adults. Thus, not all teachers, not even all outstanding teachers, are qualified to be internship staff. In addition, it will eventually be important for intern supervisors to have served as developers or readers for new licensing assessments so they are credible in their roles and knowledgeable about the standards their interns will encounter. Ultimately, all licensed teachers will have passed the performance-based licensing examinations and completed an internship so familiarity with these standards will not be a problem.

In addition, it may ultimately be desirable for professional development school (PDS) faculty (both school-based and university-based faculty) to be NBPTS certified as "highly accomplished" teachers. Given the nature of the NBPTS assessment process, such a requirement is likely to help ensure that incoming teachers will be exposed to state-of-the-art practices used by teachers who are able to reflect upon their work and articulate what they are doing and why. The ability to enact as well as articulate good teaching decisions is important for those who would teach other would-be teachers. In addition, veteran teachers who have experienced the pilot assessments of the NBPTS report that completing the portfolio and assessment center exercises constitutes one of the most powerful professional development experiences they have encountered in the course of their careers. Having experienced such a powerful approach to learning, these teachers are likely to be more able to construct powerful approaches to learning for interns.

Being a member of the internship staff need not imply a new and permanent change in role, although it will involve a change in responsibilities. As envisioned here, a school district need not create a "career ladder" in order to institute the internship program. The spirit of the internship program is that it should be an educational experience for all participants. Early experience with internship programs suggests that mentors learn as they supervise. The culture of the programs, as well as their organizational features, should encourage learning by all participants. Thus, much of the "training" of the internship staff will be its own collectively designed and implemented staff development.

Professional Development Schools

Although an internship program can be implemented in traditional schools, it can likely be more effectively conducted in professional development or clinical schools. As noted earlier, the traditional school requires that the cost of supervision be over and above the cost of instruction. Restructuring the school so it performs the dual mission of educating both students and future educators could provide many benefits. In addition to allowing for cohort training, on-site seminars for PDS faculty and interns, and ongoing inquiry into teaching and learning by site-based and university-based faculty, a restructured school organization can permit mixes of senior and junior staff to deliver instruction in such a way that the cost of instruction need be little higher than that in other schools in the district.

A strong case can be made for locating professional development schools in school buildings that currently experience high faculty turnover and hire a large number of beginning teachers (Wise, Darling-Hammond, and Berry, 1987). These buildings already function as "professional development schools," although not by design and generally not well. Moreover, the students in these buildings, often those most in need of expert instruction, do not receive it.

Urban school districts considering the creation of professional development schools should study teacher transfer and turnover patterns. Transfer patterns will locate the high turnover schools. Overall turnover patterns will help the district to anticipate the numbers of new teachers to be hired and inducted. It must be noted, though, that districts will need to help build the capacity of local schools, particularly high turnover schools, to conduct high-quality internships. This would include providing attractions for hiring, retaining highly qualified teachers, and offering supports for professional development—including libraries, professional materials, and structures conducive to teacher collaboration.

The Role of the Internship in Teacher Preparation

A final issue is how soon the internship should be implemented as part of the teacher training process. As we have envisioned it in this document, the internship would be embedded within a larger licensing process. At present, the formal assessments that precede and follow the internship are in the early stages of development. But there is no reason to defer the implementation of the internship until such examinations are ready. The internship can stand alone as an improvement in teacher education and licensing. Moreover, the internship requires significant organization in the case of traditional schools and substantial reorganization in the case of professional development schools. Thus, the full implementation of internship programs will take some time. By the time the internship is fully operational, some states are likely to have performance assessments ready for general administration.

One issue that is sure to arise is whether the internship outlined here could be a substitute for, rather than an extension of, traditional teacher education. The internship is designed to improve the practical preparation of teachers. Although internships will have a substantial didactic component in which teaching theory and research will be reviewed, the time devoted to direct teaching will be too limited to convey the breadth and depth of pedagogical and other professional knowledge new teachers must have. As we note in Chapter 2, the limited number of cases in which university-based teacher education is married to a supervised internship produce more able teachers than either component alone can achieve.

The goals to be accomplished in the internship and the abilities to be demonstrated on performance tests will not be attainable without prior professional education that includes both an understanding of theory embedded in a broad knowledge base and practical skills. In short, the internship by itself will not substitute for that portion of the intellectual preparation for teaching that occurs most efficiently in the university setting.

The internship represents a rearrangement of institutional roles and responsibilities for teacher education and induction. It involves the state, through its board of teaching, in regulating teacher education in a new way. It cannot simply be mandated, as is often the case with educational innovations. To expect school districts or schools of education to absorb the costs is unrealistic. To mandate that they implement the program without new funds is to beg for superficial compliance that, in the end, will discredit the idea. It is important that internships, as with many other educational innovations, not be "proved" ineffective before they are ever really implemented.

Implementing Performance Assessments

In developing a performance test for licensing, a number of practical concerns arise. These include issues of validity, reliability, bias, administrative conditions and procedures, scoring criteria and standards, scoring procedures, reader selection and training, methods for combining scores across tasks, establishing pass-fail standards, performance reporting procedures and policies, and test disclosure policies. We next discuss possible solutions to problems raised by each of these concerns.

Validity Studies

Concerns about validity are central to the implementation of any examination that will be used in licensure decisions. In the case of the performance assessments we have proposed, at least two types of validity studies should be conducted: expert-novice studies and content validation studies. These should establish whether the assessments are measuring the kinds of knowledge and skills that are important to assess and that are a function of developed expertise in teaching and are not measuring something else that is irrelevant.

The expert-novice, or "known-group," procedure involves giving the prototype to two groups: (a) highly motivated "novices" (such as those just entering teacher training), and (b) "experts" (such as teachers who are recognized as being highly competent in their field). Within the context of such studies, validity is indicated by the extent to which the expert's scores are higher than the novice's scores and by the degree to which the distribution of novice scores overlaps the distribution of expert scores: The smaller the overlap, the higher the validity. A study by Klein (1986a; 1988) illustrated this procedure for the California Bar exam on which law school graduates do in fact score higher than comparably intelligent but untrained entering law students.

This kind of study is especially important for validating tests of teaching knowledge given the criticisms of existing teacher tests that they mostly measure general aptitude and test-taking ability rather than a body of knowledge about teaching. The conventional wisdom generated by journalists and other lay persons who have taken teacher tests and scored well despite not knowing anything about teaching is reinforced by studies (described in Chapter 3) that find high correlations among general aptitude tests and NTE scores but no evidence of predictive validity. If teacher tests are measuring a specialized body of knowledge and skills, they should differentiate between those who are well prepared in that body of knowledge and those who are eager but unprepared.

A content validity study would involve a panel of experts making judgments about whether the types of tasks included on the prototype are representative of the important kinds of tasks beginning teachers would be expected to perform in practice. To be content valid, the prototype does not have to cover all of the important skills a beginning teacher would be expected to have. Instead, the issue is whether it measures a reasonable sample of the skills that are necessary and important, which is all a test can purport to do. Nevertheless, a job analysis would be an important benchmark for a content validity study.

Reliability Studies

Four types of reliability can be assessed: intra-reader, inter-reader, inter-task, and parallel form. Each of these is discussed next.

Intra-reader reliability refers to the degree to which a reader assigns the same score to an answer on different occasions. For example, the reader would grade a given set of ten answers toward the beginning and again toward the middle and the end of the two-week grading process. Differences in the grades the reader assigned to an answer across occasions could result from chance, fatigue, or possible changes in grading criteria and standards. Intra-reader reliability is indicated by the correlation coefficient between the scores on the different occasions in which the common set of answers was graded as well as by t-tests of differences between means between occasions.

Inter-reader reliability refers to the degree to which different readers assign the same score to an answer. Differences among readers could be caused by chance (such as fatigue), context effects (i.e., the order in which the answers were graded), or systematic differences in the readers' scoring criteria or standards that were not eliminated during the training process. If only two readers evaluate each answer, then inter-reader reliability is indicated by the correlation coefficient between the scores assigned by these readers on the set of answers they graded in common. If more than two readers evaluate a common set of answers (e.g., all five members of a reading team independently grade the same set of thirty answers), then the reliability of a single reader and that of the average of all the readers' scores can be assessed through the use of the analysis of variance procedures described by Winer (1971) or Cronbach et al. (1972). These methods also can be used to test for differences in means among readers. A large difference between inter-reader and intra-reader reliability would suggest that there are systematic, idiosyncratic differences among readers.

Even after extensive calibration and numerous training sessions, the correlation between readers on bar examination answers is usually only about .75, which is why in many states the answers written by candidates that are near the pass-fail line are read again by a different grader. Following this additional reading, the average of the scores is used in making final pass-fail decisions. Some testing programs statistically correct the scores assigned if readers differ in mean score (i.e., one reader is more lenient than another), but there is no way to adjust for differences in how readers rank-order answers. Such differences result from chance factors or readers focusing on different aspects of the
. . . . . sis in reader training programs should be on estab-
. . . . . sessment of the relative quality of the answers. And
. . . . . ining is indicated by the reliability coefficients dis-

. . . . . refers to the degree to which a candidate's score on one
. . . . . te with that candidate's score on other tasks. The com-
. . . . . his procedure also shows how well the scores on each task
. . . . . sum of the scores on the other tasks combined, which is
. . . . . g whether the candidates who do well on one task tend to do
. . . . . others. The average of the inter-task correlations can be used with standard analysis of variance procedures to estimate the overall internal consistency reliability of the entire test (coefficient alpha). A key assumption underlying this estimate is that the tasks are a random sample from a common pool of tasks that measure the same general skill (an assumption that may not hold in this context if having the skills needed to perform some tasks is not correlated with having the skills required to perform other tasks).

Parallel form reliability refers to the degree to which the candidates' scores on one version of the test correlate with their scores on another version. This is the most important of the four kinds of reliabilities to be assessed because it is used to calculate the likelihood that a candidate's pass-fail status on the exam is affected by chance or by the particular version of the test taken rather than by the candidate's skills (which, ideally, are the only factors that should influence pass-fail decisions). The test development plan presented in Chapter 6 greatly facilitates measuring parallel form reliability because superficially quite different tasks can be generated from the same task shell or blueprint.

Minimizing Bias

As we note later, to minimize bias the readers should be completely blinded to the ethnicity, gender, age, handicapping condition, native language, and other extraneous characteristics of the candidates whose answers they grade. In addition, all of the instructions and materials presented to candidates should be reviewed for potential bias by an expert panel of consultants for such things as insensitivity and stereotyping. Any problems they note will be corrected prior to the final pilot testing of the tasks.

Once the test becomes operational, a questionnaire could be distributed with the licensing packet that would ask candidates to indicate their ethnic group, gender, age, undergraduate college, and most recent educational institution. They would be advised that this information will be used solely for research purposes and that their names will not be linked with these data. These data can be used to examine adverse impact in two ways. First, they can be used to assess whether some readers systematically down-grade candidates with certain background characteristics relative to how other readers grade these same answers. This kind of investigation would be even more important if some of the tasks allow evaluators to see or interact with candidates—for example, through videotapes or interviews. If this occurs, additional blind re-reading (or other rescoring) would be required to obtain unbiased scores.

Overall results may show that some groups tend to do better on some tasks than others. For instance, analysis of a set of answers may show that women score higher than men and older candidates do less well than younger candidates. If this occurs, we will want to see whether it happens on all tasks or just a few. If some tasks show a larger adverse effect than others, and if this variation is not simply an artifact of differences in task reliability, then the solution is to try to design tasks that are more like the ones with the least adverse impact.

If the problem is more general, then the question will be whether the difference between groups on the test tends to be larger or smaller than what appears between them in their undergraduate grades or other external criteria. In short, does the prototype tend to widen or narrow the gap that previous research and other measures suggest may already exist between these groups prior to their taking the exam? Such an analysis requires a sophisticated design and data from several administrations of the prototype because of the need to have an adequate sample of candidates in each gender, age, ethnic, or other subgroup to be studied and because different groups may react differently to different tasks. (See Klein, 1993, for an example of this type of study.)

Administrative Conditions and Procedures

When the test becomes operational, all candidates for a given administration will be assessed at the same time and on the same day. There could be, for instance, one session of three hours in the morning and another session of about three hours in the afternoon. Two or three tasks would be given in the morning session with the remaining tasks administered in the afternoon session.

Assuming, as our pilot tasks do, that written response modes will be used, candidates would write their answers to the tasks in blue books or on specially prepared forms. The answer to each task would be written in a separate book (or on a separate form). The answer book would have a removable tab in the upper right-hand corner of the cover page. Candidates would put their admission ticket numbers on this tab, as well as print and sign their names on it. After the answers were turned in, staff would stamp a randomly generated candidate code number on both the book and the tab. The tab would then be removed and a link file prepared of code numbers with admission ticket numbers and names. The link file would be stored in a safe and be used to match grades to individuals only after all the scoring is completed.

Because of these procedures, a reader would have no idea whose book was being graded, nor could a candidate alert a reader to be on the lookout for a certain identification number. This double-numbering system is the procedure that is used on the bar examination in most states. The administrative conditions required for the proposed test are also the same as those needed for other group-administered paper-and-pencil tests. These conditions include standardized test administration procedures (time limits, instructions, and similar factors) that are documented in administration manuals, positive control of all test materials (e.g., numbering of the booklets containing te questions and ensuring security over their printing and distribution), a quate lighting and seating for candidates (and enough space between sea preclude copying), trained proctors, prearranged seating assignment procedures to verify candidate identification. Alternate arrangements made for candidates with disabilities or other special needs.

If in some versions of the exam candidates employ a videotape room, additional arrangements will have to be made to have an number of video monitors in the room where testing is done, a ce station, and related equipment and arrangements. An experimer such a task for the bar exam was found to be quite feasible to develor. ister, and score.

Scoring Criteria and Standards

Scoring criteria refers to the aspects (dimensions) of a candidate's answer that will be attended to in assigning a grade to that answer. Scoring standards refers to the level of quality of a candidate's response on a given dimension that merits a certain score (or score category, such as superior, acceptable, or unsatisfactory).

The scoring criteria for a task are specified at two levels: the shell level and the specific item level. For example, one task might ask candidates to evaluate a set of student answers, identify the common problem(s) in this answer set, and plan how to deal with these problems in subsequent lessons and assignments. The specific scoring criteria for a task that is developed from this shell will, therefore, consider the nature of the unique and common problems that were built into each answer. For instance, did the candidate recognize problem x in answer 1? Was the candidate's comment on this problem constructive as indicated by saying x, y, or z? In short, tasks are designed to test or elicit specific kinds of identifiable knowledge and skill. Therefore, criteria are also very specific and, hence, readily scorable.

Scoring standards also have to be devised within the context of the task, such as what candidates would have to say in their answers to show that they recognized the common problem, what they would need to do (or not do) to illustrate their use of appropriate feedback on student papers, and similar issues. In summary, the scoring criteria are tied to both the general and specific nature of each task, whereas the performance standards are inextricably linked to the specific task materials and instructions. Thus, criteria and standards are operationally defined in terms of the specific problems that were built into these materials and instructions. They are not global, amorphous, ambiguous, or generalized concepts (such as "shows an appreciation of diverse student needs"). Instead, criteria and standards are tied directly to observable and well-defined characteristics of the task and the candidates' responses to that task.

This orientation to scoring criteria and standards is extremely important because it greatly enhances the reliability and validity of the grading process. It also facilitates concrete communication with candidates as to what is expected of them.

Scoring Procedures

The readers should use an analytic or holistic scoring guide that is tailor-made to the task. This guide should be conceptually developed from the standards that articulate what teachers should know and be able do and be concretely linked to the specific task, having been developed at the time the task is constructed. However, this guide could be revised during reader calibration to better accommodate unanticipated candidate responses.

A reader would score the candidate's answer on each of the dimensions in the guide. No marks would be made on the answer itself (especially because some answers will be graded by a second reader). The candidate's total score on the task would be the sum or weighted sum of these separate scores, although provision might be made for adding a general overall dimension. To maximize reliability and to better handle unexpected candidate responses in a consistent manner, all of the reader training and grading should be done at one location so questions can be taken up among the readers at the time the scoring is taking place. Efforts should also be made to reduce halo effects in the grading process.

Candidates who, on the basis of their total score, came close to passing but failed, as well as those who came close to failing but passed, should have their answers reread. The decision to reread a candidate's examination should be based on the total score (rather than the score on each task) because the final pass-fail decision is based on total scores. The second (or third) reader on an answer should not know the score assigned to that answer by the first reader; nor should the second reader know whether the candidate's total score after the first reading was above or below the pass-fail line. The average of the two scores assigned to an answer would constitute the candidate's final score on the task. Large differences between the two readers would be resolved.

Once readers are trained and experienced with the scoring guide, they should be able to grade about ten answers per hour, depending on the extensiveness of the task. This estimate is based on experience in grading answers to the one-hour essay questions and three-hour performance test problems on the bar examination. Thus, if there are five readers per task and six hundred answers per reader (including the answers that are reread), each reader will spend about sixty hours grading answers. However, readers often cannot work all day grading answers. Thus, the grading process has to be spread out over a longer period of a week or more.

Reader Selection and Training

We anticipate that using five readers per team represents the best tradeoff among the fixed costs associated with each additional reader (such as training costs), the speed with which the answers are graded and the results reported to candidates, the greater difficulty of obtaining agreement among readers in the grades they assign to a given answer as the number of readers increases, and the greater flexibility afforded as this number goes up (such as when a reader becomes ill or cannot keep pace with the others). Applications to become a reader would be disseminated through schools and professional associations. The readers for a performance assessment in English–language arts would be chosen from among those who have taught secondary school English for at least five years. Ideally, these would be teachers who are active in their professional association and current with the literature on teaching in their field. They should be well recommended in terms of the quality of their own teaching practice. We would also recommend the use of a short job sample task to see if prospective readers can apply consistent grading standards to a specially selected set of answers.

As a group, the selected readers for each team should reflect the cultural diversity of the state's teachers and students. The training program should involve the readers reviewing the task and scoring guide, discussing these materials, then independently evaluating a common set of about three answers; that is, all five readers would grade the same set of three answers and, on a separate form, note their tentative scores on each dimension to be evaluated on each answer. They would then discuss their grades and resolve any differences. This process would be continued with several subsequent sets of answers until there is a reasonably high degree of agreement among the readers as to what score should be assigned to each answer. In short, readers cannot agree to disagree.

Combining Scores Across Tasks

A candidate will receive a total score on each task that reflects that candidate's performance over the various dimensions of that task. We anticipate that these dimensions will be weighted; that is, some will carry more influence than others in determining the candidate's total score on the task. These weights will be assigned at the time the task is developed, but they may on occasion be revised after reviewing a sample of candidate responses. Experience with similar tasks on the bar exam has indicated that for some but not all tasks, a single holistic grade on an answer is just as reliable and valid as the use of an analytic ("score card") grading approach. This is especially so when the analytic approach simply reflects a large halo effect in grading.

Once a score is obtained on each task, the problem then becomes how to combine these scores into a total score. There are several choices. For instance, a rule can be established in advance, such as: Candidates who pass at least three of the five tasks will pass overall. Alternatively, the candidate's total score could be a weighted composite of the sum of the five separate task scores. We prefer the latter approach because it makes greater use of all of the information obtained (i.e., it is more precise). However, we recognize that it may require standardizing the scores on each task before they are weighted and combined to form a total score. (Otherwise, the tasks will be weighted by their respective standard deviations.)

Establishing Pass-Fail Standards

Several methods for establishing pass-fail standards have been described in the psychometric literature (Livingston and Sieky, 1982). This literature also contains an extensive array of articles on test score equating; that is, how to maintain the standards once they are established and in a way that controls for possible variations across administrations in the difficulty of the questions asked (Angoff, 1971). However, all of the standard setting methods, such as those developed by Angoff (1971) and Nedelsky (1954), assume the use of selected response (multiple-choice) measures. The same is true for the equating procedures.

Klein (1986c, 1991) has developed an approach that can be used with constructed response measures. This procedure involves expert panels making judgments about whether specific candidate responses on the individual tasks should be considered passing or failing, relating these judgments to total test scores, and then linking these total scores, and, thereby, standards to another measure that is routinely given to all candidates and that can be equated across administrations using the well-proven, standard techniques that are applicable to multiple-choice measures. In the case of the SKOPE skills test we describe in Chapter 6, the skills section will constitute one part of a two-part examination. The SKOPE test of common core knowledge would be taken by all candidates (i.e., not just English teachers) and could therefore serve as the link test in the Klein procedure. This link test also could be used to achieve another important goal: ensuring comparability and thereby fairness of pass-fail standards across fields. For example, it should be no more difficult for an English teacher to pass the skills test in English than it is for a science teacher to pass the skills test in Science.

The procedure for doing this is analogous to the one described by Angoff (1971) for converting the scores for various subject-matter tests (such as French and Physics) on the Graduate Record Examination (GRE) to a common scale of measurement through a link test that is taken by virtually all examinees (namely, the GRE verbal and quantitative reasoning section). As a result of the Angoff procedure, the difficulty of achieving a 600 in French can be considered reasonably comparable to the difficulty of earning a 600 in Physics. In short, converting the scores on different tests to a common scale of measurement by means of a relevant link test controls for possible differences in both the level of difficulty of the various specialty exams and the average ability level of the candidates who take them.

Within the context of a licensing process for teachers, this methodology would involve the following steps: (1) Tally the scores on the link test for all of the candidates who took a particular skills test, (2) compute the mean and standard deviation of these candidates' scores on the link test, (3) compute the mean and standard deviation of these same candidates' scores on the skills test, (4) use the following equation (or a nonlinear transformation) to convert the scores on the skills test to the same score distribution as that used on the link test, and (5) use the same scaled score as the pass-fail line across all fields. Note that in this procedure, a given candidate's score on a skills test is not changed as a function of that candidate's score on the link test.

Skills Test Scaled Score $= [(A - B)/C][D] + E$
Where: A = Candidate's score on the skills test
   B = Mean of the scores on the skills test
   C = Standard Deviation of the scores on the skills test
   D = Standard Deviation of the scores on the link test
   E = Mean of the scores on the link test

Performance Reporting Procedures and Policies

Our suggestions regarding score reporting policies are summarized below. A candidate's total score would be a weighted sum of that candidate's raw or standardized score on the five tasks. Thus, a high score on one task can offset a low score on another. Pass-fail decisions would be based on the total score. Candidates who pass the exam will be notified accordingly, but they will not be told their scores. They will only be told that they passed. Their scores would also not be released to school districts. This proposed policy is in keeping with the principle that the licensing exam is a test of basic competency and that those with very high scores are not necessarily better overall teachers than those with only moderate (but still passing) scores.

Candidates who fail the exam would be given their score on each task, their total score, and the percentile equivalents of these scores (so they could see on which tasks they did well versus poorly after controlling for possible differences in difficulty or grading standards among tasks). Failing candidates would also be informed about pertinent aspects of the scoring process so they could calculate their total scores from the information provided. More detailed scores within a task would not be reported because they would not likely be reliable enough for this purpose.

Teacher education institutions that had more than twenty of their graduates sit for the exam would be informed about the average of these students' scores and their passing rate. Schools would not be given the scores of the individual graduates. The purpose of the information provided is to help schools identify general areas of strengths and weaknesses in their programs and to alert potential students to the success rate at different institutions.

Test Disclosure Policies

As with virtually all constructed response measures, once they are administered on a high-stakes licensing exam, the specific questions employed cannot be used again because security is too easily compromised. It would be simple for a commercial test preparation course to debrief the candidates after the exam in order to give the next group a leg up on how to answer. Thus, it is fairer to all candidates to release all of the test questions. Candidates should have ample information about the types of tasks that will appear on the test and the quality of the answers that will be expected in order to pass.

The best information in this regard is actual past questions and a selection of answers. For these reasons, the State Bar of California publishes all of the constructed response questions and a sample set of answers after each exam. Students find these materials invaluable in preparing for the exam. In addition, providing clear indications of the nature of the tasks on the examination should help teacher education programs understand and address the kinds of knowledge and skills their graduates will be expected to have mastered. The implementation of this policy requires that students sign a release that allows the testing agency to publish their answers (but not the names of who wrote them). Samples of multiple-choice items are released periodically, but most are kept secure because many will be used again to equate future versions of the exam. We suggest adopting the same policy.

Conclusions

In this report, we have proposed and defended a new system for teacher licensing. Although our original work for Minnesota was grounded in the needs and policies of that particular state, we believe the results are largely generalizable and that only minimal changes would need to be made by another state wishing to implement a similar system.

In summary, we have proposed a three-part assessment program: a test of the common core of teaching knowledge, a one-year supervised internship in a professional development school setting, and a performance assessment of teaching skills. We have also noted that professional accreditation of teacher preparation institutions will support this process by assuring teacher candidates of the quality of their institutions and assuring the public and the profession that candidates are prepared to begin their careers as interns.

We began by making a case for an outcomes-based professional licensing system, suggesting that such a system represents a means of gaining leverage in the process of promoting educational change. By establishing rigorous and professional standards for entry into the teaching profession, we create incentives for systemic change in teacher preparation, enhanced professional capacity to support systemic change in elementary and secondary education, more widespread use of good teaching practices—especially in schools and for children who have been least well served—and a warranted public confidence in teaching as a respected and responsible profession.

The consequences of this system for the future of the teaching profession should be manifold and mutually reinforcing. As teacher competence increases and licensing loopholes are closed, salaries are likely to rise commensurately. Talented students who might otherwise have avoided the profession will be encouraged to pursue it by the increased rigor of preparation and respect for the profession, as well as monetary rewards. As the general caliber of teachers' knowledge is improved and the wide disparities among teachers' skills are reduced, states and districts may begin to allow teachers to make major decisions about school management and educational practice. This, in turn, should permit schools to solve educational problems more effectively while reinforcing the encouragements for talented students to enter the profession.

The system we have proposed here offers a means of meeting the three basic objectives an assessment system for professional licensure should meet: articulating standards, encouraging acquisition of skills and knowledge, and reliably and validly sorting those prepared for practice from those not pre-pared. Further developing this work should engender growing consensus about what teachers should know and how they should be assessed, as well as stimulating greater debates about these issues. Just as debates continue in ar-chitecture and medicine about whether particular sorts of knowledge should be required of all future professionals, a perfect consensus should never be reached. The liveliness of the debate will itself engage members of the profes-sion in continually defining and refining standards and will create an engine for professional improvement.

Nonetheless, we believe that as in other professions, a working consensus can be reached about a core of knowledge that most teachers and teacher edu-cators would agree must be mastered by any individual who wishes to practice responsibly as a professional teacher. This growing consensus also includes a conception of teaching as based on the integration of many areas of knowl-edge, characterized by the use of multiple skills appropriately applied to particular situations and dependent upon considerations of students and subjects.

The structure, content, and approach of new assessments, once articulated, should encourage institutions of teacher education to provide their students with opportunites to encounter the knowledge and skills to be assessed and, it is hoped, to do so in a way that promotes analysis, reflection, and consider-ation of consequences for students. As a result, the knowledge professionals within the field of teaching have deemed essential to practice—along with a conception of teaching as thinking work—will permeate the curricula of pro-spective teachers throughout the state. Furthermore, students will be moti-vated to develop these capacities, since passing the examination will be a pre-requisite to practice.

None of this will happen overnight. Indeed, the investment of both time and money required to implement the kind of system we propose will probably not produce tangible results of the type we describe for many years. Nonetheless, eventually, we believe, this approach to educating, assessing, and licensing teachers could become embedded within the cultural fabric much as the licen-sure processes in other professions—medicine, law, psychology, architecture, engineering—have become accepted.

This kind of approach is appropriate and necessary to fields that require ex-pertise and provide services to the public. Public confidence that entrants un-derstand what to do and know how to do it is essential if teaching is to argue for the right to educate practitioners and regulate entry in accordance with professional standards. In the long run, this kind of confidence from the pub-lic is necessary if a public educational system that educates all children is to survive in the face of growing skepticism, discontent, and disinvestment.

More important, if all children are to be well educated, all teachers must possess the kinds of understanding, skill, and commitment we have described.

Packaged curricula and standardized school procedures cannot guarantee that all children will learn. In fact, the more standardized these alternatives to skilled teachers become, the less likely they are to meet the wide-ranging needs of nonstandardized students. Investing in knowledgeable and skillful teachers who are both willing and able to do what is right for children is the only sure way to create successful education for all.

APPENDIX A
Minnesota's Vision
for Teacher Education—
Recommended Program Outcomes
of Future Teacher Education:
Dispositions, Skills, Knowledge[1]

HISTORICALLY, teacher education has been described and evaluated by re-source criteria such as the number of courses in pedagogy or philosophy of education, and the number of faculty and their degrees. Unfortunately, de-scribing or measuring program resources provides no information about the results or consequences of the program for students, nor does it describe how the program is implemented. Defining, describing, and evaluating the results, or outcomes, of a program make it possible to judge whether the program pro-duces teachers who effectively facilitate learning for students. Defining, de-scribing, and evaluating the methods and procedures used also make judg-ments possible about the process of delivering teacher education. Current evidence suggests that teacher education should be characterized by program outcomes and process as well as input (Taylor, 1979).

Based on the task force review of the most recent knowledge of effective learning and teaching, this chapter defines and describes a minimum set of standards for the outcomes and the processes of teacher education. The first section provides the dispositions, skills, and knowledge that graduates of teacher education programs should demonstrate. Necessary elements of de-livery systems for implementing recommended programs are identified to conclude the chapter.

Introduction

Teachers should be thoughtful, creative persons who use a set of principles and strategies derived from an informed personal philosophy of education and the multiple demands of learning contexts. The descriptions of future

---

1. From *Minnesota's Vision for Teacher Education: Stronger Standards, New Partnerships*, Chapter 5. Minnesota Task Force on Teacher Education and Minnesota Higher Education Coordinating Board.

learners and teachers create a picture of education which focuses on developing learners' minds so that they can use available and changing knowledge in a variety of learning contexts.

These concepts of learners and teachers have been too infrequently realized both within schools and teacher preparation programs. Additionally, teacher education programs seldom use an ideally defined concept of a teacher as the basis for developing coherent, integrated curriculum and structure (Howey, 1984).

Several barriers to developing and implementing programs based on these concepts exist. In part, education has historically endorsed a "learn the facts and do the job" approach. This perspective permeates teaching at all levels (Nolan, 1985).

Too, educators within colleges and schools have used limited interactive instructional strategies (Cross and Beidler, 1986). For the most part, college and classroom learning behavior exemplifies the passive learner phenomenon (Katz and Raths, 1982). These obstacles affect decisions about what prospective teachers should learn and how they should learn.

Expected dispositions of beginning teachers must stem from the concept of an ideal teacher. The identified dispositions determine the range of skills needed by beginning teachers. Finally, the knowledge necessary for building the skills is defined. All are necessary to teaching regardless of grade level or subject area.

Dispositions

The goals of teacher education programs should include not only the acquisition of skills and knowledge, but also the promotion of certain dispositions. Effective teachers are intentionally disposed to act in particular ways that best facilitate learning and can explain their patterns of behavior (Green, 1964). The frequency of particular actions within specified categories or circumstances determines the particular disposition (Katz and Raths, 1984). The task force recommends that teacher education programs should be redesigned to foster the following dispositions in beginning teachers.

Dispositions Toward Self

Teachers will be disposed to:

- Understand their strengths, needs, values, and beliefs
- Reflect on their own teaching and its effects on learners
- Develop a personal philosophy of education
- Appreciate the responsibility of serving as a positive model for students
- Share decision making with learners and colleagues
- Accept change, ambiguity, and uncertainty

Dispositions Toward the Learner

Teachers will be disposed to:

- Support positive learner self-concept by fostering learner success
- Acknowledge and use the relationship between expectations and performance by learners
- Recognize and use learner readiness and motivation
- Respect and value individual and cultural differences
- Establish emphathic, cooperative relationships with and among learners
- Assist learners in clarifying beliefs, attitudes, and values
- Promote the fullest possible growth and development of all students

Dispositions Toward Teaching

Teachers will be disposed to:

- Engage with learners in joint exploration of ideas and structures of knowledge
- Use a variety of teaching strategies supported by research
- Engage in critical and divergent thinking and problem solving with learners
- Demonstrate global perspectives with a sense of responsibility for involvement

Dispositions Toward the Profession

Teachers will be disposed to:

- Act as part of a team which is informed and involved in the broader educational environment
- Engage in professional responsibilities within the building, the district, professional organizations, and the community
- Inform themselves of current professional literature

Skills

Effective teaching is more than the transmission of basic skills; it is the ability to release people to learn how to learn (Green, 1983). Teachers make multiple and continuous decisions in guiding effective, formal learning. Therefore, future teachers must acquire complex and elaborate teaching strategies. Teachers must have the skills to create environments that provoke students to ask questions and seek answers on their own. The specific skills listed are representative and not exhaustive. They are, however, essential to effective teaching. The task force recommends that teacher education programs should be redesigned to assure that beginning teachers possess and can demonstrate the following learning and teaching skills.

Intellectual Skills

Teachers serve as models to students. Therefore, they must:

- Be articulate, creative and precise in the regular use of speaking, listening, reading, writing, and mathematics
- Be disciplined in the use of analytical, critical, and problem solving strategies

Assessment Skills

Successful learning depends upon teachers' knowledge of the students. Teachers must be able to analyze and interpret both objective and subjective information about students' learning characteristics, attitudes, and backgrounds. Teachers must understand and respond to each student individually and personally. Therefore, teachers must:

- Be systematic in observing and interpreting learner behavior and dynamics which cause the behavior
- Identify levels of readiness in student learning and development
- Identify student learning style, strengths, and needs
- Identify levels and sources of learner motivation
- Identify relevant aspects of learner background and experience

Planning Skills

A significant part of effective teaching consists of making judgments and decisions about what students have learned, should learn, and are learning (Clark, 1983). Teacher planning contributes to the content and quality of instruction (Smith and Sendelbach, 1979; Clark and Elmore, 1981). Additionally, planning influences the opportunity to learn, the instructional grouping, and overall focus of the learning environment processes (Clark, 1983). Planning shapes the broad outline of what is possible and is used to manage transitions by integrating information from one activity to another. Teachers must:

- Define the purpose and goals of learning activities based on designed curriculum, learner assessment, and knowledge of learning effectiveness research
- Translate goals into integrated curricular objectives, relevant activities, and evaluation procedures based on learner need
- Select learning objectives for individual and group learning
- Establish learning priorities, develop learning plans and prescriptions for learning based on learner strengths and needs
- Select learning materials, activities, and strategies to achieve learning objectives for each learner

- Plan the course of activities for immediate, short-term and long-term goals
- Plan and design evaluation tools and strategies for assessing learner outcomes

Instructional Skills

Instruction involves the application of intentional acts aimed at promoting the learning of skills, knowledge, and values (Hyman, 1974). Achieving that goal requires balancing learning objectives, student characteristics, teaching strategies, and curriculum objectives. The teacher is responsible for blending these aspects of teaching through careful judgment and decision making (Clark and Joyce, 1981). The decisions teachers make affect their behavior and the behavior of their students in both the long and short term. Instructional skills allow teachers to make effective decisions. Teachers must:

- Use multiple learning and teaching strategies
- Provide clear, individually appropriate learning expectations
- Expect and maintain active, successful learning participation
- Expect and support self-directed learning
- Listen, reflect, and probe for learner understanding and ask for clarification
- Support, critique, and expand learner expression in speaking and writing
- Explore academic information as well as personal feelings and relationships through discussion
- Foster critical and divergent thinking and problem solving among learners
- Guide cooperative learning, independent study, and field study among learners
- Use state of the art communication technology and information systems

Evaluation Skills

Teaching and learning are reciprocal by nature; teaching influences learning and learning affects teaching. Therefore, evaluation must account for this interaction. Some forms of evaluation should be ongoing, and other forms should be periodic. Teachers must:

- Monitor and evaluate student learning through a variety of methods
- Monitor and evaluate their own behavior in relation to changes in achievement
- Modify learning objectives, plans, and instructional behavior based on evaluation results

Social Behavior Management Skills

Environments that are conducive to productive learning and promote active learner participation require the instructional strategies outlined above. Additionally, teachers need specific skills to manage the social behavior of the learners and themselves. Teachers should:

- Provide clear and appropriate behavioral expectations and establish corresponding rules and routines
- Diagnose and identify causes of antisocial, counter-productive, or nonproductive behaviors in the learning environment
- Recognize and respond to opportunities for fostering learner self-discipline
- Employ tested behavior modification and behavioral analysis principles for producing desirable behavior
- Employ strategies to alter the social-emotional climate of the learning environment in collaborative, individualistic, or cooperative structures
- Alter physical and environmental aspects of the learning environment to promote desired social development

Role Modeling Skills

Through their own behavior, teachers should demonstrate:

- Courtesy and respect for others
- Enthusiasm for learning
- Self-discipline and control
- Consistency between intention and action

Knowledge

Teaching has been described as "an art informed by science" (Gage, 1985). Thus, the education of teachers should reflect the combination of liberal education and the science of learning and teaching.

Liberal arts education is concerned with comprehensive development of the mind in acquiring knowledge. The aim is to achieve knowledge and understanding of experience in many different ways. Prospective teachers must acquire not only information, but also knowledge of complex conceptual schemes, of the arts, and of different types of reasoning and judgment (Hist, 1982). Liberal arts studies introduce the relationships among basic bodies of knowledge and the range of knowledge as a whole. The aim of liberal education must be kept in mind in the selection of disciplines studies in the liberal arts curriculum. The task force recommends that teacher education programs should be redesigned to include the following bodies of knowledge.

Knowledge About People

Future teachers must understand how social organizations function and influence people and how people influence organizations. They must comprehend the challenges and the opportunities facing people in culturally diverse societies and understand how to work with people in complex social settings. They must have knowledge which allows them to make informed judgments about issues in professional ethics. This body of knowledge should include the social and behavioral sciences, the natural sciences, the humanities, and philosophic values and belief systems.

Knowledge About Cultures

Future teachers must understand the origins and the development of western and non-western civilizations and cultures. They must understand past and present ideas and debates in the sciences and humanities. They must learn to examine issues, trends, and forecasts that may affect future thinking, behavior, and institutions. This body of knowledge should include not only social, literary, and linguistic knowledge, but also the political, religious, historical, scientific, and technological evidence that defines cultures.

Knowledge About Epistemology

Prospective teachers must gain an appreciation of differing viewpoints and theories within disciplines and of associated methods of inquiry. They must learn to evaluate explanations advanced to account for phenomena. From this experience, future teachers must understand how knowledge persistently changes and evolves over time. In liberal education, pursuit of knowledge must be complemented with learning the various "ways of knowing."

Knowledge in a Specific Discipline

Prospective teachers should understand the scope, structure, and relationship of a body of knowledge to the world. Future teachers must develop a sense of personal scholarship through in-depth study in one or more core liberal arts disciplines. They must identify sufficiently with scholars in the area(s) of concentration so that they appreciate and respond to the changing nature of knowledge. Such academic concentration must provide future teachers with knowledge that will apply in future learning and teaching environments.

Knowledge About Human Growth and Development

Future teachers must learn how the acquisition of knowledge relates to development of an individual's learning, thinking, feeling, and believing. Teachers must understand their own levels of development, learning style, and motivational habits. They must acquire this knowledge as the basis for diagnostic and prescriptive teaching that will allow them to respond to learners' individual styles, strengths, and needs. They must learn to translate theory into practical learning application and to translate practice into theory. The knowledge should include information about human learning derived from current and emerging developmental theories of the mind, body, and emotions, within and across cultures in the following areas:

- Affective/social, cognitive, moral, and physical development
- Motivational development
- Individual learning styles and modes

Knowledge About Communication and Language

Future teachers must appreciate and understand the complexities of human communication. This knowledge allows them to determine how various communication strategies and styles cause learning in a variety of contexts. The knowledge provides prospective teachers with the basis for making decisions about their own and their students' communication and language. The knowledge should include theoretical and developmental information about:

- Nonverbal communication
- Oral language and communication (listening and speaking)
- Written language and communication (reading and writing)
- Technological language and communication

Knowledge of Scientific Inquiry

Future teachers must learn methods of scientific inquiry that will provide them with a variety of problem solving strategies for addressing the difficulties and complexities of students' learning. They must learn to understand and value critical thinking and self-directed learning as intellectual habits of mind. They must learn scientific methodology and use it systematically to identify problems and create effective learning environments. Methods to be learned include:

- Descriptive procedures
- Experimental procedures

Knowledge of Literature
on Effective Learning and Teaching

Informed by the literature, teachers will learn to articulate and explain their own and their students' learning behavior. They must learn to interpret and apply research findings. Knowledge of the literature on effective learning and teaching should include:

- Learning
- Curriculum and resources
- Pedagogy
- Technology
- Organizational development

Program Delivery

To achieve desired outcomes, programs should include regular and systematic experiential activities that relate to the acquisition of dispositions, skills, and knowledge.

From the beginning of the teacher education program, future teachers must engage in regular and systematic observation, reflection, and feedback using a variety of methods; these might include videotape analysis of their behavior by themselves, their peers, faculty, and cooperating teachers. The observation should be integrated with experiences in human growth and development and communication.

Throughout the teacher education program, future teachers must observe and interpret human behavior in clinical and field settings. They must observe and work with small and large groups of learners in a wide range of real or simulated settings. In field settings, to support student growth, teacher education students and their supporting resources should be clustered within a limited number of cooperating schools.

Throughout the teacher education program, future teachers must have regular and systematic practice and use of communication technology and data-based information systems.

From the beginning, future teachers must routinely integrate scientific methods of analysis and problem solving in all field experiences and practices.

Part of the program delivery system should be a formal, structured induction period following graduation. During this time, employed beginning teachers would be required to demonstrate increased levels of the dispositions, skills, and knowledge attained in the preparation program.

Summary

After completing teacher education programs, beginning teachers should have attained the recommended dispositions, skills, and knowledge sufficiently well to teach effectively in a variety of learning environments. The task force also recommends a program delivery system to ensure that teacher education students acquire and demonstrate the recommended outcomes as they progress through the program. The outcomes and the system of program delivery should be used by teacher educators to guide curriculum redesign and implementation.

Model Standards for Beginning Teacher Licensing and Development— Interstate New Teacher Assessment and Support Consortium[1]

Principle #1: The teacher understands the central concepts, tools of inquiry, and structures of the discipline(s) he or she teaches and can create learning experiences that make these aspects of subject matter meaningful for students.

Knowledge

[Detailed standards for discipline-based knowledge will be included in the subject matter standards to be developed in the next phase of this project.]

The teacher understands major concepts, assumptions, debates, processes of inquiry, and ways of knowing that are central to the discipline(s) he teaches.

The teacher understands how students' conceptual frameworks for an area of knowledge, conceptions, and misconceptions can influence their learning.

The teacher can relate her disciplinary knowledge to other subject areas.

Dispositions

The teacher realizes that subject matter knowledge is not a fixed body of facts but is complex and ever-evolving. He seeks to keep abreast of new ideas and understandings in the field.

The teacher appreciates multiple perspectives and conveys to learners how knowledge is developed from the vantage point of the knower.

The teacher has enthusiasm for the discipline(s) she teaches and sees connections to everyday life.

The teacher is committed to continuous learning and engages in professional discourse about subject matter knowledge and children's learning of the discipline.

---

1. Excerpted from INTASC, 1992.

Performances

The teacher effectively uses multiple representations and explanations of disciplinary concepts that capture key ideas and link them to students' prior understandings.

The teacher can represent and use differing viewpoints, theories, "ways of knowing," and methods of inquiry in his teaching of subject matter concepts.

The teacher can evaluate teaching resources and curriculum materials for their comprehensiveness, accuracy, and usefulness for representing particular ideas and concepts.

The teacher engages students in generating knowledge and testing hypotheses according to the methods of inquiry and standards of evidence used in the discipline.

The teacher develops and uses curricula that encourage students to see, question, and interpret ideas from diverse perspectives.

The teacher can create interdisciplinary learning experiences that allow students to integrate knowledge, skills, and methods of inquiry from several subject areas.

Principle #2: The teacher understands how children learn and develop and can provide learning opportunities that support their intellectual, social, and personal development.

Knowledge

The teacher understands how learning occurs—how students construct knowledge, acquire skills, and develop habits of mind—and knows how to use instructional strategies that promote student learning.

The teacher understands that students' physical, social, emotional, moral, and cognitive development influences learning and knows how to address these factors when making instructional decisions.

The teacher is aware of expected developmental progressions and ranges of individual variation within each domain (physical, social, emotional, moral, and cognitive), can identify levels of readiness in learning, and understands how development in any one domain may affect performance in others.

Dispositions

The teacher appreciates individual variation within each area of development, shows respect for the diverse talents of all learners, and is committed to help them develop self-confidence and competence.

The teacher is disposed to use students' strengths as a basis for growth and errors as an opportunity for learning.

Performances

The teacher assesses individual and group performance in order to design instruction that meets learners' current needs in each domain (cognitive, social, emotional, moral, and physical) and that leads to the next level of development.

The teacher stimulates student reflection on prior knowledge and links new ideas to already familiar ideas, making connections to students' experiences, providing opportunities for active engagement, manipulation, and testing of ideas and materials, and encouraging students to assume responsibility for shaping their learning tasks.

The teacher accesses students' thinking and experiences as a basis for instructional activities by, for example, encouraging discussion, listening and responding to group interaction, and eliciting samples of student thinking orally and in writing.

Principle #3: The teacher understands how students differ in their approaches to learning and creates instructional opportunities that are adapted to diverse learners.

Knowledge

The teacher understands and can identify differences in approaches to learning and performance, including different learning styles, multiple intelligences, and performance modes, and can design instruction that helps use students' strengths as the basis for growth.

The teacher knows about areas of exceptionality in learning—including learning disabilities, visual and perceptual difficulties, and special physical or mental challenges.

The teacher knows about the process of second language acquisition and about strategies to support the learning of students whose first language is not English.

The teacher understands how students' learning is influenced by individual experiences, talents, and prior learning, as well as language, culture, family, and community values.

The teacher has a well-grounded framework for understanding cultural and community diversity and knows how to learn about and incorporate students' experiences, cultures, and community resources into instruction.

Dispositions

The teacher believes that all children can learn at high levels and persists in helping all children achieve success.

The teacher appreciates and values human diversity, shows respect for students' varied talents and perspectives, and is committed to the pursuit of "individually configured excellence."

The teacher respects students as individuals with differing personal and family backgrounds and various skills, talents, and interests.

The teacher is sensitive to community and cultural norms.

The teacher makes students feel valued for their potential as people, and helps them learn to value each other.

Performances

The teacher identifies and designs instruction appropriate to students' stages of development, learning styles, strengths, and needs.

The teacher uses teaching approaches that are sensitive to the multiple experiences of learners and that address different learning and performance modes.

The teacher makes appropriate provisions (in terms of time and circumstances for work, tasks assigned, communication, and response modes) for individual students who have particular learning differences or needs.

The teacher can identify when and how to access appropriate services or resources to meet exceptional learning needs.

The teacher seeks to understand students' families, cultures, and communities, and uses this information as a basis for connecting instruction to students' experiences (e.g., drawing explicit connections between subject matter and community matters, making assignments that can be related to students' experiences and cultures).

The teacher brings multiple perspectives to the discussion of subject matter, including attention to students' personal, family, and community experiences and cultural norms.

The teacher creates a learning community in which individual differences are respected.

Principle #4: The teacher understands and uses a variety of instructional strategies to encourage students' development of critical thinking, problem solving, and performance skills.

Knowledge

The teacher understands the cognitive processes associated with various kinds of learning (e.g., critical and creative thinking, problem structuring and problem solving, invention, memorization, and recall) and how these processes can be stimulated.

The teacher understands principles and techniques, along with advantages and limitations, associated with various instructional strategies (e.g., cooperative learning, direct instruction, discovery learning, whole group discussion, independent study, interdisciplinary instruction).

The teacher knows how to enhance learning through the use of a wide variety of materials as well as human and technological resources (e.g., computers, audio-visual technologies, videotapes and discs, local experts, primary documents and artifacts, texts, reference books, literature, and other print resources).

Dispositions

The teacher values the development of students' critical thinking, independent problem solving, and performance capabilities.

The teacher values flexibility and reciprocity in the teaching process as necessary for adapting instruction to student responses, ideas, and needs.

Performances

The teacher carefully evaluates how to achieve learning goals, choosing alternative teaching strategies and materials to achieve different instructional purposes and to meet student needs (e.g., developmental stages, prior knowledge, learning styles, and interests).

The teacher uses multiple teaching and learning strategies to engage students in active learning opportunities that promote the development of critical thinking, problem solving, and performance capabilities and that help students assume responsibility for identifying and using learning resources.

The teacher constantly monitors and adjusts strategies in response to learner feedback.

The teacher varies his or her role in the instructional process (e.g., instructor, facilitator, coach, audience) in relation to the content and purposes of instruction and the needs of students.

The teacher develops a variety of clear, accurate presentations and representations of concepts, using alternative explanations to assist students' understanding and presenting diverse perspectives to encourage critical thinking.

Principle #5: The teacher uses an understanding of individual and group motivation and behavior to create a learning environment that encourages positive social interaction, active engagement in learning, and self-motivation.

Knowledge

The teacher can use knowledge about human motivation and behavior drawn from the foundational sciences of psychology, anthropology, and sociology to develop strategies for organizing and supporting individual and group work.

The teacher understands how social groups function and influence people, and how people influence groups.

The teacher knows how to help people work productively and cooperatively with each other in complex social settings.

The teacher understands the principles of effective classroom management and can use a range of strategies to promote positive relationships, cooperation, and purposeful learning in the classroom.

The teacher recognizes factors and situations that are likely to promote or diminish intrinsic motivation, and knows how to help students become self-motivated.

Dispositions

The teacher takes responsibility for establishing a positive climate in the classroom and participates in maintaining such a climate in the school as a whole.

The teacher understands how participation supports commitment, and is committed to the expression and use of democratic values in the classroom.

The teacher values the role of students in promoting each other's learning and recognizes the importance of peer relationships in establishing a climate of learning.

The teacher recognizes the value of intrinsic motivation to students' lifelong growth and learning.

The teacher is committed to the continuous development of individual students' abilities and considers how different motivational strategies are likely to encourage this development for each student.

Performances

The teacher creates a smoothly functioning learning community in which students assume responsibility for themselves and one another, participate in decisionmaking, work collaboratively and independently, and engage in purposeful learning activities.

The teacher engages students in individual and cooperative learning activities that help them develop the motivation to achieve, by, for example, relating lessons to students' personal interests, allowing students to have choices in their learning, and leading students to ask questions and pursue problems that are meaningful to them.

The teacher organizes, allocates, and manages the resources of time, space, activities, and attention to provide active and equitable engagement of students in productive tasks.

The teacher maximizes the amount of class time spent in learning by creating expectations and processes for communication and behavior along with a physical setting conducive to classroom goals.

The teacher helps the group to develop shared values and expectations for student interactions, academic discussions, and individual and group responsibility that create a positive classroom climate of openness, mutual respect, support, and inquiry.

The teacher analyzes the classroom environment and makes decisions and adjustments to enhance social relationships, student motivation and engagement, and productive work.

The teacher organizes, prepares students for, and monitors independent and group work that allows for full and varied participation of all individuals.

Principle #6: The teacher uses knowledge of effective verbal, nonverbal, and media communication techniques to foster active inquiry, collaboration, and supportive interaction in the classroom.

Knowledge

The teacher understands communication theory, language development, and the role of language in learning.

The teacher understands how cultural and gender differences can affect communication in the classroom.

The teacher recognizes the importance of nonverbal as well as verbal communication.

The teacher knows about and can use effective verbal, nonverbal, and media communication techniques.

Dispositions

The teacher recognizes the power of language for fostering self-expression, identity development, and learning.

The teacher values all of the ways in which people communicate and encourages many modes of communication in the classroom.

The teacher is a thoughtful and responsive listener.

The teacher appreciates the cultural dimensions of communication, responds appropriately, and seeks to foster culturally sensitive communication by and among all students in the class.

Performances

The teacher models effective communication strategies in conveying ideas and information and in asking questions (e.g., monitoring the effects of messages, restating ideas and drawing connections, using visual, aural, and kinesthetic cues, being sensitive to nonverbal cues given and received).

The teacher supports and expands learner expression in speaking, writing, and other media.

The teacher knows how to ask questions and stimulate discussion in different ways for particular purposes, for example, probing for learner understanding, helping students articulate their ideas and thinking processes, promoting risk-taking and problem-solving, facilitating factual recall, encouraging convergent and divergent thinking, stimulating curiosity, helping students to question).

The teacher communicates in ways that demonstrate a sensitivity to cultural and gender differences (e.g., appropriate use of eye contact, interpretation of body language and verbal statements, acknowledgment of and responsiveness to different modes of communication and participation).

The teacher knows how to use a variety of media communication tools, including audio-visual aids and computers, to enrich learning opportunities.

Principle #7: The teacher plans instruction based upon knowledge of subject matter, students, the community, and curriculum goals.

Knowledge

The teacher understands learning theory, subject matter, curriculum development, and student development and knows how to use this knowledge in planning instruction to meet curriculum goals.

The teacher knows how to take contextual considerations (instructional materials, individual student interests, needs, and aptitudes, and community resources) into account in planning instruction that creates an effective bridge between curriculum goals and students' experiences.

The teacher knows when and how to adjust plans based on student responses and other contingencies.

Dispositions

The teacher values both long term and short term planning.

The teacher believes that plans must always be open to adjustment and revision based on student needs and changing circumstances.

The teacher values planning as a collegial activity.

Performances

As an individual and a member of a team, the teacher selects and creates learning experiences that are appropriate for curriculum goals, relevant to learners, and based upon principles of effective instruction (e.g., that activate students' prior knowledge, anticipate preconceptions, encourage exploration and problem-solving, and build new skills on those previously acquired).

The teacher plans for learning opportunities that recognize and address variation in learning styles and performance modes, e.g., aural, visual, kinesthetic.

The teacher creates lessons and activities that operate at multiple levels to meet the developmental and individual needs of diverse learners and help each progress.

The teacher creates short-range and long-term plans that are linked to student needs and performance, and adapts the plans to ensure and capitalize on student progress and motivation.

The teacher responds to unanticipated sources of input, evaluates plans in relation to short- and long-range goals, and systematically adjusts plans to meet student needs and enhance learning.

Principle #8: The teacher understands and uses formal and informal assessment strategies to evaluate and ensure the continuous intellectual and social development of the learner.

Knowledge

The teacher understands the characteristics, uses, advantages, and limitations of different types of assessments (e.g., criterion-referenced and norm-referenced instruments, traditional standardized and performance-based tests, observation systems, and evaluations of student work) for evaluating how students learn, what they know and are able to do, and what kinds of experiences will support their further growth and development.

The teacher knows how to select, construct, and use assessment strategies and instruments appropriate to the learning outcomes being evaluated and to other diagnostic purposes.

The teacher understands measurement theory and assessment-related issues, such as validity, reliability, bias, and scoring concerns.

Dispositions

The teacher values ongoing assessment as essential to the instructional process and recognizes that many different assessment strategies, accurately and systematically used, are necessary for monitoring and promoting student learning.

The teacher is committed to using assessment to identify student strengths and promote student growth rather than to deny students access to learning opportunities.

Performances

The teacher appropriately uses a variety of formal and informal assessment techniques (e.g., observation, portfolios of student work, teacher-made tests, performance tasks, projects, student self-assessments, peer assessment, and standardized tests) to enhance her or his knowledge of learners, evaluate students' progress and performances, and modify teaching and learning strategies.

The teacher solicits and uses information about students' experiences, learning behavior, needs, and progress from parents, other colleagues, and the students themselves.

The teacher uses assessment strategies to involve learners in self-assessment activities, to help them become aware of their strengths and needs, and to encourage them to set personal goals for learning.

The teacher evaluates the effect of class activities on both individuals and the class as a whole, collecting information through observation of classroom interactions, questioning, and analysis of student work.

The teacher monitors his or her own teaching strategies and behavior in relation to student success, modifying plans and instructional approaches accordingly.

The teacher maintains useful records of student work and performance and can communicate student progress knowledgeably and responsibly, based on appropriate indicators, to students, parents, and other colleagues.

Principle #9: The teacher is a reflective practitioner who continually evaluates the effects of his/her choices and actions on others (students, parents, and other professionals in the learning community) and who actively seeks out opportunities to grow professionally.

Knowledge

The teacher understands methods of inquiry that provide him/her with a variety of self-assessment and problem-solving strategies for reflecting on his/her practice, its influences on students' growth and learning, and the complex interactions between them.

The teacher is aware of major areas of research on teaching and of resources available for professional learning (e.g., professional literature, colleagues, professional associations, professional development activities).

Dispositions

The teacher values critical thinking and self-directed learning as habits of mind.

The teacher is committed to reflection, assessment, and learning as an ongoing process.

The teacher is willing to give and receive help.

The teacher is committed to seeking out, developing, and continually refining practices that address the individual needs of students.

The teacher recognizes his/her professional responsibility for engaging in and supporting appropriate professional practices for self and colleagues.

Performances

The teacher uses classroom observation, information about students, and research as sources for evaluating the outcomes of teaching and learning and as a basis for experimenting with, reflecting on, and revising practice.

The teacher seeks out professional literature, colleagues, and other resources to support his/her own development as a learner and a teacher.

The teacher draws upon professional colleagues within the school and other professional arenas as supports for reflection, problem-solving and new ideas, actively sharing experiences and seeking and giving feedback.

Principle #10: The teacher fosters relationships with school colleagues, parents, and agencies in the larger community to support students' learning and well-being.

Knowledge

The teacher understands schools as organizations within the larger community context and understands the operations of the relevant aspects of the system(s) within which he or she works.

The teacher understands how factors in the students' environment outside of school (e.g., family circumstances, community environments, health and economic conditions) may influence students' life and learning.

The teacher understands and implements laws related to students' rights and teacher responsibilities (e.g., for equal education, appropriate education for handicapped students, confidentiality, privacy, appropriate treatment of students, reporting in situations related to possible child abuse).

Dispositions

The teacher values and appreciates the importance of all aspects of a child's experience.

The teacher is concerned about all aspects of a child's well-being (cognitive, emotional, social, and physical), and is alert to signs of difficulties.

The teacher is willing to consult with other adults regarding the education and well-being of his/her students.

The teacher respects the privacy of students and confidentiality of information.

Performances

The teacher participates in collegial activities designed to make the entire school a productive learning environment.

The teacher makes links with the learners' other environments on behalf of students, by consulting with parents, teachers of other classes and activities within the schools, counselors, and professionals in other community agencies.

The teacher can identify and use community resources to foster student learning.

The teacher establishes respectful and productive relationships with parents and guardians from diverse home and community situations, and seeks to develop cooperative partnerships in support of student learning and well-being.

The teacher talks to and listens to the student, is sensitive and responsive to clues of distress, investigates situations, and seeks outside help as needed and appropriate to remedy problems.

The teacher acts as an advocate for students.

APPENDIX C
Minnesota Licensure Standards for Teachers of English and Language Arts

8700.3810 Teachers of English/Language Arts

Subpart 1. Licensure requirements. A candidate recommended for licensure to teach English/language arts in secondary schools shall hold a baccalaureate degree and shall complete the requirements of item A or B.

  A. Major preparation requires satisfactory completion of an English/language arts teacher preparation program approved by the Board of Teaching, consisting of a minimum of 54 quarter hours or the equivalent that must include all knowledge and skills specified in subpart 2.
  B. Minor preparation requires satisfactory completion of an English/language arts teacher preparation program approved by the Board of Teaching, consisting of a minimum of 27 quarter hours or the equivalent that must include knowledge and skills specified in subpart 2, item A selected by the preparation institution; knowledge and skills specified in subpart 2, item B, subitems (1) and (2), (2) and (3); or (1) and (3) selected by the preparation institution; and all knowledge and skills specified in subpart 2, item C.

Subpart 2. Program requirements. A program leading to the licensure of teachers of English/language arts shall provide candidates recommended for licensure with the knowledge, skills and understanding set forth in items A to C:

  A. Knowledge and skills applicable to the major responsibilities of teachers of English/language arts:
   (1) to teach language and writing:
      (a) knowledge of theories of language development from early childhood onward with emphasis on the adolescent and of the effects of social, cultural, and economic environment on the acquisition and use of language;

      (b) knowledge of the phonological, grammatical, and semantic functions of language, the uses of language, and the process of development and change in language particularly as applied to the English language;

      (c) knowledge of the various traditional and modern descriptions of the grammatical structure of the English language;

      (d) knowledge of the elements of the writing process, the uses of writing, and research in written composition;

      (e) knowledge of the methodologies for teaching writing and the importance of logic and reasoning to both the writing process and the written product;

      (f) knowledge of a variety of strategies for efficient yet effective evaluation of student writing;

      (g) the skill of writing effectively as a model for students;

      (h) the skill of providing instruction and activities that will enable students to write grammatically and to adapt strategies and forms of writing to various contexts, audiences, and purposes; and

      (i) the skill of responding specifically, constructively, and efficiently to students' writing for the purpose of revising and improving the writing; responding to considerations of audience, purpose, and context; and diagnosing problems in reasoning, form, structure, usage, and style as well as in syntax, diction, spelling, punctuation, and legibility.

   (2) to teach literature:

      (a) knowledge of a representative body of American and British literature, past and present, written for adults and for adolescents by majority and minority male and female authors, and some of the major works, in translation, if necessary, of continental and non-Western authors;

      (b) knowledge of the value of literature as an art as well as the enjoyment derived from a variety of experiences and viewpoints encountered in literature. . . .

Subpart 4. Continuing licensure. A continuing license shall be issued and renewed according to rules of the Board of Teaching governing continuing education/relicensure.

Subpart 5. Effective date. This part is effective July 1, 1989, for an applicant for entrance licensure as a teacher of English/language arts.

MS § 125.05 and 1; 125.185 subd 411 SR 48

APPENDIX D
Sample Questions for an Examination of Teaching Knowledge

Task 1. Analysis of Students' Conceptual Difficulties

Task Prompt

Candidate is presented with a description of a class in terms of age, subject area, achievement level, and other salient characteristics. The previous lessons are also described, so that the candidate realizes that the teacher has spent a given number of class periods teaching a particular concept using specific methods. Candidates may also be presented with artifacts of lesson plans, videotaped segments of lessons, previous assignments, and student work demonstrating what students are doing and appear to understand. Three examples of situations that might be presented to candidates follow.

Situation 1

A heterogeneously grouped second-grade class has spent three class periods learning fractions by drill and practice. The artifacts will show that the teacher has given brief lectures on fractions followed by seatwork in which students work individually on worksheets that call for matching a notation for a fraction with a picture showing shaded portions of shapes. Student work samples show that although many students have finished the worksheets, only two can independently demonstrate (in response to questions and on a written test) how to divide objects into fractions or how to add or subtract fractions within the context of problems that require this kind of work.

Situation 2

An eighth-grade class, composed of students whose reading achievement level is low, is part of a general science program that uses a survey approach to learning basic concepts about physical and natural sciences. Having recently finished covering the textbook (a copy of which is one of the artifacts for the task), the teacher has just spent four class periods teaching a new theory of

plate tectonics from *Scientific American* using lecture and readings. Class artifacts show the teacher's lecture notes, taken closely from the *Scientific American* issue, and assigned readings with questions for students to complete
based on the readings. Students work individually on the questions following
the lectures each day in class.

Situation 3

A twelfth-grade Honors U.S. History class has spent one class period learning
about similarities and differences between the Magna Carta and the U.S. Constitution by discovery and discussion. Class artifacts show the assignment students were asked to complete, examining the two documents and looking for
ways in which they share common ideas and ways in which they diverge in
their views of human rights and governmental responsibilities. Following this
class period, students were asked to present their conclusions. Their work is
sketchy, indicating superficial understanding of the two documents and the
ideas underlying them.

Question A

Given your understanding of the cognitive development of children and generally accepted pedagogical principles, what would most likely explain why the
children have not yet learned (Concept Y)?

Question B

What alternative strategy or strategies, if any, would probably have been more
successful than the one the teacher tried? Explain your answer, and give an example of what you would do.

Situation 1 (Second-grade fractions)

Candidates' responses should indicate an understanding that the teacher's
pedagogical strategy is inappropriate for preoperational thinkers. Students
would gain a deeper understanding of what fractions are and how to work with
them by using manipulatives, creating and using models to solve problems,
and talking about their thinking as they work. Candidates might propose working in heterogeneous small groups on active tasks that involve manipulating
materials as one appropriate strategy. Having students think aloud about
problems in class discussions, presenting hypotheses and testing them, would
also be an appropriate suggestion. One would expect to see suggestions for
connecting the work to personal experiences and familiar items (splitting a
pizza among a family of five, for example).

Situation 2 (Eighth-grade plate tectonics)

Candidates' responses should indicate that the concept is likely to be a difficult one for a group at this age level, especially given the superficial background in earth sciences incorporated in the science curriculum and the text

students have been using. Furthermore, the teacher's lectures have not provided the scaffolding needed to create a base of knowledge on which to build an understanding of plate tectonics. Readings from *Scientific American* are not likely to be easily accessible for a group at this grade level whose reading skills are not highly developed, and failure to use any concrete activities allowing for active learning will not help overcome this difficulty. Lecturing without use of models, visual aids, or hands-on experiences for students is not likely to prove an effective means for instruction. Suggestions might include building models that demonstrate the ways in which the earth's subsurfaces operate, involving students in guided group work that enables them to pursue specific questions together, using a wider range of reading materials, including graphics and illustrations, and connecting the unit to things the students may have heard about or experienced (e.g., recent California earthquakes).

Situation 3 (Twelfth-grade Constitution)

Candidates' responses should indicate that although the topic is not conceptually problematic and the use of the inquiry method is promising, more time is required for students to closely examine the documents, discuss their ideas with their peers, and formulate their arguments. Suggestions may include ways for the teacher to provide more scaffolding for the task, linking it to students' prior knowledge and personal views (e.g., about individual rights), and ways to use additional time for students to explore the documents more fully, guided by thought-provoking questions and a performance task that requires them to apply their analysis in a concrete way.

Task 2: Identifying Students for Further Assessment

Task Prompt

Following are various descriptions of students. Indicate whether you would refer each student for further assessment and the reason for your decision. Keep in mind that referral resources are limited but should be used promptly if needed. (If you adopt a "wait-and-see" approach, indicate what you would be waiting to see, what you would do, and how long you would let the current situation persist before taking further action.)

[Note that another way to present a prompt for this task would be to provide samples of Jan's written work and perhaps a videotape or running record of Jan's oral reading as well. Then the candidate would need to be able to identify the kind of errors Jan is making as well as decide how to address them.]

Question 1A

Jan, a six-year-old child in first grade, reverses "b"s, "p"s, and "d"s in her writing. She also writes her name backward (i.e., reversing the sequence of the letters). She frequently misreads words such as "saw" for "was" and "on" for "no."

Response 1A

The response should indicate that this is not unusual at this age level and is often a nonproblematic stage in the development of literacy skills. The candidate may indicate that she or he will watch over the period of the year to see if the problem is correcting itself, if the child uses context clues while reading to return to a word and correctly decode in order to make sense of a sentence, and if greater visual discrimination is developing over time. The candidate may suggest strategies to help Jan develop visual-perceptual skills, including tactile work with letter shapes and puzzles, aural readalongs with big books and books on tape, and other developmentally appropriate approaches that simultaneously encourage skill development and growth of familiarity and self-confidence with written notation. The candidate should not suggest that the situation is alarming, a sign of intellectual inadequacy on the part of the child, or a cause for referral to special education. Similarly, the candidate should not indicate that she or he would immediately correct the child's reading or writing each time the problem occurred, as this would be an overreaction likely to undermine Jan's self-confidence and her developing independence as a reader and a writer. A suggestion for extensive drill in writing letters or misspelled words correctly (e.g., writing the letter "d" or the word "was" one hundred times) would also be an inappropriate response given current knowledge about child development and the development of literacy skills.

Question 1B

What if Jan were a ten-year-old child in fourth grade?

Response 1B

In this case the candidate's response should be different, given the greater age of the student. Given normal development, this situation is grounds for likely referral to a specialist for further assessment. The candidate should recognize that dyslexia or another visual-perceptual difficulty is a possibility. The candidate may suggest some additional investigation of the student's performance to further evaluate the nature of the problems (e.g., Are there similar problems in number reversal in mathematics? Does Jan appear to have difficulty seeing smaller as opposed to larger print? Does Jan like to read, or does she avoid reading?)

As with Response 1A, a suggestion that Jan's mispronunciations or misspellings should be corrected each and every time they occur is not appropriate; nor is overly extensive drill, such as writing misspelled words one hundred times. These methods would be likely to undermine interest and confidence in reading and writing in a student who may already be experiencing negative feelings about engaging in these activities. However, some more modest amount of focused skill work, alongside further assessment by a specialist, would be appropriate.

APPENDIX E

Secondary English–Language Arts Performance Assessment

Task 1: Evaluation and Planning Skills— Evaluating Student Papers and Planning Instruction

Context

Seventh-grade English class with thirty students, mid-November. Class mixed with respect to ability level and includes students from diverse first-language backgrounds. Previous lessons dealt with topic sentence and supporting details. Students were given an assignment to write a one-paragraph, one hundred–three hundred-word character sketch of Johnny Tremain. They were told to begin with a topic sentence and support it with adequate evidence (examples and details). They have turned in the first of three drafts of this paper. All of the students in the class are able to use the word processor.

Materials

Candidate is given eight of the first drafts of these papers and is told they are representative of the sketches that were written by the class. These first drafts vary in overall quality, and most (but not all) share a common problem (lack of supporting details). Answers are typed double-spaced. The eight papers are characterized as follows.

1. Model paper—strong topic sentence and at least five supporting details but has some nonagreement of subject and verb as well as spelling errors.
2–4. Strong topic sentence—for example, "Johnny Tremain was immature at the beginning of the novel but matured later"—but with few supporting details. Paper 3 has the following additional characteristics: immature sentence patterns, more spelling errors, verb-tense shifts.
5–7. Strong topic sentence but unrelated supporting details; for example, "Johnny was really arrogant. He had a burned hand."

8. No topic sentence and lots of unrelated details; for example, "I liked this book and I liked Johnny. I didn't like Becky. Rab was OK. Johnny's hand is grose. I was mad that Rab got killed at the end."

Task 1

On rough draft 1, write the response you would give to the writer of this paper as if this student were in your seventh-grade class. Do the same for papers 3, 5, and 8.

Scoring Criteria 1

Candidate gives specific praise for strong aspects of the students' work (such as good topic sentence and supporting details). For instance, candidate could say: Paper #1: "You did a good job in supporting your topic sentence when you said _____" and "This is a good detail to support your main point." Paper #3: "Your topic sentence raises an interesting point. You gave one good detail to support your thesis. Can you think of others, such as how he treated Becky?" Paper #5: "Your topic sentence is very strong. But does the fact that Johnny burned his hand show that he is arrogant? How else can you demonstrate his arrogance?" Paper #8: "I can tell that you read and enjoyed the book. Could you list some of the things about Johnny that made you like him?"

General, nonspecific praise is less appropriate; for example, "Good, except you made a lot of spelling errors" or simply "very good." Caustic comments or nonspecific criticisms should be avoided; for example, "What does this have to do with anything?" "I do not like this example." "ONLY ONE DETAIL ???? !!!!" "See me." "Where have you been?"

Candidate should evaluate how and when to call attention to mechanical errors so as to provide guidance when students are developmentally ready for it in ways that are helpful and not demoralizing. Candidate should not mark all mechanical errors but in a strong paper like #1 could say something like "Be sure to check your spelling and grammar before turning in your final draft." In other papers, the teacher may choose to focus on noting one type of recurring problem for feedback or for future teaching (see Task 2) or may use a nonintrusive marking system to note some things she or he would like the student to look at for editing in a subsequent draft.

Task 2

Describe the strengths and weaknesses of specific papers. How, if at all, would your analysis and feedback differ if this paper had been written by a limited English proficient (LEP) student?

Scoring Criteria 2

Candidate is able to distinguish between discourse-level aspects of the papers and use of conventions. The candidate should give specific praise to the LEP student about progress the student has made in language acquisition and should pay attention to the discourse aspects of her or his communication rather than focusing only on grammatical concerns. The candidate can analyze patterns of mechanical problems in ways that allow her or him to teach principles of English usage to students whose first language is not English. The candidate may further note that the feedback for the LEP student regarding the mechanical problem should be oral rather than written, focusing on teaching principles of language use rather than merely identifying errors without explanation.

Task 3

Evaluate the answers as a set in order to plan the next lesson. Based on this representative set of first drafts, what would you focus on in your next few lessons and assignments? What is the rationale for your answer?

Scoring Criteria 3

In a good answer, the candidate

- Identifies the common problem (lack of supporting details)
- Acknowledges the acquisition of the concept of topic sentences
- Suggests appropriate strategies to deal with the common problem; for example, before students start their second drafts, provide additional class instruction on supporting details through whole-class instruction, brainstorming about specific points raised in student papers, peer review, individual writing conferences, guided practice, and modeling
- Does not suggest focusing on a topic other than the one assigned or eliminating the revision process

Further Possibilities

Other tasks could draw upon the following types of unique and common problems in writing development.

Reasoning—logic, argumentation, clarity
Considerations of audience and purpose
Persuasiveness
Form and structure—main idea, topic sentence, paragraphing, organization, and similar elements
Grammar—syntax, spelling, and punctuation
Word usage (appropriate and vivid use of words)
Developing a personal voice
Use of evidence

Task 2: Assessment and Instruction Skills— Selecting an Appropriate Book for an Individual Student

Context

You are teaching an eleventh-grade class in world literature. The class is work-ing on independent book reports. One student comes to you for advice regard-ing a book to read for his report. This student is not particularly engaged in class: He is bright but has low regard for school, he is interested in motorcycles and cars, he does not finish assignments, and his overall academic achieve-ment does not reflect his ability level.

Materials

Candidate is given a list of twelve books selected from a longer list of thirty–-fifty books, poems, stories, and plays that will be distributed to all candidates six–eight weeks prior to the test. Sample list might be:

Pride and Prejudice
Ramona the Pest
The Scarlet Letter
Lord of the Flies
One Hundred Years of Solitude
Great Expectations
That Was Then, This Is Now
Beloved
Are You There God? It's Me, Margaret.
Native Son
The Chocolate War
Red Pony

Task

1. Select three books from the attached list that you would recommend to the student.
2. Give a brief summary of what you would say to the student about each book.
3. Give your rationale for your recommendations.

Scoring Criteria

1. Candidate should choose books that meet the following standards: The reading level and theme are not too immature for a student of this grade level; however, the book should be reasonably short to engage the student's attention and not be too daunting at this stage of his reading development. Given his interests, positive features of a

book might be an action-oriented plot, a strong protagonist, and a relevant theme. From the list suggested, appropriate choices could include *Lord of the Flies; That Was Then, This Is Now; Native Son.*

2. Candidate should demonstrate basic familiarity with the plot of the book (e.g., "It's a story about a group of boys marooned on an island") and should present the book so it would appeal to an unenthusiastic reader (e.g., do not say "you should read this book to be an educated citizen").

3. Rationale should include some of the criteria in (1) above and should address issues of motivation and engagement as well as reading level.

Task 3: Management and Instruction Skills— Observing and Managing a Classroom Discussion

Context

The candidate observes on videotape an eleventh-grade discussion of *The Scarlet Letter* after the class has finished reading the novel. The discussion is designed to use the novel to focus on the principle that a person's actions have consequences.

Materials

Videotape of a classroom lesson. Tape is divided into one- to four-minute segments. Each segment is shown twice to candidates, who are then asked to respond as described here. Response modes for this type of stimulus could include at least the following.

- Identification: Asking the candidate to observe teacher behavior and identify appropriate and inappropriate aspects of it. "What is the teacher doing here? Is it useful? Why or why not?"
- Critique: Asking the candidate to critique a behavior identified by the examiner. "The teacher is trying to engage the disengaged students. Is her technique appropriate? Why or why not?"
- Production: Asking the candidate to put himself or herself in the teacher's place. "What would you do in this situation, and why?"

Scenarios and Tasks

Excerpts could include a variety of examples of useful or less useful strategies or classroom situations about which candidates are asked to comment. Illustrative examples include:

Segment 1: Shows the start of the lesson. After a few minutes the tape is stopped and candidates are asked to comment about what they have seen thus far in terms of how well the teacher has framed the discussion. Video segments can depict examples of good practice—the teacher starts with a question about the students' own experiences with personal consequences and subsequently ties them to the goal of the lesson—or less appropriate practices—the teacher just says "today we are going to discuss *The Scarlet Letter*" and launches into a monologue that is not related to the goal of the lesson, finally returning to the topic with a vague general question (e.g., "So, what did you think of the book?").

Criteria 1: Candidate should notice that the teacher has begun in a useful or less than useful manner and should be able to describe how the start of the lesson does or does not provide a sense of purpose and goals, as well as a connection to the students' experiences.

Segment 2: Class has run for several minutes. In the course of the discussion, the tape indicates to a careful viewer that some students are tuning out.

Task 2: Videotape is stopped. Candidate is asked, "What would you do at this point in the lesson?"

Criteria 2: Candidate should notice that some students are not engaged and make appropriate suggestions to engage those students in a manner that involves them in a way that builds self-esteem and is nonpunitive. The tape could also show the teacher continuing to call on only a few students, even though others are raising their hands (or have raised their hands and then given up and begun to tune out).

Appropriate responses would include suggestions such as directing a relevant question to one of the non-engaged students to which she could respond easily, standing next to a tuned-out student and drawing him into the discussion, asking all of the students to write a brief answer to a question such as "list something that happened to Hester or Dimmesdale because of their own actions" or "briefly describe something that happened to you as a result of something you did. Did the consequence seem fair?" (This task is good because it engages all students in the activity.) Have students read their answers.

Inappropriate responses would include ignoring the tuned-out students, shaming students into participation, calling attention to the superior performance of students who are participating (e.g., "Is Sally the only one here who has read the book?"), or letting only a few students continue to monopolize the conversation.

Segment 3: Teacher is shown responding to student answers. The teacher has asked the class, "What happened to Hester because of her actions?" A student responds, "The community shunned her because she violated the moral code." The videotape is stopped.

Task 3a: Candidate is asked, "What would you do or say?"

Criteria 3a: Illustrate understanding of principle of giving informative, constructive, specific feedback that extends the discussion. Examples of appropriate answers: "So, going against the community's standards has consequences. Do you think that is fair?" "Yes, the community certainly did. Do you think that kind of reaction would happen today?"

Inappropriate answers (or video excerpts that are critiqued by candidates) include responses that are not specific and do not extend the discussion—for example, "That is a good answer." "Thank you, I can always count on you." "You're just as smart as your older brother." "I wish I had thirty of you in this class."

Task 3b: Student responds with inadequate answer; for example, "Hester had to wear the letter A." The candidate may be asked either to produce a response or to critique the teacher's response.

Video might include appropriate responses, such as "Yes, and what did that stand for? Why did she have to do that?" "Yes. How do you think this made Hester feel?" Inappropriate responses could include, "Well we know that, tell us something new," or "OK"; then the teacher calls on someone else with an unrelated question.

Criteria 3b: The candidate should notice that the teacher's response is appropriate or inappropriate and should illustrate an understanding of the principle of acknowledging an answer and extending discussion on the point.

Task 3c: Student responds with wrong or confused answer; for example, "Hester marries Dimmesdale." Candidate is asked, "What would you do or say?" or critiques teacher responses shown on the videotape.

Criteria 3c: Illustrate understanding of principles of not discouraging students from participating but not letting class remain confused.

Examples of appropriate responses: "Well, I can understand how you might get that idea because Dimmesdale fell in love with Hester, but he never married her." "Can anyone help us clarify the relationship between Hester and Dimmesdale?"

Examples of inappropriate responses: "You missed the most important point here about the relationship between Hester and Dimmesdale. You obviously did not finish the book. Who has the right answer?" "Right" (or any response that suggests that the candidate does not know the correct facts). Ignore student response and ask someone else the same or a different question.

Other segments could examine candidate's ability to discern more and less useful classroom management strategies (e.g., teacher using unobtrusive technique, such as placing hand quietly on a student's shoulder when he starts to whisper to a neighbor rather than disrupting the class to deal with a minor problem); to identify errors associated with subject-matter knowledge (e.g., show teacher making factual errors or giving incorrect information); or to communicate well with students (e.g., to rephrase questions when students do not understand the question as it was asked or to build on student responses in class discussions).

APPENDIX F
Code of Ethics for Minnesota Teachers

Standards of Professional Conduct[1]

1. A teacher shall provide professional educational services in a non-discriminatory manner.
2. A teacher shall make reasonable effort to protect the student from conditions harmful to health and safety.
3. In accordance with state and federal laws, a teacher shall disclose confidential information about individuals only when a compelling professional purpose is served or when required by law.
4. A teacher shall take reasonable disciplinary action in exercising the authority to provide an atmosphere conducive to learning.
5. A teacher shall not use professional relationships with students, parents, and colleagues to private advantage.
6. A teacher shall delegate authority for teaching responsibilites only to licensed personnel.
7. A teacher shall not deliberately suppress or distort subject matter.
8. A teacher shall not knowingly falsify or misrepresent records or facts relating to that teacher's own qualifications or to other teachers' qualifications.
9. A teacher shall not knowingly make false or malicious statements about students or colleagues.
10. A teacher shall accept a contract for a teaching position that requires licensing only if properly or provisionally licensed for that position.

---

1. Excerpted from chapter 9, sec. 3.130, of the Minnesota Code.

References

Adams, R. D., S. Hutchinson, and C. Martray (1980). "A Developmental Study of Teacher Concerns Across Time." Paper presented at the annual meeting of the American Educational Research Association, Boston, Mass.

Adelman, Nancy E. (1986). *An Exploratory Study of Teacher Alternative Certification and Retraining Programs.* Washington, D.C.: Policy Study Associates.

American Association of State Psychology Boards (a). *Entry Requirements for Professional Practice of Psychology.* Montgomery, Ala.: American Association of State Psychology Boards.

——— (b). *Licensing/Certification Requirements.* Montgomery, Ala.: American Association of State Psychology Boards.

——— (c). *Information for Candidates: Examination for Professional Practice in Psychology.* Montgomery, Ala.: American Association of State Psychology Boards.

Anderson, C. S. (1982). "The Search for School Climate: A Review of the Research." *Review of Educational Research* 52 (3): 368–420.

Anderson, C. W. (1991). "Policy Implications of Research on Science Teaching and Teachers' Knowledge." In M. M. Kennedy (ed.), *Teaching Academic Subjects to Diverse Learners.* New York: Teachers College Press, pp. 5–30.

Anderson, R. C., E. H. Hiebert, J. Scott, and I.A.G. Wilkinson (1984). *Becoming a Nation of Readers: A Report of the Commission on Reading.* Washington, D.C.: National Institute of Education.

Andrews, J. W., C. R. Blackmon, and A. Mackey. (1980). "Preservice Performance and the National Teacher Examinations." *Phi Delta Kappan* 6 (5): 358–359.

Andrews, T. (1984). *Teacher Competency Testing: 1984.* Olympia, Wash.: State Department of Education.

Angoff, W. H. (1971). "Scales, Norms, and Equivalent Scores." In R. L. Thorndike (ed.), *Educational Measurement.* 2d ed. Washington, D.C.: American Council on Education.

Apple, M. W. (1987). "The De-skilling of Teaching." In F. S. Bolin and J. M. Falk (eds.), *Teacher Renewal.* New York: Teachers College Press, pp. 59–75.

Armor, D. J., P. Conroy-Oseguera, M. Cox, N. King, L. McDonnell, A. Pascal, E. Pauly, and G. Zellman (1976). *Analysis of the School Preferred Reading Program in Selected Los Angeles Minority Schools.* Santa Monica: RAND Corporation.

Ashton, Patricia, and Linda Crocker (1986). "Does Teacher Certification Make a Difference?" *Florida Journal of Teacher Education* 3: 73–83.

——— (1987). "Systematic Study of Planned Variations: The Essential Focus of Teacher Education Reform." *Journal of Teacher Education* May–June: 2–8.

Athanases, S. Z. (1990). *Assessing the Planning and Teaching of Integrated Language Arts in the Elementary Grades.* Technical Report no. L3. Stanford: Stanford University School of Education, Teacher Assessment Project.

Ayers, J. B., and G. S. Qualls (1979). "Concurrent and Predictive Validity of the National Teacher Examinations." *Journal of Educational Research* 73 (2): 86–92.

Ayers, W. (1988). "Fact or Fancy: The Knowledge Base Quest in Teacher Education." *Journal of Teacher Education* 39: 24–29.

Bacharach, S. B. (1985). *Teacher Shortages, Professional Standards, and Hen House Logic*. Ithaca: Organizational Analysis and Practice, July 1985.

Baratz-Snowden, J. (1991). "Performance Assessment for Identifying Excellent Teachers: The National Board for Professional Teaching Standards Charts Its Research and Development Course." *Journal of Personnel Evaluation in Education* 5: 133–145.

Begle, E. G. (1979). *Critical Variables in Mathematics Education*. Washington, D.C.: Mathematical Association of America and National Council of Teachers of Mathematics.

Begle, E. G., and W. Geeslin (1972). *Teacher Effectiveness in Mathematics Instruction*. National Longitudinal Study of Mathematical Abilities Reports, no. 28. Washington, D.C.: Mathematical Association of America and National Council of Teachers of Mathematics.

Bents, Mary, and Richard Bents (1990). "Perceptions of Good Teaching Among Novice, Advanced Beginner and Expert Teachers." Paper presented at the annual meeting of the American Educational Research Association, Boston, Mass.

Berliner, D. (1984). "Remarks to the Governor's Task Force on Teacher Education." Tucson: University of Arizona, February 16, 1984.

——— (1987). "In Pursuit of the Expert Pedagogue." *Educational Researcher* 15: 5–13.

——— (1992). "Exemplary Performances: Studies of Expertise in Teaching." *Collected Speeches*. National Art Education Association Convention, 1992.

Berliner, D. C., P. Stein, D. Sabers, P. B. Clarridge, K. Cushing, and S. Pinnegar (1988). "Implications of Research on Pedagogical Expertise and Experience for Mathematics Teaching." In D. A. Grouws and T. J. Cooney (eds.), *Perspectives on Research on Effective Mathematics Teaching*. Reston, Va.: National Council of Teachers of Mathematics.

Berman, P., and M. W. McLaughlin (1977). *Federal Programs Supporting Educational Change. Vol. 7: Factors Affecting Implementation and Continuation*. Santa Monica: RAND Corporation.

Berry, B., and R. Ginsberg (1988). "Legitimizing Subjectivity: Meritorious Performance and the Professionalization of Teacher and Principal Evaluation." *Journal of Personnel Evaluation in Education* 2: 123–140.

Bird, T., and B. King (1990). *Report on the Use of Portfolios to Assess Biology Teachers*. Technical Report no. B1. Stanford: Stanford University School of Education, Teacher Assessment Project.

Bledsoe, J. C., J. V. Cox, and R. Burnham (1967). *Comparison Between Selected Characteristics and Performance of Provisionally and Professionally Certified Beginning Teachers in Georgia*. Washington, D.C.: U.S. Department of Health, Education, and Welfare.

Borko, H. (1986). "Clinical Teacher Education: The Induction Years." in J. V. Hoffman and J. Edwards (eds.), *Reality and Reform in Teacher Education*. New York: Random House, 1986.

Borko, H., and C. Livingston (1988). "Expert and Novice Teachers' Mathematics Instruction: Planning, Teaching and Post-Lesson Reflections." Paper presented at the meetings of the American Educational Research Association, New Orleans, La., April.

Brookover, W. (1977). *Schools Can Make a Difference*. East Lansing: College of Urban Development, Michigan State University.

Brophy, J. E., and C. M. Evertson (1974). *Process-Product Correlations in the Texas Teacher Effectiveness Study: Final Report*. Austin: Research and Development Center for Teacher Education.

——— (1976). *Learning from Teaching: A Developmental Perspective*. Boston: Allyn and Bacon.

——— (1977). "Teacher Behavior and Student Learning in Second and Third Grades." In G. D. Borich (ed.), *The Appraisal of Teaching: Concepts and Process*. Reading, Mass.: Addison-Wesley.

Bush, R. N. (1979). "Implications of the BTES." *The Generator* 9, no. 1: 15.

Bussis, A., T. Chittenden, and M. Amarel (1976). *Beyond the Surface Curriculum: An Interview Study of Teachers' Understandings*. Boulder: Westview Press.

Butcher, P. M. (1981). "An Experimental Investigation of the Effectiveness of a Value Claim Strategy Unit for Use in Teacher Education." Ph.D. diss. Macquarie University, Sydney, Australia.

Byrne, C. J. (1983). "Teacher Knowledge and Teacher Effectiveness: A Literature Review, Theoretical Analysis and Discussion of Research Strategy." Paper presented at the meeting of the Northeastern Educational Research Association, Ellenville, N.Y.

Carey, S. (1986). "Cognitive Science and Science Education." *American Psychologist* 41 (10): 1123–1130.

Carnegie Forum on Education and the Economy (1986). *A Nation Prepared: Teachers for the 21st Century*. Washington, D.C.: Carnegie Forum on Education and the Economy, Task Force on Teaching as a Profession.

Carter, K. (1986). "Teachers' Knowledge and Learning to Teach." In W. Houston (ed.), *Handbook of Research on Teacher Education*. New York: Macmillan, pp. 291–310.

——— (1992). "Creating Cases for the Development of Teacher Knowledge." In T. Russell and H. Munby (eds.), *Teachers and Teaching: From Classroom to Reflection*. London: Falmer, pp.109–123.

Carter, K., W. and Doyle (1987). "Teachers' Knowledge Structures and Comprehension Processes." In J. Calderhead (ed.), *Exploring Teacher Thinking*. London: Cassell, pp.147–160.

Centra, J. A., and D. A. Potter (1980). "School and Teacher Effects: An Interrelational Model." *Review of Educational Research* 50 (2): 273–291.

Chapman, D. W. (1984). "Teacher Retention: The Test of a Model." *American Educational Research Journal* 21 (3): 645–659.

Clandinin, J. (1986). *Classroom Practice: Teacher Images in Action*. London: Falmer Press.

Clark, C. M. (1983). "Research on Teacher Planning: An Inventory of the Knowledge Base." In D. Smith (ed.), *Essential Knowledge for Beginning Educators*. Washington, D.C.: AACTE, ERIC Clearinghouse on Teacher Education.

Clark, C. M., and J. L. Elmore (1981). "Teacher Planning in the First Weeks of School." Research Series No. 56. East Lansing, Michigan: Michigan State University Institute for Research on Training.

Clark, C. M., and B. R. Joyce (1981). "Teacher Decisionmaking and Teaching Effectiveness." In B. R. Joyce, Brown, and L. Peck. (eds.), *Flexibility for Teaching*. New York: Longman.

Clarridge, P. B. (1988). "Alternative Perspectives for Analyzing Expert, Novice, and Postulant Teaching." Ph.d. diss., University of Arizona, Tucson.

Coker, H., D. Medley, and R. Soar (1980). "How Valid Are Expert Opinions About Effective Teaching?" *Phi Delta Kappan* 62: 131–134, 149.

Coley, R. J., and M. E. Thorpe (1985). *Responding to the Crisis in Math and Science Teaching: Four Initiatives*. Princeton: Educational Testing Service.

Copley, Patrick O. (1974). *A Study of the Effect of Professional Education Courses on Beginning Teachers*. Springfield: Southwest Missouri State University. ERIC Document no. ED098 147.

Cronbach, L. J., (1975). "Beyond the Two Disciplines of Scientific Psychology." *American Psychologist* 30 (2): 116–127.

Cronbach, L. J., and R. E. Snow (1977). *Aptitudes and Instructional Methods: A Handbook for Research on Interactions*. New York: Irvington.

Cronbach, L. J., G. C. Gleser, H. Nanda, and N. Rajaratnam (1972). *The Dependability of Behavioral Measurements: Theory of Generalizability of Scores and Profiles*. New York: John Wiley.

Cross, K. P., and P. Beidler (1986). "Taking Teaching Seriously." Paper presented at the American Association for Higher Education National Conference, Washington, D.C., March 12–15, 1986.

Darling-Hammond, L. (1984). *Beyond the Commission Reports: The Coming Crisis in Teaching.* Santa Monica: RAND Corporation.

————— (1986a). "Teaching Knowledge: How Do We Test It?" *American Educator* 10 (3): 18–21, 46.

————— (1986b). "A Proposal for Evaluation in the Teaching Profession." *Elementary School Journal* 86 (4): 1–21.

—————. (1989a). "Accountability for Professional Practice." *Teachers College Record* 91 (1): 59–80.

————— (1989b). "Teacher Supply, Demand, and Standards." *Educational Policy* 3 (1): 1–17.

————— (1990a). "Achieving Our Goals: Structural or Superficial Reforms?" *Phi Delta Kappan* 72 (4): 286–295.

————— (1990b). "Teacher Professionalism: Why and How." In Ann Lieberman (ed.), *Schools as Collaborative Cultures: Creating the Future Now.* Philadelphia: Falmer Press, pp. 25–50.

————— (1990c). "Teacher Supply, Demand and Quality: A Mandate for the National Board." Paper prepared for the National Board for Professional Teaching Standards.

————— (1992). "Teaching and Knowledge: Policy Issues Posed by Alternative Certification for Teachers." *Peabody Journal of Education* 67 (3): 123–154.

————— (1994). *Professional Development Schools: Schools for Developing a Profession.* New York: Teachers College Press.

Darling-Hammond, L., and B. Berry (1988). *The Evolution of Teacher Policy.* Santa Monica: RAND Corporation.

Darling-Hammond, L., with E. Sclan (1992). "Policy and Supervision." In Carl Glickman (ed.), *Supervision in Transition.* Alexandria, Va: Association for Supervision and Curriculum Development, pp. 7–29.

Darling-Hammond, L., T. Gendler, and A. E. Wise (1990). *The Teaching Internship.* Santa Monica: RAND Corporation.

Darling-Hammond, L., L. Hudson, and S. N. Kirby (1989). *Redesigning Teacher Education: Opening the Door for New Recruits to Science and Mathematics Teaching.* Santa Monica: RAND Corporation.

Darling-Hammond, L., A. E. Wise, and S. Pease (1983). "Teacher Evaluation in the Organizational Context: A Review of the Literature." *Review of Educational Research* 53 (3): 285–328.

Davis, C. R. (1964). "Selected Teaching-Learning Factors Contributing to Achievement in Chemistry and Physics." Ph.D. diss., University of North Carolina, Chapel Hill.

Delandshere, G. and A. Petrosky (1992). "Capturing Teachers' Knowledge: Performance Assessment." Paper presented at the annual meeting of the American Educational Research Association, San Francisco, Calif.

Dennison, George M. (1992). "National Standards in Teacher Preparation: A Commitment to Quality." *Chronicle of Higher Education,* December 2, A40.

Denton, J. J., and L. J. Lacina (1984). "Quantity of Professional Education Coursework Linked with Process Measures of Student Teaching." *Teacher Education and Practice:* 39–64.

Dewey, John (1929). *The Sources of a Science of Education.* New York: Horace Liveright.

Doyle, W. (1978). "Paradigms for Research on Teacher Effectiveness." in L. S. Shulman (ed.), *Review of Research in Education.* Vol. 5. Itasca, Ill: F. E. Peacock.

————— (1979). "Classroom Tasks and Students' Abilities." In P. L. Peterson and H. J. Walberg (eds.), *Research on Teaching.* Berkeley: McCutchan, pp. 183–209.

————— (1986). "Content Representation in Teachers' Definitions of Academic Work." *Journal of Curriculum Studies* 18: 365–379.

————— (1990). "Classroom Knowledge as a Foundation for Teaching." *Teachers College Record* 91 (3): 247–260.

Druva, C. A., and R. D. Anderson (1983). "Science Teacher Characteristics by Teacher Behavior and by Student Outcome: A Meta-Analysis of Research." *Journal of Research in Science Teaching* 20 (5): 467–479.

Dunkin, M. J., and B. J. Biddle (1974). *The Study of Teaching*. New York: Holt, Rinehart, and Winston.

Ebmeier, H., S. Twombly, and D. J. Teeter (1991). "The Comparability and Adequacy of Financial Support for Schools of Education." *Journal of Teacher Education* 42 (3): 226–235.

Educational Testing Service (ETS) (1984). *A Guide to the NTE Core Battery*. Princeton: ETS.

———— (1992). *Praxis III: Classroom Performance Assessment. Assessment Criteria*. Princeton: ETS.

Elbaz, F. L. (1983). *Teacher Thinking: A Study of Practical Knowledge*. London: Croom Helm.

Ellett, C. D., W. Capie, and C. E. Johnson (1981). *Teacher Performance and Elementary Pupil Achievement on the Georgia Criterion Referenced Tests*. Athens: Teacher Assessment Project, University of Georgia.

Erekson, T. L., and L. Barr (1985). "Alternative Credentialing: Lessons from Vocational Education." *Journal of Teacher Education* 36 (3): 16–19.

Evertson, C., W. Hawley, and M. Zlotnik (1985). "Making a Difference in Educational Quality Through Teacher Education." *Journal of Teacher Education*, 36 (3): 2–12.

Feiman-Nemser, S., and M. B. Parker (1990). *Making Subject Matter Part of the Conversation or Helping Beginning Teachers Learn to Teach*. East Lansing: National Center for Research on Teacher Education.

Ferguson, R. F. (1991). "Paying for Public Education: New Evidence on How and Why Money Matters." *Harvard Journal on Legislation* 28 (2): 465–498.

Floden, R. E., and H. G. Klinzing (1990). "What Can Research on Teacher Thinking Contribute to Teacher Preparation? A Second Opinion." *Educational Researcher* 19 (5): 15–20.

Florida Coalition for the Development of a Performance Evaluation System (1983). *Domains of the Florida Performance Measurement System*. Tallahassee: Florida Department of Education.

Florida State Department of Education (1989). *Manual for Coding Teacher Performance on the Screening/Summative Observation Instrument: Florida Performance Measurement System*. Tallahassee: Florida Department of Education.

Fox, S. M., and T. J. Singletary (1986). "Deductions About Support Induction." *Journal of Teacher Education* 37: 12–15.

Frazier, C., and P. Callan (n.d.). *What State Leaders Can Do to Help Change Teacher Education. Advancing the Agenda for Teacher Education in a Democracy: A Guide for State Leaders*. Washington, D.C.: American Association of Colleges for Teacher Education.

Frederiksen, J. R., and A. Collins (1989). "A Systems Approach to Educational Testing." *Educational Researcher* 18 (9): 27–32.

French, R. L., D. Hodzkom, and B. Kuligowski (1990). "Teacher Evaluation in SREB States. Stage I: Analysis and Comparison of Evaluation Systems." Paper presented at the annual meeting of the American Educational Research Association, Boston, Mass.

Gage, N. (1985). "Hard Gains in the Soft Sciences: The Case for Pedagogy." *Phi Delta Kappan*.

Gage, N. L. (1978). *The Scientific Basis of the Art of Teaching*. New York: Teachers College Press.

Gage, Nathaniel L., and P. H. Winne (1975). "Performance-Based Teacher Education." In Kevin Ryan (ed.), *Teacher Education: The Seventy-Fourth Yearbook of the National Society for the Study of Education*. Chicago: University of Chicago Press.

Garibaldi, A. M. (1987). *Quality and Diversity in Schools: The Case for an Expanded Pool of Minority Teachers*. Racine: American Association of Colleges for Teacher Education.

Ginsberg, R., and B. Berry (1990). "Experiencing School Reform: The View from South Carolina." *Phi Delta Kappan* 71: 549–552.

Gitlin, A., and J. Smyth (1990). "Toward Educative Forms of Teacher Evaluation." *Educational Theory* 40 (1): 83–94.

Glaser, R. (1990). *Testing and Assessment: O Tempora! O Mores!* Pittsburgh: University of Pittsburgh, Learning Research and Development Center.

Glassberg, S. (1980). "A View of the Beginning Teacher from a Developmental Perspective." Paper presented at the annual meeting of the American Educational Research Association, Boston, Mass.

Goertz, M. E. (1988). *State Educational Standards in the 50 States: An Update.* Princeton: Educational Testing Service.

Goertz, M. E., and B. Pitcher (1985). *The Impact of NTE Use by States on Teacher Selection.* Princeton: Educational Testing Service.

Goldenberg, C., and R. Gallimore (1991). "Local Knowledge, Research Knowledge, and Educational Change: A Case Study of Early Spanish Reading Improvement." *Educational Researcher* 20 (8): 2–14.

Gomez, Deberie L., and Robert P. Grobe (1990). "Three Years of Alternative Certification in Dallas: Where Are We?" Paper presented at the annual meeting of the American Educational Research Association, Boston, Mass.

Good, Thomas L. (1983). "Recent Classroom Research: Implications for Teacher Education." In David C. Smith (ed.), *Essential Knowledge for Beginning Educators.* Washington, D.C.: American Association of Colleges for Teacher Education, ERIC Clearinghouse on Teacher Education.

Good, Thomas S., and Jere E. Brophy (1986). *Educational Psychology.* 3rd ed. White Plains: Longman.

Goodlad, J. I. (1990). *Teachers for Our Nation's Schools.* San Francisco: Jossey-Bass Publishers.

Graham, P. A. (1987). "Black Teachers: A Drastically Scarce Resource." *Phi Delta Kappan* (April): 598–605.

Green, M. (1983). "Student Teaching as Human Project." In G. A. Griffin and S. Edwards (eds.), *Student Teaching: Problems and Promising Practices.* Austin: University of Texas at Austin, Research and Development Center for Teacher Education.

Green, T. F. (1964). "Teaching, Acting and Behaving." *Harvard Educational Review* 34 (4): 507–509.

Greenberg, J. D. (1983). "The Case for Teacher Education: Open and Shut." *Journal of Teacher Education* 34 (4): 2–5.

Griffin, G. A. (1986). "Clinical Teacher Education." In J. V. Hoffman and S. A. Edwards (eds.), *Reality and Reform in Clinical Teacher Education.* New York: Random House, pp. 1–24.

Grimmett, P., and A. Mackinnon (1992). "Craft Knowledge and the Education of Teachers." In G. Grant (eds.), *Review of Research in Education, Volume 18.* Washington, D.C.: American Educational Research Association, pp. 385–456.

Grossman, P. L. (1988). "A Study in Contrast: Sources of Pedagogical Content Knowledge for Secondary English." Ph.D. diss., Stanford University.

——— (1989). "Learning to Teach Without Teacher Education." *Teachers College Record* 91 (2): 191–208.

——— (1990). *The Making of a Teacher: Teacher Knowledge and Teacher Education.* New York: Teachers College Press.

Grover, B. (1989). "Scoring a Semi-Structured Interview: Quantifying Quality." Paper presented at the meeting of the American Educational Research Association, New Orleans, La., April.

Guyton, Edith, and Elizabeth Farokhi (1987). "Relationships Among Academic Performance, Basic Skills, Subject Matter Knowledge and Teaching Skills of Teacher Education Graduates." *Journal of Teacher Education* (September–October): 37–42.

Haberman, Martin (1984). "An Evaluation of the Rationale for Required Teacher Education: Beginning Teachers with or without Teacher Preparation." Prepared for the National

Commission on Excellence in Teacher Education, University of Wisconsin–Milwaukee, September 1984.

Haertel, E. H. (1990). "Performance Tests, Simulations, and Other Methods." In Jason Millman and Linda Darling-Hammond (eds.), *The New Handbook of Teacher Evaluation: Assessing Elementary and Secondary School Teachers.* San Francisco: Sage, pp. 278–294.

———— (1991). "New Forms of Teacher Assessment." In Gerald Grant (ed.), *Review of Research in Education.* Vol. 17. Washington, D.C.: American Educational Research Association, pp. 3–29.

Haney, W., G. Madaus, and A. Kreitzer (1987). "Charms Talismanic: Testing Teachers for the Improvement of American Education." *Review of Research in Education* 14: 169–238.

Hansen, Jan Bergquist (1988). "The Relationship of Skills and Classroom Climate of Trained and Untrained Teachers of Gifted Students." Ph.D. diss., Purdue University.

Hawk, Parmalee, Charles R. Coble, and Melvin Swanson (1985). "Certification: It Does Matter." *Journal of Teacher Education* 36 (3): 13–15.

Hawkins, A., and T. Sharpe (forthcoming). "Field System Analysis: In Search of the Expert Pedagogue." *Journal of Teaching in Physical Education.*

Hawley, Willis, and Susan Rosenholtz (1984). "Good Schools: What Research Says About Improving Student Achievement." *Peabody Journal of Education* 61 (4): 1–178.

Hazi, H. M. (1989). "Measurement Versus Supervisory Judgment: The Case of *Sweeney v. Turlington.*" *Journal of Curriculum and Supervision* 4 (3): 211–229.

Henderson, J. (1988). "A Curriculum Response to the Knowledge Base Reform Movement." *Journal of Teacher Education* 39: 13-17.

Hice, J.E.L. (1970). "The Relationship Between Teacher Characteristics and First-Grade Achievement." *Dissertation Abstracts International* 25 (1): 190.

Hillocks, G. (1986). *Research on Written Composition: New Directions for Teaching.* New York: National Institute for Education.

Hist, P. H. (1982). "Liberal Education and the Nature of Knowledge." In R. F. Dearden, P. H. Hist and R. S. Peters (eds.), *Education and the Development of Reason.* London, England, Routledge and Kegan Paul.

Hollingsworth, S., M. Dybdahl, and L. Minarik (1993). "By Chart and Chance and Passion: The Importance of Relational Knowing in Learning to Teach." *Curriculum Inquiry* 23 (1): 5–35.

Holmes Group (1986). *Tomorrow's Teachers: A report of the Holmes Group.* East Lansing: Holmes Group.

———— (1989). *Work in Progress: The Holmes Group One Year On.* East Lansing: Holmes Group.

———— (1990). *Tomorrow's Schools: Principles for the Design of Professional Development Schools.* East Lansing: Holmes Group.

Hoover, N. L., and L. J. O'Shea (1987). "The Influence of a Criterion Checklist on Supervisors' and Interns' Conceptions of Teaching." Paper presented at the annual meeting of the American Educational Research Association, Washington, D.C.

Housner, L. D., and D. C. Griffey (1985). "Teacher Cognition: Differences in Planning and Interactive Decision Making Between Experienced and Inexperienced Teachers." *Research Quarterly for Exercise and Sport* 56: 44–53.

Howey, K. R. (1984). "The Next Generation of Teacher Education Programs." Paper prepared for the National Commission for Excellence in Teacher Education.

Howey, K. R. and N. L. Zimpher (1993). "Patterns in Prospective Teachers: Guides for Designing Preservice Programs." Draft manuscript. Columbus: Ohio State University.

Huling-Austin, L., and S. C. Murphy (1987). "Assessing the Impact of Teacher Induction Programs: Implications for Program Development." Paper presented at the annual meeting of the American Educational Research Association, Washington, D.C.

Hyman, R. T. (1974). *Ways of Teaching.* New York: J. B. Lippincott & Co.

Imig, David G. (1992). "The Professionalization of Teaching: Relying on a Professional Knowledge Base." Paper presented at the American Association of Colleges for Teacher Education Knowledge-Base Seminar, St. Louis, Mo.

Interstate New Teacher Support and Assessment Consortium (INTASC) (1992). *Model Standards for Beginning Teacher Licensing and Development: A Resource for State Dialogue.* Washington, D.C.: Council for Chief State School Officers.

Johnson, R. T., and D. W. Johnson (1985). "Student-Student Interaction: Ignored but Powerful." *Journal of Teacher Interaction* 36 (4): 22–26.

Joyce, B. R., and M. Weil (1972). *Models of Teaching.* Englewood Cliffs: Prentice-Hall.

Katz, L. and J. D. Raths (1982). "The Best Intention for Education of Teachers." *Action in Teacher Education* 4 (1): 8–16.

Katz, L., and J. D. Raths (1984). "Teachers' Dispositions as Goals for Teacher Education." Paper presented at the annual meeting of the American Educational Research Association. Chicago, Illinois. March 31, 1985, Session 3.11: Impacts in Teacher Education: Skills and Dispositions.

Kennedy, M. (1990). *A Survey of Recent Literature on Teachers' Subject Matter Knowledge.* East Lansing: National Center for Research on Teacher Education, Michigan State University.

——— (ed.) (1991a). *Teaching Academic Subjects to Diverse Learners.* New York: Teachers College Press.

Klein, S. P. (1982). "An Analysis of the Relationship Between Clinical Skills and Bar Examination Results." A report prepared for the Committee of Bar Examiners of the State Bar of California.

——— (1984). "Measuring Trial Practice Skills on a Bar Examination." Paper presented at the meetings of the American Educational Research Association, New Orleans, La., April.

——— (1986a). "The Performance of Novice Law Students and Law School Graduates on the Bar Examination." A report prepared for the Committee of Bar Examiners of the State Bar of California.

——— (1986b). "Establishing Pass/Fail Standards." *Bar Examiner* 55: 16–24.

——— (1988). "When Novices Take a Licensing Test." Paper presented at the meetings of the American Educational Research Association, March.

——— (1991). "Setting Pass/Fail Standards on Constructed Response Licensing Tests." Paper presented at the annual meetings of the National Council on Measurement in Education, Chicago, Ill.

——— (1993). *Summary of Research on the Multistate Bar Examination.* Chicago: National Conference of Bar Examiners.

Klein, S. P., and B. Stetcher (1991a). "Developing a Prototype Licensing Examination for Secondary School Teachers." *Journal of Personnel Evaluation in Education* 5: 169–190.

——— (1991b). *Final Report for English/Language Arts Tasks.* Santa Monica: RAND Corporation.

Knapp, M. S. (1982). *Toward the Study of Teacher Evaluation as an Organizational Process: A Review of Current Research and Practice.* Menlo Park: Educational and Human Services Research Center, SRI International.

Lareau, A. (1985). *A Comparison of Professional Examinations in Six Fields: Implications for the Teaching Profession.* Stanford: Stanford University.

Leinhardt, G. (1988). "Situated Knowledge and Expertise in Teaching." In J. Calderhead (ed.), *Teachers' Professional Learning.* Basingstoke: Falmer, pp. 146–168.

Lenk, H. A. (1989). "A Case Study: The Induction of Two Alternate Route Social Studies Teachers." Ph.D. diss., Teachers College, Columbia University.

Lieberman, A., L. Darling-Hammond, and D. Zuckerman (1991). *Early Lessons in School Restructuring.* New York: National Center for Restructuring Education, Schools, and Teaching, Teachers College, Columbia University.

Liston, D. P., and K. M. Zeichner (1987). "Critical Pedagogy and Teacher Education." *Journal of Education* 169: 117–137.

Litt, M. S., and D. C. Turk (1983). "Stress, Dissatisfaction, and Intention to Leave Teaching in Experienced Public High School Teachers." Paper presented at the annual meeting of the American Educational Research Association, Montreal.

Livingston, S. A., and M. J. Sieky (1982). "Passing Scores: A Manual for Setting Standards of Performance on Educational and Occupational Tests." Princeton: Educational Testing Service.

Loacker, G., and P. Jensen (1988). "The Power of Performance in Developing Problem Solving and Self-Assessment Abilities." *Assessment and Evaluation in Higher Education* 13 (2): 128–150.

Lortie, D. (1975). *Schoolteacher: A Sociological Study.* Chicago: University of Chicago Press.

LuPone, L. J. (1961). "A Comparison of Provisionally Certified and Permanently Certified Elementary School Teachers in Selected School Districts in New York State." *Journal of Educational Research* 55: 53–63.

Lutz, Frank W., and Jerry B. Hutton (1989). "Alternative Teacher Certification: Its Policy Implications for Classroom and Personnel Practice." *Educational Evaluation and Policy Analysis* 11 (3): 237–254.

Lythcott, J., and F. Schwartz (1993). "Professional Development in Action." In L. Darling-Hammond (ed.), *Professional Development Schools: Schools for Developing a Profession.* New York: Teachers College Press.

MacMillan, J. B., and S. Pendlebury (1985). "The Florida Performance Measurement System: A Consideration." *Teachers College Record* 87: 69–78.

Madaus, G. F. (1988). "The Influence of Testing on the Curriculum." In L. Tanner (ed.), *Critical Issues in Curriculum.* Chicago: University of Chicago Press, pp. 83–121.

McDiarmid, G. Williamson (1989). *What Do Prospective Teachers Learn in Their Liberal Arts Courses?* East Lansing: National Center for Research on Teacher Education.

McDiarmid, G. Williamson, Deborah L. Ball, and Charles W. Anderson (1989). *Why Staying One Chapter Ahead Doesn't Really Work: Subject-Specific Pedagogy.* East Lansing: National Center for Research on Teacher Education.

McDonald, F. (1980). *The Problems of Beginning Teachers: A Crisis in Training. Vol. 1, Study of Induction Programs for Beginning Teachers.* Princeton: Educational Testing Service.

McDonald, F. J., and P. Elias (1976). *Executive Summary Report: Beginning Teacher Evaluation Study, Phase II.* Princeton: Educational Testing Service.

McKenna, B. H. (1981). "Context/Environment Effects in Teacher Evaluation." In J. Millman (ed.), *Handbook on Teacher Evaluation.* Beverly Hills: Sage Publications.

McNeil, J. D. (1974). "Who Gets Better Results with Young Children—Experienced Teachers or Novices?" *Elementary School Journal* 74: 447–451.

Medley, D. M. (1977). *Teacher Competence and Teacher Effectiveness: A Review of Process-Product Research.* Washington, D.C.: American Association of Colleges for Teacher Education.

———— (1979). "The Effectiveness of Teachers." In P. L. Peterson and M. J. Walberg (eds.), *Research on Teaching.* Berkeley: McCutchan Publications, pp. 11–27.

———— (1985). "Evaluation of Research on Teaching." In *The International Encyclopedia of Education.* Vol. 7. London: Husen and Postlethwaite, pp. 4315–4323.

Melnick, S. and D. Pullin (1987). "Testing Teachers' Professional Knowledge: Legal and Educational Policy Implications." *Educational Policy* (Spring).

Minnesota Board of Teaching (MBOT) (1986). *Minnesota's Vision for Teacher Education: Stronger Standards, New Partnerships.* St. Paul: Task Force on Teacher Education, Minnesota Higher Education Coordinating Board.

———— (MBOT) (1992). *A Report on Teacher Preparation and Licensing.* St. Paul: MBOT.

Mitchell, N. (1987). *Interim Evaluation Report of the Alternative Certification Program* (REA87-027-2). Dallas: Dallas Independent School District, Department of Planning, Evaluation, and Testing.

National Board for Professional Teaching Standards (NBPTS) (1993a). *Early Adolescence/ English Language Arts Standards.* Washington, D.C.: NBPTS.

——— (1993b). *School Site Portfolio, Early Adolescence English Language Arts.* Pittsburgh: Assessment Development Laboratory, University of Pittsburgh.

——— (n.d.). *What Teachers Should Know and Be Able to Do.* Detroit: NBPTS.

National Board of Medical Examiners (NBME) (1986). "Bulletin of Information and Description of National Board Examinations." Philadelphia: NBME.

National Council for Accreditation of Teacher Education (NCATE) (1993). "NCATE Public Opinion Poll." Washington, D.C.: NCATE.

National Council of Architectural Registration Boards (NCARB) (1987a). *Organization, Services, Procedures, Records, Certifications, and Examinations:1987 Circular of Information No. 1.* Washington, D.C.: NCARB.

——— (1987b). *The Architect Registration Examination: 1987 Circular of Information No. 2.* Washington, D.C.: NCARB.

National Council of Engineering Examiners (n.d.). *Why Become a P.E.? The NCEE Guide to Registration.* Clemson, S.C.: National Council of Engineering Examiners.

National Institute of Education (NIE) (1977). *Violent Schools—Safe Schools: The Safe School Study Report to Congress.* Washington, D.C.: NIE.

——— (1979). *Beginning Teachers and Internship Programs.* Report no. 78-0014. Washington, D.C.: U.S. Department of Education.

Nedelsky, L. (1954). "Absolute Grading Standards for Objective Tests." *Educational and Psychological Measurement* 14: 3–19.

Nelson, K. R. (1988). "Thinking Processes, Management Routines, and Student Perceptions of Expert and Novice Physical Education Teachers." Ph.D. diss., Louisiana State University, Baton Rouge.

Nolan, J. (1985). "Professional Laboratory Experiences: The Mission Link in Teacher Education." *Journal of Teacher Education* 33(4): 49–53.

Odell, S. (1986). "Induction Support of New Teachers: A Functional Approach." *Journal of Teacher Education* 37: 26–30.

Olsen, Dwayne G. (1985). "The Quality of Prospective Teachers: Education vs. Noneducation Graduates." *Journal of Teacher Education* 36 (5): 56–59.

Palladino, J. (1980). *The Charade of Testing Teacher Competency: Relevant Criticism for the New York State Education Commissioner's Task Force on Teacher Education and Certification.* New York: Marymount Manhattan College.

Pearson, P. D., R. Barr, M. L. Kamil, and P. Mosenthal, eds. (1984). *Handbook of Reading Research.* New York: Longman.

Pecheone, R., and N. Carey (1989). "The Validity of Performance Assessments for Teacher Licensure: Connecticut's Ongoing Research." *Journal of Personnel Evaluation in Education* 3: 115–141.

Pecheone, R. L., J. B. Baron, P. D. Forgione, and S. Abeles (1988). "A Comprehensive Approach to Teacher Assessment: Examples from Math and Science." In A. Champagne (ed.), *This Year in School Science, 1988.* Washington, D.C.: American Association for Advancement of Science.

Perkes, V. A. (1967–1968). "Junior High School Science Teacher Preparation, Teaching Behavior, and Student Achievement." *Journal of Research in Science Teaching* 6 (4): 121–126.

Peterson, K., and D. Kauchak (1982). *Teacher Evaluation: Perspectives, Practices, and Promises.* Salt Lake City: Center for Educational Practice, University of Utah.

Peterson, P. L. (1976). "Interactive Effects of Student Anxiety, Achievement Orientation, and

Teacher Behavior on Student Achievement and Attitude." Ph.D. diss., Stanford University, Palo Alto.

Peterson, P. L., and M. A. Comeaux (1987). "Teachers' Schemata for Classroom Events: The Mental Scaffolding of Teachers' Thinking During Classroom Instruction." *Teaching and Teacher Education* 3: 319–331.

——— (1989). "Evaluating the Systems: Teachers' Perspectives on Teacher Evaluation." Paper presented at the annual meeting of the American Educational Research Association, San Francisco, Calif.

Pitcher, B. (1962). "The Relation of Academic Success in College Preparatory Curricula to Scores on the NTE Common Examinations." *ETS Statistical Report.* Princeton: Educational Testing Service.

Pitsch, M. (1991). "Senate Moving to Revamp Louisiana's Teacher-Evaluation System." *Education Week,* May 29, p. 16.

Pugach, M. C., and J. D. Raths (1983). "Testing Teachers: Analysis and Recommendations." *Journal of Teacher Education* 34 (1): 37–43.

Quirk, T. J., B. J. Witten, and S. F. Weinberg (1973). "Review of Studies of the Concurrent and Predictive Validity of the National Teacher Examination." *Review of Educational Research* 43: 89–114.

Resnick, L. B. (1987). *Education and Learning to Think.* Washington, D.C.: National Academy Press.

Reynolds, M. C. (1989). *Knowledge Base for the Beginning Teacher.* New York: Pergamon.

Romberg, T. A., and T. P. Carpenter (1985). "Research on Teaching and Learning Mathematics." In M. C. Wittrock (ed.), *Handbook of Research on Teaching.* 3rd ed. New York: Macmillan, pp. 850–873.

Rosenholtz, S. J. (1989). *Teachers' Workplace: The Social Organization of Schools.* New York: Longman.

Rosenshine, B., and N. Furst (1971). "Research on Teacher Performance Criteria." In B. O. Smith (ed.), *Research in Teacher Education: A Symposium.* Englewood Cliffs: Prentice-Hall.

Roth, Robert A. (1986). "Alternate and Alternative Certification: Purposes, Assumptions, Implications." *Action in Teacher Education* 8 (2): 1–6.

Rottenberg, C. J., and D. C. Berliner (1990). "Expert and Novice Teachers' Conceptions of Common Classroom Activities." Paper presented at the annual meeting of the American Educational Research Association, Boston, Mass.

Roupp, R., J. Travers, F. Glantz, and C. Coelen (1979). *Children at the Center: Summary Findings and Their Implications.* Cambridge, Mass.: Abt Associates.

Rutter, M., B. Maughan, P. Mortimore, and J. Ouston (1979). *Fifteen Thousand Hours: Secondary Schools and Their Effects on Children.* Cambridge, Mass.: Harvard University Press.

Ryan, K. (1980). "Toward Understanding the Problem: At the Threshold of the Profession." In K. Howey and R. Bents (eds.), *Toward Meeting the Needs of Beginning Teachers.* Minneapolis: U.S. Department of Education/Teacher Corp.

Schalock, D. (1979). "Research on Teacher Selection." In D. C. Berliner (ed.), *Review of Research in Education.* Vol. 7. Washington, D.C.: American Educational Research Association.

Schwartz, H. (1988). "Unapplied Curriculum Knowledge." In L. N. Tanner (ed.), *Critical Issues in Curriculum.* The Eighty-Seventh Yearbook of the National Society for the Study of Education. Chicago: University of Chicago Press, pp. 35–59.

Sciacca, Johnny Robert (1987). "A Comparison of Levels of Job Satisfaction Between University-Certified First-Year Teachers and Alternatively Certified First-Year Teachers." Ph.D. diss., East Texas State University.

Sclan, E., and L. Darling-Hammond (1992). *Beginning Teacher Performance Evaluation: An*

Overview of State Policies. Washington, D.C.: ERIC Clearinghouse on Teacher Education, American Association of Colleges for Teacher Education.

Sedlak, M., and S. L. Schlossman (1986). *Who Will Teach? Historical Perspectives on the Changing Appeal of Teaching as a Profession.* Santa Monica: RAND Corporation.

Shavelson, R. (1973). "What Is *the* Basic Teaching Skill?" *Journal of Teacher Education* 14: 144–151.

Shavelson, R., and N. Dempsey-Atwood (1976). "Generalizability of Measures of Teacher Behavior." *Review of Educational Research* 46: 553–612.

Shepard, L. (1993). "Evaluating Test Validity." In L. Darling-Hammond (ed.), *Review of Research in Education.* Vol. 19. Washington, D.C.: American Educational Research Association, pp. 405–450.

Shulman, Lee S. (1986). "Those Who Understand: Knowledge Growth in Teaching." *Educational Researcher* 15 (2): 4–14.

——— (1987). "Knowledge and Teaching: Foundations of the New Reform." *Harvard Educational Review* 57 (1): 1–22.

——— (1991). *Final Report of the Teacher Assessment Project.* Palo Alto: Stanford University, Teacher Assessment Project.

——— (1992). "Toward a Pedagogy of Cases." In J. Shulman (ed.), *Case Methods in Teacher Education.* New York: Teachers College Press, pp. 1–29.

Shulman, L. S., and G. Sykes (1986). "A National Board for Teaching? In Search of a Bold Standard." Paper commissioned for the Task Force on Teaching as a Profession, Carnegie Forum on Education and the Economy.

Skipper, Charles E., and Richard Quantz (1987). "Changes in Educational Attitudes of Education and Arts and Science Students During Four Years of College." *Journal of Teacher Education* (May–June): 39–44.

Smith, E. L., and N. B. Sendelbach (1979). "Teacher Intentions for Science Instructions and Their Antecedents in Program Materials." Paper presented at the Annual Meeting of the American Educational Research Association, April 8–12, San Francisco.

Soar, R. S. (1972). *Follow-Through Classroom Process Measurement and Pupil Growth.* Gainesville: Institute for Development of Human Resources, College of Education, University of Florida.

Soar, R., D. Medley, and H. Coker (1983). "Teacher Evaluation: A Critique of Currently Used Methods." *Phi Delta Kappan* 65: 239–246.

Southern Regional Education Board (SREB) (1982). *Teacher Testing and Assessment: An Examination of the National Teacher Examinations (NTE), the Georgia Teacher Certification Test (TCT), and the Georgia Teacher Performance Assessment Instrument (TPAI) for a Selected Population.* Atlanta: SREB.

Stallings, J. A. (1977). "How Instructional Processes Relate to Child Outcomes." In G. D. Borich (ed.), *The Appraisal of Teaching: Concepts and Process.* Reading, Mass.: Addison-Wesley.

Starr, Paul (1982). *The Transformation of American Medicine.* New York: Basic Books.

Stodolsky, S. S. (1984). "Teacher Evaluation: The Limits of Looking." *Educational Researcher* 13 (9): 11–18.

Summers, A. A., and B. L. Wolfe (1975). *Equality of Educational Opportunity Quantified: A Production Function Approach.* Philadelphia: Department of Research, Federal Reserve Bank of Philadelphia.

Sykes, G. (1990). "Sources of Justification for Knowledge Claims in Teaching." In *The Assessment of Teaching: Selected Topics.* Amherst, Mass.: National Evaluation Systems, pp. 11–29.

Taylor, J. A. (1979). "A Better Way: Quality Assurance for Professional School Personnel." Unpublished paper.

Taylor, J. K., and R. Dale (1971). *A Survey of Teachers in the First Year of Service.* Bristol: University of Bristol, Institute of Education.

Taylor, T. W. (1957). "A Study to Determine the Relationships Between Growth in Interest and Achievement of High School Students and Science Teacher Attitudes, Preparation, and Experience." Ph.D. diss., North Texas State College, Denton.

Thornton, G. C., and W. C. Byham (1982). *Assessment Centers and Managerial Performance.* New York: Academic Press.

Tisher, R. (ed.) (1978). *The Induction of Beginning Teachers in Australia.* Melbourne: Monash University.

Tyack, D. (1974). *The One Best System.* Cambridge: Harvard University Press.

Tyson-Bernstein, H. (1987). "The Texas Teacher Appraisal System: What Does It Really Appraise?" *American Educator* 11 (1): 26–31.

Valli, L., and A. R. Tom (1988)."How Adequate Are the Knowledge Base Frameworks in Teacher Education?" *Journal of Teacher Education* 39: 5–12.

van Manen, M. (1984). "Reflections on Teacher Experience and Pedagogic Competence." In E. C. Short (ed.), *Competence: Inquiries into Its Meaning and Acquisition in Educational Settings.* Lanham: University Press of America.

Veenman, S. (1984). "Perceived Problems of Beginning Teachers." *Review of Educational Research* 54: 143–178.

Walberg, H. J., and H. C. Waxman (1983). "Teaching, Learning, and the Management of Instruction." In D. C. Smith (ed.), *Essential Knowledge for Beginning Educators.* Washington, D.C.: American Association of Colleges for Teacher Education and ERIC Clearinghouse on Teacher Education.

Waxman, H. C., and M. J. Eash (1983). "Utilizing Students' Perceptions and Context Variables to Analyze Effective Teaching: A Process-Product Investigation." *Journal of Educational Research* 76 (6) (July–August): 321–325.

Wilson, S. M., and S. S. Wineburg (1993). "Wrinkles in Time and Place: Using Performance Assessments to Understand the Knowledge of History Teachers." *American Educational Research Journal* 30: 729–769.

Wilson, S. M., L. S. Shulman, and A. E. Richert (1987). "150 Different Ways of Knowing: Representations of Knowledge in Teaching." In J. Calderhead (ed.), *Exploring Teachers' Thinking.* Sussex: Holt, Rinehart, and Winston.

Winer, B. J. (1971). *Statistical Principles in Experimental Design.* 2d ed. New York: McGraw-Hill.

Wise, A. E. (1979). *Legislated Learning.* Berkeley: University of California Press.

Wise, A. E., and L. Darling-Hammond (1987). *Licensing Teachers: Design for a Teaching Profession.* Santa Monica: RAND Corporation.

Wise, A. E., and J. Leibbrand (1993). "Accreditation and the Creation of a Profession of Teaching." *Phi Delta Kappan* 5 (2): 133–136, 154–157.

Wise, A. E., L. Darling-Hammond, and B. Berry (1987). *Effective Teacher Selection: From Recruitment to Retention.* Santa Monica: RAND Corporation.

Wise, A. E., L. Darling-Hammond, M. W. McLaughlin, and H. T. Bernstein (1984). *Teacher Evaluation: A Study of Effective Practices.* Santa Monica: RAND Corporation.

Wright, David P., Michael McKibbon, and Priscilla Walton (1987). *The Effectiveness of the Teacher Trainee Program: An Alternate Route into Teaching in California.* Sacramento: California Commission on Teacher Credentialing.

Zeichner, K. (1993). *Reflections on the Career-Long Preparation of Teachers in Wisconsin.* Madison: University of Wisconsin.

About the Book and Authors

A License to Teach speaks directly to the quality-of-education debate now focused on public schools. The authors show that reform of teacher education and licensing are needed to ensure that teachers are prepared for the classroom. A well-conceived licensing system that supports high-quality teacher preparation would ultimately support the more demanding learning goals now expected of students and would give parents and policymakers greater confidence that teachers are being prepared to practice their profession responsibly.

The authors propose a comprehensive plan for licensing analogous to those in other professions. An extensive analysis of licensing examination and preparation grounds specific proposals for new assessments for teachers based on complex, real-life teaching tasks. The book also describes the kind of rigorous preparation program teachers should experience along with a well-designed and supervised internship in specially-designated professional development schools.

This book offers much-needed, practical advice on how to prepare and evaluate teachers for the challenging work they must accomplish. Agreement on standards for teacher preparation and licensing—among teachers, policymakers, and lay people—would go a long way toward improving the quality of education for children while also strengthening and improving the teaching profession itself.

Linda Darling-Hammond is William F. Russell Professor of Education and codirector of the National Center for Restructuring Education, Schools, and Teaching at Teacher's College, Columbia University. **Arthur E. Wise** is president of the National Council for Accreditation of Teacher Education. **Stephen P. Klein** is senior social scientist at the RAND Corporation.

Index